THE
FINAL
DIVE

THE
FINAL
DIVE

THE LIFE AND DEATH OF
'BUSTER' CRABB

DON HALE

First published in the United Kingdom in 2007 by
Sutton Publishing, an imprint of NPI Media Group Limited
Cirencester Road · Chalford · Stroud · Gloucestershire · GL6 8PE

British Library Cataloguing in Publication Data
A catalogue record for this book is available from the British Library.

Hardback ISBN 978-0-7509-4574-5

Typeset in Photina.
Typesetting and origination by
NPI Media Group Limited.
Printed and bound in England.

To Kath and absent friends

Contents

List of Illustrations

Foreword

Noel Cashford RNVR, MBE

It is with great pleasure that I write this foreword.

My good friend, the late Cdr Gordon Gutteridge RN, OBE, FRSA, frequently worked with Lionel Crabb during the Second World War and during the postwar years. He probably knew Crabb better than anyone else – yet he knew very little about Crabb's past. I, too, was in the company of Cdr Crabb infrequently.

Lionel Crabb always bordered on the eccentric and remained very secretive. It was Gordon's wish for us to collaborate and to try and write the definitive story. Planning meetings had already taken place but sadly Gordon died.

Now, my author friend, Don Hale, whose track record in investigative journalism is well proven, has used his meticulous research to bring this amazing story to fruition, so that it can now be told in full. Crabb's final dive at Portsmouth in April 1956 was never easy to research but despite often having his inquiries blocked by intrigue, constant cover-ups and government bureaucracy, coupled with threats relating to the Official Secrets Act, Don has now been able to reveal the facts relating to this fascinating and complex case.

Let me end with Gordon's last words regarding the 'Crabb affair':

It is, I'm afraid, the story of an ill-conceived Intelligence project, most unlikely to have a useful end product, which was sloppily executed, using inadequate resources. The pity is that our rabidly anti-Communist, down at heel and blinkered monarchist has been denied, in his advancing years, the regard of his peers and the enjoyment of Scotch and beer chasers with his diving chums. But then, it was as much his fault as anyone's and he never would come in from the cold!

Noel Cashford RNVR, MBE
Ex Lt RNVR Bomb and Mine Disposal Officer 1941–7

Note

Lt Noel Cashford RNVR was awarded the MBE (Military Division) for his wartime work of rendering safe mines and bombs. He joined the Navy aged seventeen and a half and spent many years involved with interesting, exciting and highly dangerous incidents as an RNVR Bomb and Mine Disposal Officer. At 5ft 6in he was precisely the same height and build as Lionel Crabb, and he trained and worked with Crabb during the war. Noel also became a well-known, highly respected and much decorated young officer, honoured by the King. While working in the Navy, he made safe over 200 devices, including fifty-seven in just three days, during a colourful six-year career with the bomb disposal squad. Noel was also one of the first men ashore during the daring Liberation of Jersey in the Channel Islands in May 1945. He worked as a key member of the team with Operation 'Nestegg' and Task Force 135, when the German-occupied Channel Islands finally surrendered after five harsh years.

Preface

For fifty years, Cdr Lionel 'Buster' Crabb's sudden, bizarre and mysterious disappearance has continued to fascinate. His final dive in April 1956 took place amid fears and anxieties from the Soviet Union during the Cold War and still ranks high on the list of the world's most notable conspiracy stories. A host of famous authors, politicians, conspiracy theorists and others have added their own theories without actually solving the riddle. It is a story that, unlike its subject, will probably never die.

My own involvement came about purely by chance. I happened to be working with a former diving colleague of Crabb, Noel Cashford MBE, who had worked with Crabb during wartime training as a diver and with the Bomb and Mine Disposal Unit. Noel had asked for my help in publishing his memoirs, and as we discussed Crabb's role in Noel's life, he confirmed that, unbeknown to many people, the case was reviewed by several former senior naval officers more than thirty years after Crabb disappeared.

I was curious to see what, if anything, had been discovered, and more importantly, why the Navy failed to publish all its findings. Noel put me in touch with some of Crabb's former colleagues, but sadly as time went by there were fewer and fewer people still living who had direct knowledge of Crabb and his final dive.

I did, however, talk with the senior naval officer who commissioned the review, with several of Crabb's diving colleagues, and with many friends and family members who had mixed views and opinions of the man, his life, his extraordinary work, and sudden disappearance. I also studied the confidential files.

It soon became clear that despite government restrictions, Crabb's family, friends and former colleagues still wanted to know the truth about his final dive. They seemed particularly concerned by press reports and repeated allegations that Lionel may have defected, turning his back on a country that he had served with distinction for decades.

Others questioned whether he had simply outsmarted everyone and operated as a Soviet spy or a double agent, as some of his friends and former associates before him, such as Anthony Blunt, Guy Burgess, Donald Maclean, John Cairncross, Kim Philby, and perhaps even Lord Rothschild.

I must admit that I found the idea of Crabb's defection almost impossible to believe. There seemed little or no supporting evidence, and why, if Crabb genuinely had defected, had not the Russians triumphantly paraded him through Moscow's Red Square, as they had with other acclaimed double agents?

I also found it strange that the British government had deliberately and continually blocked any further examination of Crabb's operational files for so long. Why had so many former naval personnel claimed that they too had been threatened by the authorities and still remained concerned about the Official Secrets Act?

I found it difficult to understand such secrecy after all this time and, encouraged by my sources' obvious desire to set the record straight, accepted a challenge to make further investigations.

Some of those I interviewed have since died and I would like to thank them and their families for their cooperation in helping reveal some of the key elements to this extraordinary mystery.

I believe that I have most, if not all, of the missing names and important facts from the puzzle, and hope to be able to explain the many hows, whens and wherefores of a truly fascinating case.

For more than a decade, Cdr Lionel Kenneth Philip Crabb GM, OBE, RNVR, was Britain's best-known frogman spy. Many of his highly dangerous undersea operations were later publicised throughout the world – with some even made into films and TV documentaries.

Crabb's heroic actions quite rightly earned him two national accolades for his outstanding bravery and devotion to his country. He became a loyal servant to certain members of the royal family, and also a friend, colleague and confidant to top politicians, naval officials, the rich and famous of the day, and even to members of the notorious Cambridge spy ring.

Crabb's character and his remarkable, at times eccentric, wartime exploits became the inspiration for his former Naval Intelligence (NI) boss, Ian Fleming's fictional hero, James Bond in Fleming's now famous series of spy books set against the backdrop of the Cold War. Although worlds apart from Bond in terms of physique, Crabb's controversial activities in Gibraltar, Italy, Egypt, Malta, Israel and elsewhere no doubt generated many ideas for plots and storylines. In this book, I will reveal other surprising links to Fleming's Agent 007.

Lionel Crabb was a natural diver. He was physically strong and completely fearless. Yet he had his own very personal demons, which from early in his adult life he fought with a combination of adventure and hard living. He was an undisputed war hero and an experienced spy, who remained a complex character. He was also a loner who suffered recurring bouts of depression, and had a lifelong passion for gambling, alcohol, tobacco and women – not necessarily in that order.

With luck, 'Crabbie', or 'Buster' Crabb, as the public knew him, could have continued in service for many years and perhaps would have become a household name. His diving skills and vast experience of Intelligence operations and undersea warfare techniques were legendary, and he could no doubt have influenced, inspired and educated many generations of naval and diving recruits.

Crabb was undoubtedly a most unusual character. At times he was stubborn, pig-headed and foolish. He was a man never quite satisfied with his life who, mainly through his famous Second World War exploits, became both well known and well connected. His legendary status was no doubt enhanced by his sudden and mysterious disappearance so that his life and exploits still attract worldwide controversy and speculation.

Some reports claim Crabb was shot, stabbed, electrocuted, strangled, kidnapped, captured or that he deliberately defected to the Russians from Portsmouth harbour. Others suggest he allowed himself to be taken, and worked for decades in the Soviet Union as a double agent and Red Navy diving instructor. As the years since Crabb's disappearance have gone by, so the exaggerated tales from certain ex-colleagues have continued to surface.

I was fascinated by Crabb's turbulent family background and the contrast in lifestyle and opportunity between his father's (Crabb) and mother's (Jarvis) sides of the family. I was also keen to find the answers to a number of contradictions surrounding his early life. In particular, I wanted to know why a man who supposedly hated exercise and was a poor swimmer with an acknowledged eye defect should volunteer for a succession of highly dangerous underwater missions. I also wondered what had transformed this once modest, reserved youngster into a fearless and unstoppable war hero, constantly prepared to risk life and limb for his country.

I became intrigued by whether Crabb had been manipulated, persuaded or deliberately coerced into adopting this shady world of international espionage and counter-espionage, and whether his family links may have contributed towards this unusual and risky career path.

I was fascinated, too, by his illustrious war record and his diving achievements with fairly primitive equipment. How, in freezing, dark, dangerous waters, did Crabb withstand the extremes of water pressure and temperature as he searched out enemy mines, booby traps and other perils lurking in the deep? I wanted to discover what made this extraordinary man tick.

Several people who knew Lionel Crabb well initially suggested that he had a troubled childhood and mentioned his ambition from an early age to seek a career at sea. It was clear that many aspects of his life and career were rife with myths, rumours and speculation. I wanted to determine which, if any, were true, and particularly to investigate the key events leading up to his disappearance and the subsequent discovery of a decapitated, handless body more than a year later in Chichester harbour.

The following chapters are based on sources ranging from interviews, research notes and secret intelligence files to personal letters, general correspondence, archive material, his mother's scrapbook, emails, family photograph albums and many other personal recollections. They also include important extracts from official and unofficial records, the private and personal testimony of many high-ranking senior and former naval officials and personal friends and relatives, which could not be told within their lifetime.

This account, based on four years' research, is my investigation into the extraordinary life and death of Lionel 'Buster' Crabb, and what really happened.

Introduction

In the spring of 1956, Lionel Crabb received an urgent summons to meet Lord Louis Mountbatten, the First Sea Lord, at Cowdray Park, Sussex. He was invited to undertake a special joint mission organised by British and American Intelligence agencies.

A few weeks later, Crabb began visiting and corresponding with friends and relatives, many of whom he had not seen for years. In a brief note home to his mother, 'Daisy', he confirmed that he was 'off to do another little job in Portsmouth'. He also instructed her to destroy the note once she had read it. And unusually, just before this particular assignment, Lionel asked his fiancée, Pat Rose, to accompany him on the train south. She explained:

On the journey down to Portsmouth I threatened to break off our engagement if he didn't tell me what was really going on . . . Finally he admitted he was going to look at the bottom of the Russian cruiser. At Portsmouth, Crabbie said we couldn't stay in the same hotel because he had to leave to meet with Matthew Smith, an American agent. He said that if he didn't phone tomorrow, he would call sometime in the evening. That was the last I saw of him.

This is a reconstruction of events leading up to Crabb's final dive on Thursday 19 April 1956.

For the umpteenth time the two naval officers synchronised their watches. It was just a few minutes to 7 a.m., and the start of a difficult mission. They sat hunched in a small launch positioned about 80 yards offshore. There was a freshening wind and yet the whole area was shrouded in a swirling mist that hovered a few inches above the choppy waters of Portsmouth harbour. It was cold and damp, and the bitter chill made both men anxious to begin their task.

Cdr Crabb was an experienced diver and was already dressed and prepared for action. He wore his favourite Heinke diving suit. His colleague, Lt George Albert Franklin – better known as 'Frankie' – checked Crabb's oxygen tank and watched as the diver puffed away on a hand-rolled cigarette. He coughed and spluttered before Franklin tried to distract him by handing over a new Admiralty underwater test camera. Crabb took one long last drag on his cigarette before hurling the smoking stub overboard and grabbing the camera firmly in his right hand.

Franklin was a good friend and former diving colleague, who had assisted Crabb as he prepared for this dive, helping Crabb put on his diving suit while he himself was dressed in warm casual clothing, and waterproofs. The attendant flicked the primer switch on this experimental new camera, which Crabb was to use to film the hull, rudder and screws of some visiting Russian warships. Franklin checked his watch again. It was now 7 a.m. precisely.

Crabb nodded and smiled nervously. He gave his colleague the thumbs-up and slipped quietly and efficiently over the side into the dark foaming waters. A trickle of small bubbles drifted towards the intended target. Frankie turned, scanned the shoreline, and waved across towards his American minder, Matthew Smith, a CIA liaison officer. It was Smith's job to guard their spare gear on the quayside, and to keep a watchful eye on any other unexpected activities.

On the launch, the boat rocked violently with the buffeting wind, and a heavy swell on the ebb tide. Franklin wiped his eyes and cleared his head. Across to shore, he could see Smith shuffling his feet to keep warm. It was another twenty minutes before Crabb returned. There was a sudden surge of bubbles on the port side, and Franklin watched anxiously as his colleague clung desperately to the side of the boat.

Until that point, the mission had followed a similar pattern to the brief test dive the day before. This time, however, Crabb seemed flushed, impatient, and out of sorts. His breathing was also slightly laboured. He snapped at his colleague before demanding more weights for his footwear. Crabb also ordered Franklin to check his oxygen levels again. Little had been used, and the attendant told Crabb that all was well.

Cdr Crabb, though, was angry. He dumped the bulky camera back in the boat, and started to curse his equipment. He complained of limited visibility, the dreadful stench of the water, and the bitter cold. Franklin was concerned and asked Crabb if he was well enough to continue. The diver rejected any suggestion of aborting the mission and both understood that timing was critical.

For a few seconds, as Crabb struggled to regain his breath, his mind may have gone back to the start of his day when he was awoken in pitch darkness at 5.30 a.m. by the shrill sound of his alarm clock at the nearby Sallyport Hotel. It had only seemed an hour or so since he had returned to his room from a night out with friends in a local bar. Crabb had had a good few too many drinks and his mouth was bone dry. He had stayed at the hotel with Smith, who occupied an adjacent room on the top floor. Through Crabb's small window he had had a bird's eye view of the harbour and could just see the Russian vessels in the distance.

In his anxiety to start work, Crabb had knocked on Smith's door before descending the stairs to listen to the early morning shipping forecast in the hotel reception. He remembered punching the air when he heard there would be more fog in the Channel, and hoped it would spread to cover his daylight dive.

Smith and Crabb then left on foot and travelled the short distance to the dock gates where, as arranged the previous day, they met Police Superintendent Jack Lamport, and a CID colleague, who escorted them through the security checkpoint.

As they cleared the gate, Lt Franklin drove the party the few hundred yards across to the King's Stairs, a small flight of stone steps that led down to their launch. Franklin had already stowed much of their essential gear, before dragging some heavier items out of Crabb's nearby storage shelter. The policemen bade them good luck, and left before Smith provided a final briefing.

Now on the dive, Crabb's hands were shaking. Torn between the desperate need for a cigarette and the knowledge that he must continue, Crabb decided he just wanted to get the job done and go home. He told Franklin he was OK and, biting hard on his mouthpiece, vanished into the murky depths.

Ahead and beyond, perhaps little more than a hundred yards or so, and partially blanketed in this rolling mist, the attendant could make out the rough outline of the three visiting Russian warships. They had berthed along-side at the Southern Railway Jetty less than twenty-four hours earlier. The ship of most interest was a very modern-looking cruiser, the *Ordzhonikidze*. She was escorted by two Soviet destroyers, *Sovershenny* and *Smotryashchi*. The ships had brought Soviet Premier Nikolai Bulganin and Communist Party Chief Nikita Khrushchev to Portsmouth at Prime Minister Anthony Eden's invitation. The Russians' arrival had been delayed due to fog the previous day, and the two leaders had entered the harbour first by launch, and then travelled to London by a special train, where Eden greeted them.

The *Ordzhonikidze* was a sister ship to the *Sverdlov*, another highly manoeuvrable Soviet cruiser that had visited these same waters less than a year before. Crabb and another diving colleague had taken the opportunity to complete a similar underwater inspection. The Soviets, however, had been made aware of Crabb's previous visit, and were now on notice of something similar happening again.

Time passed slowly and Franklin, who now worked for the HMS *Vernon* diving school, was already beginning to regret his involvement. It obviously was not, as Crabb had suggested, a quick operation. Franklin's eyes began to water from the cold, and from staring hard towards the Russian ships through powerful binoculars.

His vision also became impaired by the constant glare off the water, as the first few rays of the early morning sun shimmered along the rippling surface. The mist was rapidly diminishing. As Frankie adjusted his viewfinder, his shoulders suddenly tensed and his arms stiffened. For a brief second, he felt his heart skip a beat. Somewhere between the three ships, he thought perhaps he had seen some large dark shape – maybe even a diver – bob to the surface, and then suddenly disappear.

As he wiped his eyes again, Frankie noted some activity on the foredeck of one of the Soviet vessels. In addition, there appeared to be a slight disturbance in the water, but as he stared again, it settled. He checked his watch. It was just after 8 a.m. He knew his colleague carried less than two hours of oxygen, and he also knew that Crabb was past his peak, and that his friend smoked heavily, and had downed far more than his fair share of booze the night before. For another hour his anxious eyes scoured the surface of the water for any further signs of life. His hands were ice-cold, and he became confused and frustrated.

He had a gut feeling something had gone terribly wrong, but he had his orders to wait. Franklin wondered if the Russians had seen, attacked or even captured Crabb. He thought the latter options highly unlikely, especially in British waters, but then considered that his friend might have encountered a problem with his equipment. In addition, he knew his breathing had not been too good. He wished Lionel Crabb had heeded his advice not to continue. Worse still, knowing the perils of diving in this hazardous harbour, even in daylight, Franklin thought Crabb might have become snagged on some underwater obstruction.

He immediately considered a rescue dive, but knew it was against Crabb's orders, then asked himself where would he start to search. He looked to Smith for guidance, was unable to spot him but felt he should have been doing something more. He quickly hauled in the anchor and began patrolling the area in his launch.

Franklin went as near the Soviet ships as he dared, but after another ten minutes returned to his original position. He knew he faced a hopeless task, and as the minutes raced by, he began to appreciate the significance of the problem, and soon realised the Admiralty would be highly embarrassed, and the government compromised. Finally, at 9.15 a.m., more than two hours after the start of their operation, Franklin signalled to his colleague on shore, packed up the kit, and reluctantly abandoned the mission.

Chapter 1

Missing in Action

On a bitter, cold day in March 1918, a chill wind seemed to whistle through nearly every crack and crevice of the small house in Streatham, south London. Beatrice Crabb was well wrapped against the elements. She wore an old cardigan draped around her shoulders, a pair of warm mittens on her hands and two pairs of woollen socks on her feet.

As she pulled the curtains to lessen the draught, she suddenly stopped and dreamily watched the cold winter sun disappear below the horizon, scattering a spectacular blood-red and pale blue haze across the tops of the fir trees by the park. She knelt down and put a few of her nine-year-old son Lionel's toys away in an old tea chest. Like so many other housewives and mothers of the First World War, Beatrice was trying to keep busy to take her mind off her husband serving at the Western Front.

A few minutes earlier, she had begun preparations for supper. The table was set, with three sets of place mats, knives, forks and spoons. Several pans bubbled and hissed on the stove in the kitchen, and some plates were warming in the hearth. There was a strong, comforting smell of vegetable broth and onions, with cups and saucers set out for when the kettle boiled. Beatrice always kept her house spotlessly clean. She also maintained a demanding schedule, working part-time at a local bakery while raising her very active young boy, mainly on her own.

Unusually, Beatrice had not heard from her husband, Hugh, for more than a fortnight. He normally wrote several times a week but she knew that with this freeze, the troops were probably sheltering whenever they could. Beatrice always kept a place at the table for her husband just in case he came home unexpectedly. She was tall, attractive and slightly old-fashioned in her manner and appearance. She was, however, a very determined young woman with a positive outlook on life.

She stood for a moment at the corner of the room and smiled as she watched Lionel at play. He was well away in his own private world, completely oblivious to any distraction. She listened as he began to bark out orders to a collection of brightly coloured lead soldiers. In one hand he held a wooden sailing ship, delicately hand-carved by his father during a brief spell of home leave before this last 'Big Push'. For Lionel the ship was something special. He thought it contained magical qualities and provided essential covering fire for a land-based assault by his toy soldiers. He carefully positioned the battalion around the back of a table leg in support, waiting for the command to attack.

He called the red soldiers 'infantrymen' in recognition of his father. This latest battle may have been a fierce re-enactment of some major skirmish on the Turkish mainland as read out by Hugh from newspaper extracts, praising the bravery and heroics of his colleagues.

Beatrice yawned and suddenly felt very tired. She smoothed her long dark hair behind her ears and pulled it into a ponytail, then stared back into the room. Pulling another cloth from her apron pocket she started to wipe the top of the mantelpiece, before dusting some ornaments, and folding her ironing. She walked back towards the kitchen, knowing the kettle would soon be ready. Lionel looked up just as she left the room but remained silent. His mind was still occupied with military and maritime adventures.

Lionel could hear his mother rattling pans and cleaning up in the kitchen, when suddenly there was a loud knock at the door. Beatrice shouted that it was probably for him but that he couldn't go out, as it was too late and too dark. Lionel looked down the hallway, and when his mother opened the door, he could see a young telegraph delivery boy holding a small brown envelope, while trying to balance his bicycle. Lionel knew the boy. He was a member of the local Sunday school, the eldest son of a friend of his mother.

Beatrice had kept telling Lionel to join the boy at church, saying he always set a good example.

Lionel could see his mother staring at the boy. For some reason, she didn't want to accept the envelope. He heard her ask the boy if he had come to the right address. He couldn't hear his reply. He saw the boy turn the envelope over to read out: 'Number Four, Greyswood Street, Streatham. Mrs Beatrice Crabb?' Everyone in the street knew his mother as Daisy. Lionel told his friends that she had always hated her real name.

'Mrs Beatrice Crabb?' asked the boy again. He saw his mother hang her head. Even in the reflection of the streetlight she looked pale. She held out her hand again, and watched as the messenger turned away. She began to read the message. Lionel could see that she was struggling. Her hands were shaking. She automatically stepped back inside the house, and into the brighter light of the oil lamp in the hallway. She turned, smiled and patted Lionel on the head. He could see tears in her eyes. He asked her something but she didn't hear him and just muttered: 'No. It's not for you.'

Beatrice read the short message again. The boy asked if there was any reply. 'No, no reply.' She then gripped the boy's arm and pleaded with him to let his mother know. She closed the door and stepped back into the kitchen. She sat down heavily on a wooden stool and sighed. Lionel instinctively ran into the kitchen and stood next to her. At the top of the note he could make out an address at the War Office and below the message: 'To Mrs Beatrice Crabb, we beg to inform you that No. 25894, Lance Corporal Hugh Alexander Crabb, of the 8th Battalion East Surrey Regiment, has been reported missing in action at Pozières.'

Beatrice screwed up the telegram. Lionel didn't know what to do or say. He sensed his mother's distress but didn't really know why. His mother reached for him and hugged him tight. She held him so hard that he could hardly breathe. Neither said a word and tears streamed down their cheeks. After a few minutes she pushed him away, wiped his face, and calmly said: 'Your father's missing.'

More than thirty years later, when Lionel was sitting in a bar swathed in cigarette smoke, he would tell colleagues how he learned of his father's death. He said it had been the worst moment of his life. His eyes filled each time he told the story and he said he could feel the same sense of breathlessness whenever he faced a difficult dive. Once, he thought he even saw the ghostly face of his father rising from the ocean depths.

Lionel said his mother never gave up hope. She spoke about Hugh constantly. And as the youngster began to make his way in the world he recalled how his father talked of witnessing many acts of courage on the battlefield, and of how he had tried to cope with the loss of friends and comrades while serving his country. He said his father had written many letters home on behalf of the fallen, often mentioning the need for a 'stiff upper lip'. Just how much this really affected the early life of Lionel Crabb, one can only guess. Hugh's body was never found.

Some said it was a token final surge, which gained a few hundred yards in yet another blood-soaked, shell-holed battlefield. Others claimed it was a successful counter-attack. Crabb's father and numerous others never even enjoyed the dignity of a proper family funeral. Instead, the Imperial War Graves Commission at Pozières engraved his name among 14,644 others on the grand memorial to the fallen heroes. Hugh's date of death is shown as 22 March 1918. He was just forty years old.

For Daisy Crabb, it took a few more days for the full implication of the news to sink in. At thirty-seven, she was a war widow and a single parent. She worked part-time as a baker and later obtained additional temporary work as a cook to a large family, working at times in the early morning and late evening. Occasionally, the jobs overlapped and Lionel was left with friends, neighbours or relatives.

Daisy had little money but refused to accept charity or sympathy. However, she knew she would eventually require some financial support for Lionel's education. Her own parents and grandparents had long since died and Daisy remained thankful for the generous support of some close relatives. The strongest support came from Daisy's wealthy cousin Frank Jarvis and his wife Catherine Florence, though Frank's sister, Kate, and unofficial aunts Bessie and Ada also lent a hand. The Jarvis and Crabb family connection came through Daisy's grandfather, Joseph Adshead, who married Harriett Ross, an aunt of Frank's father, Edward. For better and worse, the wealthy Jarvis family would exert a strong influence on Lionel Crabb's upbringing and throughout his life.

Chapter 2

Family Ties

The predicament of the Crabb family at the end of the First World War was no different from countless others of the time. As Lionel later told colleagues, by the end of hostilities in November 1918 half his classmates had lost the main breadwinner. The cruelty of losing a husband so close to the end of the war was not lost on Daisy, who contacted her cousin Kate, also bereaved of her partner. For a while they comforted each other and shared the care of their children, but for society as a whole the loss of almost a whole generation of young men was incalculable. Daisy admitted to a few long periods of depression and the odd drinking spree, which she always tried to hide from Lionel.

How different life might have been if Hugh, and Daisy's brother John, had escaped from the doom and gloom of Edwardian London just a few years earlier. In 1913 the men had set off for Australia in search of a new life, having read about fantastic opportunities in the New World. They intended to find accommodation and employment Down Under before sending for Daisy and young Lionel. However, their exploratory trip was interrupted by developments in the Balkans, with the ubiquitous posters of Lord Kitchener summoning young men to war with 'Your country needs YOU!' It was believed this conflict would all be over by Christmas.

At thirty-five, Hugh thought he was too old to fight. Yet he was reluctant to be seen as a coward and saw just how many others were eager to take the 'King's shilling'. This included Daisy's brother John, who was four years younger and very keen to sign up. They decided to enlist together, and were placed in one of the new 'Pals' battalions.

Hugh was a courageous, lively, happy-go-lucky type, who quickly gained his first stripes. He was promoted to lance-corporal with the East Surreys, and when he came home on leave or wrote to Lionel and Daisy between battles, he always tried to play down the full horrors of life at the Front.

Lionel was just five years old when the First World War began, yet he was able to recall sitting on his father's knee and listening intently to his tales of heroism. For Lionel, the trappings of war were far more exciting than mere toys, and he remained fascinated by Hugh's campaign medals, his polished lapel and cap badges, uniform, helmet and rifle. For Daisy, however, the war marked the beginning of a long hard struggle to survive.

In addition to a new life in Australia, Hugh, Daisy and Lionel might also have enjoyed the security of a generous inheritance had not William James Crabb, his paternal grandfather, died suddenly at the age of 45. William had become a wealthy corn merchant, adding generously to his own status and wealth when he married the beautiful Lavinia, the daughter of a prominent London merchant.

It seems that until William's death, the family lived in relative splendour, employing at least two servants. They resided at a number of exclusive London addresses including a very fashionable detached town house, known as St Mary's Lodge, on Lordship Road, Stoke Newington. Records describe this property as one of a number of 'grand homes for gentlemen'.

William Crabb's house was designed by leading architect of the time, John Young, and featured rare arched windows and terracotta brickwork accents. In 1871, according to the deeds, 33-year-old William James Crabb moved into the property with his young wife Lavinia, their young daughter Lavinia Maud, aged three, and infant son Alfred Philips, who was later to become a well-known architect. Lionel's father, Hugh, was born six years later.

William's sudden death, twelve years after purchasing the property, affected the family business and it quickly fell into decline. His wife Lavinia died just five years later, leaving Hugh and his brother Alfred in the care of their sixteen-year-old sister, Lavinia Maud. Remarkably, the teenager performed this task admirably well, and in 1901 she married Edward Henry Lovell, enjoying a well-to-do lifestyle, even employing two servants of her own.

Upon his sister's marriage, Hugh Alexander Crabb was left to fend for himself. Having lost both parents by the time he was twelve, and with money hard to find, he had to forfeit any hopes of further education by finding work. He was always interested in art and photography, and managed to obtain a job as a travelling salesman for a firm of photographic materials merchants. It is likely he met Daisy through her father, Jonas Taylor Goodall, who was also a salesman. Hugh's occupation is listed as 'commercial traveller' in the 1901 census and the same title also appears on his death certificate.

When Lionel's father was lost in the war the boy's 'uncle', Frank Jarvis, took on a vital role in helping with the young boy's education and upbringing. At thirty-six, Frank was four years younger than Hugh, and about the same age as Daisy, with whom he had shared much of his childhood and who was a good friend. Frank had made his mark in the world of commerce some thirteen years earlier, in 1905, when he and his business partner, Howard Garner, rented some temporary premises at 13 Paternoster Row, close to St Paul's Cathedral in London.

The pair began by importing unmarked American pens for the British market. The Crabb family explained this was the beginning of a successful international production and marketing company, which eventually provided employment for several family members. For some unexplained reason, the partners called the firm Conway Stewart after two well-known musical entertainers of the period.

About a year later, Conway Stewart started to sell revolutionary self-filling and self-cleaning fountain pens, known as 'American bulb fillers'. The same year, Frank's brother Stanley joined the Conway Stewart board of directors, which enabled the founders to concentrate on marketing and producing a unique low-cost and reliable pen for the mass market. The business expanded rapidly, achieving worldwide acclaim. Some of their first pens were made from vulcanite rubber, and were produced from new premises at Upper Thames Street.

Frank's wife, Catherine Florence (née Bishop) – known as Kitty – was, like her husband, a childhood friend of Lionel's mother Daisy. The Bishop family were regular visitors to the Jarvis household and as children, Daisy, Kitty and Frank all played together.

It is perhaps not too surprising, therefore, that in later years, and at about the same time as Frank began his pen business, he and Kitty formed a romantic attachment. They married in 1907. Kitty was the daughter of Charles William Bishop and Catherine Sarah North. Her father was a chief telegraphonist, initially with the Post Office, and then within the Civil Service. He was also a Morse code expert, and an ardent union official. In the 1901 census, Kitty was listed as a 'trainee telegraphonist'. She developed some similar interests to her father and progressed rapidly through several important government departments. She had a peculiar passion for newspaper crosswords, riddles and codes, and eventually worked at the War Office and for Intelligence agencies.

Kitty later became a valued personal assistant to the Keeper of the Queen's Pictures, Anthony Blunt, working among other famous names in the world of espionage, including Guy Burgess, Donald Maclean, Kim Philby, and the creator of the James Bond character, Ian Fleming.

Frank Jarvis, meanwhile, is described by his relatives as a 'warm, sensitive and friendly man, who perhaps drank a little too much for his own good'. Apart from running a successful business, he was also a keen sportsman. He particularly enjoyed boxing, golf and greyhound racing, and at one time he bred and raced dogs. And just like Lionel Crabb, Frank had lost his father when aged nine. Frank served in the First World War as a member of the Royal Army Service Corps (RASC), and spent much of his wartime service based at Aldershot, where he was a captain and adjutant at the local army barracks. As a youth he was a good amateur boxer and also taught himself to ride, winning a number of prestigious equestrian events on a horse named Spider.

Frank said he didn't enjoy his time in the army. He became too attached to the troops, and his relatives claim that sending young men and horses into battle broke his heart, and led him to start drinking heavily.

Shortly after his discharge from the army in 1919, Frank returned to his business interests at Conway Stewart. The firm expanded its extensive pen range and in subsequent years they registered their trademark. Following the appointment of another of Frank's close relatives, Mortimer James Goodall, as chairman, the company became one of the first to introduce coloured and decorative pens. The Jarvis family became the essential 'rock' for Daisy and the impressionable young Lionel to cling to in times of need. Frank and Kitty Jarvis had three children of their own, Kenneth Charles, Eileen Catherine, and Audrey Florence.

The major family contacts, who have generously helped with my research, are all closely related to this Jarvis side of the family. They include Eileen's daughter Miss Lomond Handley, and Audrey's three daughters, Mrs Charleen Miller, Miss Glenda Hammond, and Mrs Jemma Fortune. Charleen, speaking on behalf of her sisters, explains that the Jarvis family at that time was extremely wealthy and considered 'very upper class'. She says:

> The family mixed in some very high circles. Everyone was very well spoken, smart, charming and cultured. I wouldn't say they were intellectually brainy but grandmother Kitty loved the arts. She was a member of the Arts Theatre Club and went every week to the cinema. [As well as theatre] she also loved interior design – and in later life her flat at Douglas Mansions, London, was stuffed with beautiful antiques. She shopped, partied and entertained. Kitty was always elegantly dressed, and carried a dictionary with her. She was very keen on crosswords. Wherever the family stayed it would have been the best. They always had the best of everything. And Mother said they lived in great luxury and wanted for nothing.

Charleen added that the family home – Allendale – had its own tennis court, and confirmed that her mother, Audrey, and sister Eileen, attended boarding school near Eastbourne. Charleen's cousin, Lomond Handley, remarks:

> Isn't our class system peculiar? Frank Jarvis was considered 'new money' and if he'd lived he might possibly have done the 'debutante' circuit for his daughters. Their 'coming out' parties would have cost him a fair old packet of course, and he would have had to find someone else,

who had already been presented at court, to 'present' them. He was a member of the RAC Club, which took anybody, whilst other London clubs such as Boodles, Whites, or the Athenaeum were very fussy about backgrounds. New money wasn't always enough to get people into different social circles.

In [John Galsworthy's] *The Forsyte Saga*, I remember someone saying that Eton wouldn't accept him, because his father was, or had been 'in trade'? There is also a possibility that there is Jewish blood somewhere in the Jarvis family. It was a family joke. My dad used to say that Frank and Kitty met at the synagogue, which mother denied, saying there was French ancestry. There was no unkindness meant in this family joke, and it was all in good part and may have had some truth in it. Frank looked Jewish, so did Kenneth and Lionel. Granny said that if all three children hadn't been born at home she'd have thought that my mother might have accidentally been swapped because she was tall, blonde and willowy.

Audrey said something once about Frank trying to get them into Roedean but the school's lists were full, so they went to Boston House instead. Maybe Roedean didn't want to take girls whose folks were 'new money' and were not aristocrats.

Charleen Miller forwarded me written evidence of an early friendship between Crabb's mother, Daisy, and Frank's wife, Kitty, and the stark contrast between the Crabb and Jarvis family finances immediately after the First World War. The two young women kept a 'Book of Confessions' – a most intriguing item that belonged to Charleen's grandmother, Kitty Jarvis.

The first entry completed by Kitty was made on 2 June 1903. She was nineteen and Daisy a few years older. Neither was married. Daisy married Hugh Crabb in September 1906, and Kitty, Frank, the following year. It was not until 6 August 1915 that Kitty persuaded Daisy to write down her own thoughts in the book. By then, she had been married for over nine years and her only son Lionel was six years old. The war had been raging for nearly a year and her husband was fighting overseas. Kitty had been married for eight years and had three children. However, whereas Kitty had married into a wealthy family, Daisy had to scrimp and save every penny.

The book consists of thirty-eight personal questions on a range of varied subjects and opinions relating to the best and worst in life. Daisy's replies highlight her loneliness, her constant struggle against poverty, and perhaps even a hint of jealousy. She states her ambition 'to be very rich' while Kitty confesses 'a fear of being without friends or money, and a desire to live in London with her family and friends'. Kitty's answers indicate a much higher social standing than Daisy's, and a more relaxed and contented life.

Meanwhile it appeared that just as the two women enjoyed a close friendship, a strong bond had formed between their sons, Lionel Crabb and Kenneth Jarvis. The boys were distant cousins, just a few months apart in age and remarkably similar in appearance. Although Kenneth was slightly taller and stockier than Lionel, the pair were often mistaken for brothers. They became the best of friends and Lionel was encouraged to share Kenneth's passion for collecting birds' eggs. He used to keep his collection in glass cases and wooden boxes, all neatly catalogued and labelled. There were also constant rumours that Lionel had bad eyesight, but when I asked Lomond Handley, she confirmed that although he had a lazy eye, there was no apparent sight defect. She says:

Quite the contrary. I don't know what the fitness requirements were to enter the services, but Lionel was a good shot with a catapult – as was Kenneth! Mother told me that when the boys were about six or seven, the boys were playing in the chicken run in the garden – which they weren't supposed to because there were rats, and the whole area was out of bounds. Mother naturally followed them, as they were supposed to be looking after her, and she was dressed in a beautiful white lace dress. The boys must have disturbed a rats' nest and one ran up mother's leg to her shoulder and she screamed, so Lionel immediately shot at it with his catapult, killing it instantly. There was blood all over mother's dress. Luckily the stone missed her face. The boys knew they would be in trouble if it got out that they had been in the chicken run so they pooled all their pocket money and bribed mother to keep quiet about her dress and how it became bloodstained. Granny Jarvis was obviously concerned to know how little Eileen had become covered in blood, and eventually put it down to a sudden nosebleed. Mother said she made a few shillings out of this deal and also gained a lot of sympathy.

Lionel and Kenneth spent most of their school holidays together, sharing many exciting adventures. And it seems that another young relative, a First World War orphan of a similar age, Stanley North, also joined this group at about the same time. Stanley was said to be the son of one of Kitty's uncles and did not spend quite as much time with the Jarvis family as Lionel did, but Frank determined that despite their disadvantaged backgrounds both boys should have a chance in life. Frank agreed to pay their school fees and both boys regularly joined in with family holidays and excursions. Frank became a prominent 'father figure' to Lionel, who in later years would explain to friends how he used to sit transfixed listening to Frank's tales of adventures and about business trips around Europe and America. One memory that stuck in Lionel's mind was the story of Frank's trip across the Atlantic, to attend one of the most savage and controversial World Boxing Championship fights between Jack Dempsey and Jess Willard in Toledo, Ohio, on 4 July 1919.

Despite a busy schedule and various sales and marketing trips abroad, Frank and Kitty always had time for the children. And although Frank's children attended boarding schools and enjoyed many chauffeur-driven trips, the cousins were always encouraged to play together, and despite an obvious difference in status and social background, they remained good friends.

Lomond says her grandfather loved animals and had told the family that if he'd been poor, he would have gladly worked as a zookeeper. He used to take the family on regular outings to London Zoo. She recalls:

One day he took them when the lion was fast asleep in its cage, so grandfather gave it a gentle poke through the bars with his walking stick, hoping to see some activity. To Frank, the stick was extremely precious. It was the mark of a gentleman and it had a splendid decorative silver knob on its handle. The lion didn't appreciate being poked by anything, never mind a posh stick, which grandfather still held on to.

He was being dragged nearer and nearer to the cage door, and towards a very angry beast. Consequently, he was forced to let go, whereupon the lion proceeded to scrunch it, and smash it up, much to the children's amusement. Grandfather was very upset at the loss of his stick and complained to the zoo. They said they were sorry about the loss of his stick but respectfully pointed out that Mr Jarvis should not have poked the lion in the first place.

Mother used to laugh about it. She said the speed at which the lion woke, turned, and grabbed the stick was amazing, as was the ease with which it dragged the stick through the bars.

This vivid experience and the luxury of a gentleman's walking stick remained in Lionel's memory for decades. And years later, when he, too, felt he had finally achieved something in life, he also indulged in a gentleman's fancy swordstick, this time embossed with a golden crab.

Frank always took an active interest in Lionel's education and welfare, regularly discussing with Lionel his school career, and what he planned to do in the future. Frank said he would have liked Lionel to join his pen company, but Lionel always said he wanted to go to sea. Daisy claimed this had been his ambition from the age of eight. It was perhaps sparked by that small wooden ship, carved and given to him by his father, together with Frank's tales of adventures. Certainly this passion for a career at sea developed shortly after his father's death.

Boarding schools and education played an important part in the family life of Kitty and Frank, and yet frustratingly for his mentor, Lionel remained very casual, showing no sign of academic ambitions. Kenneth Jarvis attended Berkhamsted School, while Eileen and Audrey were educated at Boston House School. Lomond says that in Lionel's later years at school, when Frank was going through one of Lionel's reports, he said: 'Well Lionel, you might not be much of a scholar, but according to this, your manners are impeccable, and I'm very proud of you.' Lomond adds that although she never met Lionel, 'The family claimed he was always smart and well presented.'

Relatives have spoken of Lionel's deep love for his mother, Daisy. Sadly no personal papers, letters or diaries remain but Charleen and Lomond's parents confirmed that Lionel would regularly write a short note to Daisy, and visited her as much as possible. It is said that he always spoke most fondly of her, despite often being chastised by her.

From recent conversations with some of Crabb's former colleagues, Lionel retained a fear of offending his mother and a passionate need to prove himself worthy of her. It seems he was always trying to live up to her expectations, and may have suffered the consequences of being compared with his father.

This might explain why Crabb appeared to carry a chip on his shoulder, and why he constantly longed for new challenges. Lionel Crabb spoke about his love of the 'high life' and his early days, sampling the luxury of the Grand Hotel in Eastbourne. He told friends how he enjoyed having his shoes cleaned, playing about in lifts, room service and cooked breakfasts. Perhaps this surreal existence gave him the taste for a lifestyle he would never quite achieve. It seems clear that whatever else he had in mind, Crabb certainly had every intention of leaving some mark on society.

By the time Crabb was fourteen, his family say he had become unsettled, ambitious and impatient. In a letter to his adoptive uncle Frank – now, like almost all of his correspondence, sadly lost – Lionel said he had become bored with traditional education. He said he had no intention of seeking a conventional career, and pleaded to be released from his educational commitments for an opportunity at sea.

This request, although perhaps half expected, was a disappointment to Frank, Kitty and the cousins, and particularly to his widowed mother. Daisy frequently criticised Lionel's attitude to life and school, yet agreed she still did not want to lose his company. She was concerned about her son spending so many months away at sea, and thousands of miles from home.

Frank shared Daisy's concern but after further discussion with the teenager agreed to cover his training costs. Lionel suggested a career in the Royal Navy, but Frank had other ideas. He was worried, not only about the fees, but also whether Lionel would stay the course. Frank's opinion eventually proved justified, although for very different reasons.

Frank knew that, though well brought up and trustworthy, Lionel was no scholar. His own experience of basic military training led Frank to believe that Lionel would definitely struggle to stay the course at Dartmouth.

Through his former service contacts Frank therefore arranged for Lionel to attend a special two-year training course with the Merchant Navy at HMS *Conway*, berthed on Merseyside.

Archive records suggest Lionel applied to join the ship as an apprentice cadet sometime between 1922 and 1924. However, he had to be at least fourteen years old to join, and it seems his course ran between 1923 and 1925. HMS *Conway* was a medium-size, nineteenth-century wooden battleship. She was almost permanently moored in the Sloyne, just off Rock Ferry, on the River Mersey and was in fact the last of a long line of specially commissioned battleships provided by the Admiralty as a specialist training ship.

In later years, Lionel told colleagues how much he had enjoyed his time at HMS *Conway* and always retained a genuine affection for the old school. He was known as a 'bit of a daredevil' and a 'show-off' – aspects of his make-up which remained with him all his days. Most either loved or loathed Crabb. It was said he always tried too hard to please and craved attention.

Lomond Handley says that on one occasion he could and should have been court-martialled. As a dare he took a monocle from inside the cabin of a visiting commanding officer (CO). To Lionel, it merely represented a silly prank. It also provided another opportunity to try to prove something to himself and to his much wealthier shipmates. It became a public school-type initiation ceremony.

The dare was executed at short notice in the early hours and in pitch darkness. Lomond confirms that the officer in question was known as something of a 'stuffed shirt', and that fortunately all went well with the dare. Crabb removed the monocle from the CO's dressing table, placed it in his top pocket and escaped while the man slept. His family do not know where Lionel actually hid the monocle or how he got away with it, but he retained this symbolic prize throughout his service days.

Lionel Crabb was not the only well-known personality to attend HMS *Conway*. Other famous names to train there include champion Channel swimmer Matthew Webb (1860–2), Poet Laureate John Masefield (1891–4), Conservative Party leader Iain Duncan Smith (1968–72) and England rugby player and team coach Sir Clive Woodward (1969–74).

While completing their basic training in Liverpool, Lionel and his fellow students were encouraged to visit shipping offices to enquire about forthcoming vacancies. Many merchant and passenger companies produced attractive posters and brochures to try to tempt passengers and crew on to round the world voyages, promising luxury, adventure, and excitement. Some companies even offered top quality accommodation at a slightly lesser tariff, aboard a freighter bound for some exotic location. Most packages were targeted at the wealthy.

Crabb studied several offers and visited Lamport & Holt, one of the major shipping and travel agents. He was particularly interested in working a regular passage to central and southern America, as it was a region that always held a particular fascination for him. Lionel was offered an apprenticeship aboard the company's new steamship, the SS *Bonheur.* Formerly registered as the *War Triumph,* this vessel was built in 1920 at the famous Harland & Wolff shipyard at Queen's Island on Belfast's River Lagan. Coincidentally, the yard also built the ill-fated passenger liner *Titanic,* which sank on her maiden voyage to New York on 10 April 1912.

Crabb was anxious to go to sea. As soon as he completed his training course at *Conway* and during the early part of 1926, he signed on, finally setting sail from Liverpool for pastures new. This, however, was where the Crabb family story started to unravel. For some strange reason, Lionel failed to complete his apprenticeship, and even quit his ship in New York about two years later. I studied numerous archive notes about his travels, yet nothing threw any light on this turn of events.

I therefore contacted family members and checked through confidential papers to see if there was a specific reason – personal, for health reasons, or discipline – that may have forced his hand. On the face of it, there seemed no clear explanation for his throwing away a golden opportunity to excel at his chosen career. I also wanted to know why, surprisingly, he later ended up in America in a host of dead-end jobs.

I wondered what routes he had taken, what cargoes he carried, and whether there were any reports or clues from former shipmates. I had plenty of questions but very few answers until I received a couple of calls which put everything into context, providing a credible reason for Crabb's early and extraordinary decisions.

Chapter 3

Life at Sea and a Scandal

One of the first of many interesting calls received during the course of my investigations came from fellow researcher Patricia Milligan, who coincidentally was busy working in Australia on a parallel project. Trish is a Briton who emigrated Down Under in the 1960s on a £10 assisted passage. She supplied me with some fascinating news and links to Crabb's overseas manifest records and crew listings relating to United States arrivals. It was a welcome contact, especially as Trish was also searching archive material about the SS *Bonheur*. More importantly, she surprisingly confirmed that her grandfather, William John Milligan, served with Crabb as Fourth Engineer on this ship in 1927–8. He worked with him on at least four round-trip voyages to and from South America, including his maiden voyage, when Crabb was just an inexperienced sixteen-year-old apprentice.

Milligan was more than thirty years Crabb's senior. He also had a very fiery temper, and a reputation to match. Trish said her grandfather joined Lamport & Holt after being dismissed by rivals Cunard for throwing a fellow crew member overboard into the Mersey. After hearing this, I felt the pair would have got along just fine.

William came from seafaring stock. His father Thomas had also served in the Merchant Navy, working as a 'greaser' and 'refrigeration attendant', as did William's younger brother, Alexander. Trish claimed that William became marooned in New York in 1930, when Lord Kylsant's shipping empire, including Lamport & Holt, suddenly went bust. She said that William and all his shipmates were left stranded and destitute, and that his family were forced to bail him out. They had to club together to pay his return fare home. The company was revived four years later but by then William had had enough of seafaring and obtained a secure job on dry land.

Some of the main references to Crabb's early maritime career on the SS *Bonheur* have recently been made available in America. They are stored at the US National Archives in Washington, DC, and relate to passenger and crew listings of vessels arriving at New York 1897–1957. There are also records and information available about the Immigration and Naturalization Service. Their database contains passenger lists and an index of all ships arriving from foreign ports 1820–1957, and confirms a 'list or manifest of aliens employed' on a particular vessel, as members of crew.

I have extracted some details from about eight of these passages just to show the extent of Crabb's travels, and his determination to gain further experience. Lionel was listed as a British subject, and signed on to work the SS *Bonheur* from Buenos Aires on 26 March 1927. The original port of departure was shown as Liverpool, with the port of destination New York. It is more than likely that he first signed on in Liverpool, and then re-signed, as was the normal practice, upon arrival in South America. He was first listed as L.K. Crabb, and the ship's papers were stamped at the American Consulate in Port of Spain, Trinidad, and at the American Consulate in Brazil and Argentina.

On arrival back in New York on 5 April 1927, Crabb re-signed for a return passage to Buenos Aires. His papers dated 20 April record his tender age, occupation and a statement by the master that the ship arrived with a total crew of forty seamen. It says eighteen men were discharged upon arrival, with a further nineteen signed on, making a crew total of forty-one for the return journey.

The ship worked under the Lamport & Holt flag and was consigned to Sanderson & Son Ltd. She was shown as berthing at Pier 14, Hoboken. The papers suggest the ship was due to sail on 23 April to Buenos Aires, via the US port of Norfolk.

During this period, the ship's register also confirms that *Bonheur* worked almost constantly between New York and Brazil, and via Argentina and Port of Spain. The register also records the development of new starters like Crabb. On beginning his sea career he was listed as a small, lightweight individual, 5ft 4in tall and weighing just 125lb. Towards the end of his apprenticeship, and more than two years later, he had grown by 2in and put on 5–10lb. *Bonheur*'s manifest papers indicate the ship returned to New York on 20 July 1927, with another mixed consignment for Sanderson & Son Ltd, this time from Rosario, Argentina.

The papers record Crabb's age as seventeen years, and credit him with one-and-a-half years' service. The next destination was the River Plate. An almost identical passage and manifest was recorded in the New York arrivals of 8 November 1927, this time showing the ship's arrival port as Santa Fe Rosario, Pemambrico, Argentina. Other reference papers confirm that Crabb was still aboard the *Bonheur* on 12 October 1928, arriving back at New York from Montevideo, in Uruguay.

I noted that his final entry showed a Lionel Kenneth Crabb recorded on a list or manifest of alien passengers travelling on the *Albertic*, sailing out of Liverpool and arriving at the port of New York on 7 January 1929. His age was shown as twenty, occupation, clerk. In letters and postcards home to his Uncle Frank and cousin Kenneth, Crabb complained about limited shore leave. However, I believe this might have been something of a blessing, and may even have saved him from getting into further trouble.

Crabb admitted having few shipmates of his own age and wrote back saying that he usually tagged along with older crewmen to find bars and other places to unwind, away from the rigours of many hard months at sea. Crabb however said he often became bored, frustrated, and at times felt very isolated. Despite his youth, he began to succumb to the dark demons of drink and gambling. He could generally hold his liquor, but sometimes the drinks were spiked by unscrupulous bar owners determined to keep their customers on the premises. This, plus the cheapness and availability of much stronger alcohol on an empty stomach, often helped create additional problems for the young sailor.

It is clear the youngster found the work tough and demanding, and well into the second year of his apprenticeship he wrote home saying he was beginning to hate the constant drudgery. On the face of it, he gave the impression of struggling to get along with some fellow crew members. In other letters, Crabb moaned about tropical storms, the poor standard of food, his fluctuating health and the lack of hygiene. But he was always known as something of a 'moaner', and at first, I considered it could have been any one or all of these problems that may have helped influence his decision to quit. Other archive papers confirm he also turned down an opportunity to take a second mate's ticket, opting to leave the ship on arrival back in New York.

I was still not convinced this was the whole story. It seemed an insufficient reason for leaving such a promising career. Surely something more serious was the cause. Following further discussion with his cousins, and after scouring additional family archive material, I finally discovered the reason. It seems there was a major scandal. Lionel's adopted aunt Kitty Jarvis had an affair with a Mr Pitt, one of her husband's best friends. Frank, and Kitty's father, Charles Bishop, tracked the couple to France. The men eventually persuaded Kitty not only to return, but also to sign a legal agreement promising not to run away again.

By modern standards this episode may not seem all that serious, but during the mid-1920s it must have been devastating for the young sailor and for his cousins back home. It must have come as a total bombshell for Crabb's mentor, Frank Jarvis, and for his close business associates and high society friends.

Unfortunately for Frank, his health began to suffer. The scandal also marked the beginning of the end for the Jarvis family as Lionel had known it. Frank and Kitty had been fun-loving surrogate parents, who shared with him their home, holidays and family outings. He could not have wished for a warmer family atmosphere.

Regular correspondence between Kenneth and Frank confirmed some more of the details, but Lionel found it all hard to believe. He had nowhere to turn, and no one he could trust or confide in. Suddenly his life was torn apart. It was too far to return home, and apart from his mother's house, he wondered if his life would ever be the same again. As for the notorious Mr Pitt, both the Crabb and Jarvis families had welcomed him so his affair with Kitty must have seemed a bitter betrayal.

Charleen Miller, Frank and Kitty's granddaughter, confirms this:

We certainly knew about Mr Pitt. Mother and Kitty used to talk about him. We never heard his Christian name used. He lived in Bushey, Hertfordshire, near to my grandparents. We knew they had gone off to France together but came home within a week. I don't think she ever met up with him again.

I don't know what he did for a living. He was definitely married, as his wife was mentioned once. But I don't think Kitty and Frank were very happy, and I never heard either Mother or Kitty talk of him at all. As far as I know there were no love letters when she died. Maybe Frank just put every waking hour into the firm, and she felt neglected, or perhaps it was because he wasn't happy that he put everything into his job. We shall never know.

Another of Kitty's granddaughters, Lomond Handley, adds:

Granny Jarvis, Frank's wife, was undoubtedly a great beauty in her day, and she was also very smart and bright. She had many admirers and had a 'fling' with one of Grandad's best friends. He was obviously very keen on her and it upset Frank very much, and probably made him drink more. Mr Pitt was a married man, and his boss was also his father-in-law, who made it clear that if 'Pitty' failed to stick by his own wife, he'd be out of a job.

After grandfather died, Granny Kitty was free – but Mr Pitt wasn't because his father-in-law threatened to sack him if he ever strayed again. I gather that at some point the couple had a tiff and both waited by their respective telephones hoping each would call to make it up. Neither did.

Lionel Crabb was ashamed and embarrassed. In further letters home, he admitted he was struggling to cope. He said that after quitting his job he felt a failure. Kitty's affair, and his decision to interrupt his seafaring career, marked a major turning point in his life. He was reluctant to return home and told Kenneth he couldn't face his mother, and listen to her 'told you so' attitude.

He opted to see something of America, and explained that he had often heard 'wonder' stories about people making their fortune in the States, and particularly in the Texan oilfields. He wondered if all the rumours were true, and later told friends that he thought it better to let the dust settle first before returning.

A couple of weeks later, his mother finally received a letter from Lionel confirming his American travel plans. Far from being angry or disappointed, Daisy was pleased to have at least received some news from him. She told Frank she understood his reasons and even sympathised.

She recalled the time when Lionel's father, Hugh, had travelled halfway round the world to Australia, trying to build a new life, just before the First World War. This time, work and money were said to be plentiful in America. Lionel just wanted to try his luck. He was convinced it would work out, but was unable to persuade anyone else from his ship to join him. His oil rush therefore became a brave solo effort, which eventually led to a unique journey of discovery.

Chapter 4

Jack of all Trades

Lionel Crabb was an exhibitionist. Throughout his life, he generally attracted a 'love–hate' relationship with most people he met. To some, he had an overbearing personality, and could be awkward, obstinate, and pompous. Others found him amusing and highly entertaining.

By late 1929, Crabb was a little man in a big hurry. Despite a promising start to his trek across America his enthusiasm waned, and when he reached a small one-horse town called Windgap, situated in the eastern district of Pittsburgh, Pennsylvania, his extraordinary adventure ground to a halt. Here, he obtained some basic accommodation in exchange for a job at a gas station owned by the Shell Eastern Petroleum Company.

This was to become the nearest he ever came towards realising his oilfields dream. Years later, he told his best chum Maitland Pendock that he loved the American social scene. Maitland said Crabb became a hard drinker, a chain smoker and a gambler. He enjoyed life to the full, and yet only remained in Pennsylvania just long enough to raise funds to pay his way back home.

Crabb told Maitland the experience had been fantastic. He said he had undertaken a variety of menial jobs but had loved every minute of it. He also said this was the place where he developed an instinct for survival, and where he had finally grown up. He accepted that most problems in life had been of his own making but in conversation with Navy colleagues Crabb admitted he always felt more at home with strangers than with family and friends.

On returning from his travels, and some considerable time after Kitty's affair, Lionel was thankful to be welcomed back by all his family. There was no animosity and Frank understood his decision to quit his apprenticeship. Lionel also told his mother that he had learned a valuable lesson. Within weeks, though, he had started to feel bored and frustrated with life in suburbia. He explained to Kenneth that he was becoming desperate for money and needed a new challenge. On one of his frequent trips back to the city to lunch with former naval colleagues, Lionel occasionally met Maitland Pendock, an old school friend. Maitland was an entrepreneur, and a well-known local businessman. Their paths were to cross many times, but for the present, Maitland spoke to him about a temporary six-month contract working for an exclusive funeral parlour in Manhattan, New York.

A deal was agreed, and with his expenses paid, Lionel soon re-crossed the Atlantic. Archive notes suggest he probably worked 'front of house', and was later taught the process of embalming. For much of the time he also remained on the wagon, and even attended a few church meetings.

When the contract expired, and with his confidence boosted, Lionel returned to England, but faced bleak prospects. He again went back to live with his mother but returned to London as often as possible. One day, quite by chance, Lionel met an old family friend, another distant cousin, who my Crabb family contacts believe was one of 'aunt' Kate and 'uncle' Thomas Honniball's four sons. Kate was Frank Jarvis's sister. The Honniballs enjoyed a very privileged lifestyle.

Crabb's cousin, Lomond Handley, says that: 'The four Honniball boys were very close to my mother's family. They all attended Epsom College and Uncle Evan was extremely wealthy and very knowledgeable. Mother never mentioned it but she knew the Jarvis family had its share of heavy drinkers.'

Mr Honniball was a director of a big city bank, and each offspring received a rather generous monthly allowance. This allowance, however, provided little incentive to work, and even funded this particular cousin's luxury apartment in central London. Lionel and the cousin chatted, drank and slowly renewed their friendship. The cousin was going through a difficult time and persuaded Crabb to stay, and later to move in with him, at least on a temporary basis.

His cousin said he wanted to introduce him to his friends, and to show Lionel the growing London social scene. This generally included going on late-night drinking sprees to gentlemen's clubs and other high-class establishments.

Here, Crabb met many influential members of the aristocracy. He also noticed how many of these so-called new friends were 'stinking rich', with plenty of time on their hands. Several were understood to be the sons of gentry, who nominally worked for respectable city law firms, or financial institutions.

Crabb felt uncomfortable and at times out of his depth. Despite his passion for socialising, he later claimed he had found it difficult to keep up. After a while Crabb said he had had enough. He spoke with his cousin Kenneth, and admitted feeling slightly ashamed of taking advantage of his Honniball cousin's generous hospitality. Lionel was making arrangements to leave when the young man's parents suddenly arrived. He expected a severe scolding, but to his utter surprise, they thanked him for his friendship. They said they understood his reasons for wanting to leave and praised the fact he had already held down a few jobs, and had travelled to many interesting parts of the world. The parents explained they wanted someone reliable to take their son away from London, and asked if he would be willing to undertake an unusual challenge, sharing a long holiday, and supported by a generous payment.

Lionel told Kenneth he had been embarrassed by their request but said the parents insisted he was the man for the job. They wanted him to accompany their son on a luxury steamboat passage to China and the Far East. The Honniball family hoped to cure their son of a growing addiction to drink and possibly drugs. Lionel, who had always been fascinated by thoughts of the Far East, accepted their proposal. But later, when Lionel raised the matter with Frank, he was shocked to learn that the Jarvises already knew all about the plans.

Lionel always travelled light. He had only limited resources and hastily stuffed his few belongings into a couple of battered old cases. The following day his well-heeled friend travelled down with him to Southampton. There, the pair watched from the top deck of the cruise ship as an army of porters struggled along the quayside with trunk after trunk of bespoke gentlemen's accessories, all considered essential for such a long journey.

His cousin also employed a valet, and Lionel's jaw dropped when he saw a huge gramophone and an oak chest packed full of records inside the prestigious cabin. Crabb couldn't help thinking just how much his life had changed in such a short space of time. And just as he had sometimes experienced in his childhood, Crabb could feel and smell the taste of pampered luxury.

As he sat up on his bed, he found a letter from his mother tucked away in his luggage. It practically repeated the comments of his cousin's parents. Suddenly the penny dropped. He now understood why he had been personally selected for this task. He also understood the smile on Frank Jarvis's face. The closeness of the two families was evident. It seemed both parties had agreed to jointly fund the trip. They thought it the best way forward for both wayward boys, but Lionel faced a huge responsibility – and hoped he might prove worthy of the trust placed in him.

The boys endured a fairly rough outward sea voyage, and later, a somewhat turbulent relationship, especially when his cousin discovered that Lionel was being paid to look after him, and had been ordered to hide the booze. Lionel felt embarrassed and pleaded with his friend to ease up on his alcohol-fuelled lifestyle. Unfortunately, though, Lionel could not watch over his cousin every minute of the day and night. Nor did he have the financial clout to prevent his cousin from bribing the crew to get him what he wanted.

At the next port of call, Lionel sent an urgent cable home asking for help and advice. He was ordered not to let his charge out of his sight. It became mission impossible, and following several manic days of desperation, and with his own nerves in tatters, Crabb finally decided: 'If you can't beat them, join them!' The two youngsters then indulged in a few all-day benders until he could stand it no more.

By the time they reached Singapore from Shanghai on the return leg, the pair were barely speaking, and Lionel decided to throw in the towel. Before sending a final message back to his cousin's worried parents, he discharged his final duty by making sure his cousin was sober and safely back on board. He handed the luggage keys to the valet, and with a huge sigh of relief wished them *bon voyage*. Crabb was more than glad to jump ship. He drew his remaining wages and secured a simple room at the local hostelry, where he began to drown his sorrows again.

Lionel Crabb stayed in Singapore for several months. He gradually curbed his dependence upon alcohol and began to make many new friends. He also attempted to learn the language. The phonetic sounds, the colourful silks and light clothing and culture all fascinated him. Unfortunately Lionel was tone deaf. As a schoolboy he had been barred from joining the choir and attending music lessons, so learning Chinese or Mandarin was always going to be a difficult task. He loved the regular street entertainment and colourful processions, and soon his own unorthodox actions and support gained him many new friends and a rather zany reputation.

Back in England, Frank Jarvis's Conway Stewart pen business continued to prosper. Frank put his heart and soul into the firm and enjoyed many successful sales trips at home and abroad. With several new brands already established, Frank decided to take out a lease on a new property at 75–82 Shoe Lane, London. This remained the Conway Stewart headquarters until 1948. However, when the Depression of the 1930s began to bite, Frank and his partners looked for additional ways to attract business. They cut back on production of their own brands and started making cheaper pens for other companies, which at least kept some cash flowing and helped to generate a lucrative alternative income.

On his return to London from the Far East, Lionel was slightly wary of going home, as by then he believed his cousin would have already claimed the moral high ground. He knew his cousin had arrived home safely, but again Crabb was jobless and penniless. He contacted Maitland Pendock to see if he could find him some work.

By this time, Maitland was involved in promoting a host of new enterprises in the field of advertising, marketing and promotions. He looked Crabb up and down. Maitland thought he looked a mess and gave him some money to buy a change of clothes. He decided, though, that he still looked fit and gave him a chance. He handed him a card with a name and address for a temporary job the following day at a Soho agency. Lionel smiled, drained his glass and put the documents in his top pocket.

Maitland said he was to be a model for gentlemen's underwear. Lionel hated the idea but was desperate for some cash. Fortunately, he always remained fairly slim throughout his life and had a small appetite to match his stature.

He was only 5ft 6in tall and had a V-shaped body, with broad shoulders, slim hips and strong, sturdy legs. He also had a couple of webbed toes, which were a source of embarrassment to Crabb and amusement to others, prompting the predictable frog or duck impressions. Because of this minor deformity, over the years his associates said Crabb detested taking his clothes off in public. However, Lionel was a generally good-looking young man with long sideburns, darkish hair and hazel eyes and the distinguishing characteristic of beard tufts on his cheeks.

The next morning, nursing a familiar hangover, Crabb walked through Soho struggling to read Maitland's instructions. He was shocked to visit Soho for the first time. Prostitutes were openly touting for business at 10 a.m. on a cold morning. On reaching the address, he gazed skywards to a top-floor window where the logo for an advertising and photographic agency was etched into the dirty glass.

With trepidation he climbed the stairs. At the door of the top office he knocked and entered. Before him stood a painfully thin man in his late fifties with a cigarette dangling freely from the corner of his mouth, and a large flash camera slung around his neck. 'Are you Crabb?' Lionel nodded and handed him Maitland's note. 'You're late. Hurry up and get changed.'

Lionel looked around for the changing rooms but the man pointed to an old wooden chair in the far corner of the room, and saw some plain-looking underclothes hanging from a rail. As Lionel argued, the man told him to 'either strip or leave'. He held up a new type of protective sports truss, and some other skimpy underwear. Crabb later claimed that attending this 'studio' and taking orders from someone like him was among the most humiliating experiences of his life. He tried on the garments but insisted on keeping his hat on.

The photographer was not bothered in the slightest. He just kept clicking away and mumbling to himself. Each time he spoke he coughed and a long trail of ash fell to the floor. When he finally said something coherent, the photographer explained that he was only interested in the underwear. He said Crabb's face would not be used. He was a man of few words. To Crabb the whole experience seemed the longest, most tortured of his life. When it was over, he rushed to change and left in such a dash that he almost forgot to get his work card signed. He raced down the stairs and out into the fresh air.

Within minutes he had a strong drink in his shaking hands, before leaving to challenge Maitland back at his office. He told him about his embarrassment and pledged 'never again'. Maitland laughed. The photographer was a pal of his. He had already been on the telephone. He only wanted a few pictures of a new sports truss and said he hadn't the heart to stop Lionel putting on his flatmate's old jock strap and underpants. As he recalled this Maitland laughed out loud – and told him that beggars couldn't be choosers! He handed him a few guineas, and then took him out for lunch.

As they chatted, Lionel explained he certainly didn't want a nine-to-five office job. He said he was now ready for something out of the ordinary. He said he really wanted something that could pay for a grand holiday in the sun, preferably by a swimming pool.

The word 'pool' struck a chord. Maitland was still grinning about Lionel's last job. He was a large man with a rosy face and a great barrel chest. He was smart but slightly eccentric. He laughed again. Maitland then told Crabb that he had just the thing – and said he could start tomorrow. When they arrived back at his office, he made a couple of phone calls before going to his filing cabinet, pulling out a small brown paper parcel and dropping it on the desk.

Ever curious, Lionel asked what it was all about. Maitland smiled again, and said this idea had come from an eccentric, if not crazy, French inventor called Louis de Corlieu. He said the man had developed a revolutionary new product called 'flippers'. He claimed they were a form of swimming aid. He carefully unpacked the parcel and stared at two large slip-on black rubber shoes. They had broad tapered ends.

Crabb remembered the hurtful remarks about ducks and suddenly became wary. He lifted them up to his nose. There was a powerful smell of strong rubber and something else, chlorine perhaps? They certainly had the smell of the local baths, where de Corlieu had been testing them.

Crabb put them back on the desk. He wrapped them back in the paper and said they looked and smelled like stale fish and chips. Crabb wondered what was coming next and saw Maitland scribble something down on another work 'chitty'. He told him it was the ideal job. 'Somewhere warm by a pool,' he laughed, adding, '11 o'clock sharp tomorrow at Marshall Street Baths.'

Maitland said the inventor would also be present for a demonstration of his flippers. Both thought they looked ridiculous, and although Lionel Crabb was not a great swimmer, he doubted any claims that they would provide extra power and direction. This time he was paid up front. He received five £1 notes and some loose change for a black 'wake-up' coffee. Lionel looked surprised when his friend explained that he would probably need it, to help him sober up. The next day, he arrived dead on time. He went to the changing rooms and put on his swimming trunks. As he came poolside, he saw the photographer from the previous shoot. He seemed to be laughing with Maitland. Lionel, who was wrapped in a dressing gown, hoped they were not laughing at his expense. Then the photographer asked if they were his trunks or his flatmate's? The joke was not funny to Crabb. He felt annoyed and acutely embarrassed, and just as he was about to give them a piece of his mind a tall foreign gentleman with a small goatee beard swept along the edge of the pool. The man was accompanied by a rather large lady in a colourful swimming costume. She had a pair of these new flippers tucked under her arm. As the inventor explained the object of the exercise and the reasons for the photographer, Lionel's heart sank again. He told Maitland that he didn't want to do any more photographs.

He claimed it was too embarrassing – especially after all the sniggering. He said it wasn't part of the deal but Maitland showed him his signature on the chitty and pointed to the cameraman who was busy demisting his lens. The photographer had another cigarette hanging from his mouth, and repeated his statement from the previous assignment, that he didn't want pictures of Crabb's face. 'Feet only this time,' he demanded.

As they spoke and exchanged grimaces, the woman dived into the water. She resurfaced, swam over to the steps and put on her flippers. She started to splash about once more. The group had to restrain themselves from laughing. She resembled a large seal. 'More splashing,' demanded the inventor, waving impatiently at the scruffy photographer.

The whole episode was hilarious, but Crabb didn't want to be any part of this freak show. As the men spoke with the woman at the far end of the baths, Crabb took his leave and left through a side door. He hastily changed and within minutes he was in the pub across the road.

A few days later, Maitland and de Corlieu turned up at Lionel Crabb's local, the Nag's Head in Kinnerton Street, Knightsbridge. They surprised him. At the time, Crabb was busy entertaining the landlord with exaggerated stories about his latest adventures. The businessmen entered with solemn faces but were soon full of smiles. The whole episode had been rigged and rehearsed. They had organised it as a huge joke. They knew he wouldn't do it – but agreed they still needed someone else to test out this flipper invention. Maitland demanded that Crabb should pay for the next round, as he had already pocketed the fee.

He then introduced the Frenchman. Crabb quickly put his anger aside and took to the man straight away. Lionel apologised for leaving the demonstration. The man accepted his apology, and said it didn't really matter, as he wanted to talk about something else. The inventor carried a small suitcase packed with samples.

He told Crabb he needed someone to help promote his new ideas. He said he had produced some unusual new material from a special type of thread called 'Sewing Kapok'. He said that through his overseas contacts he had developed this revolutionary new thread from naturally grown, lightweight fibres. For once Crabb was speechless.

He had seen and admired some similar silks in China and Singapore. He marvelled at their delicate touch. A few drinks later and de Corlieu gave Lionel a list of potential customers in and around London. He offered him the sample case and asked him to come to his office for a demonstration the next day. The Frenchman said there was no reason why Crabb couldn't work for him on commission.

Lionel thought for a few seconds and then turned him down. He said he was no mug, and told the inventor it would have to be a partnership, or no deal. Crabb had recognised a bargain. And with his experience of delicate lightweight silks, he believed he might at last be on to a winner. The inventor screwed up his face and looked back at Maitland, who smiled and nodded. After muttering a few choice words in French, the inventor agreed. They all shook hands, and this time it was the Frenchman who ordered another round.

Maitland winked at Crabb and gave him a pat on the back. His friend had already agreed to underwrite any start-up costs, and was acting as an agent for other potential investors. 'You're learning!' Maitland told him. Within days, the former merchant sailor was on his way to becoming a super-salesman. He began visiting dress shops, clothing designers and fashion stores with samples of pillows, bedding and insulation products. Everyone admired the quality and shared his enthusiasm.

Crabb felt happy and contented. Within weeks sales were booming, and when he arrived back one day with an extremely large order and another important new contract, the Frenchman threw his arms around Crabb and kissed him on both of his hairy cheeks. For possibly the first time in his life, he felt part of a quite unusual success story.

At the beginning of December 1932, the Jarvis family received the first of two mortal blows that were to mark the end of their close-knit family group. On the third of the month, Frank Jarvis died from typhoid fever at his home near Watford. He was just fifty-one years old. He had been the linchpin of Conway Stewart and the company consequently suffered a huge financial loss.

Following Frank's death, his brother Stanley became responsible for the day-to-day running of the business, working alongside partners and fellow founders Rex Gardner and Bob Fry. Tensions mounted however, and family rifts occurred. The firm began to reorganise, and a short time later, Frank's only son Kenneth joined the board. He was introduced to sales and began to travel extensively, adding a calm hand to maintain a strong family influence. Lomond Handley recalls:

My grandfather loved oysters and drinking Guinness. Unfortunately, he ate a duff batch of them one evening from a stall in a London market just after leaving a Conway Stewart board meeting. Regrettably, grandfather Jarvis drank too much when he'd made his money, which weakened his constitution. When he contracted typhoid fever from these oysters his system failed. And according to my mother, the family GP, Dr Davidson – who was a great family friend – said if Frank hadn't been a drinker, he might have survived.

Family archives suggest that Frank started to drink more heavily following Kitty's affair with his friend Mr Pitt. The family also agree that by then, alcoholism had become a familiar problem for other members of the family. Not long after Frank's death, Kitty was forced to sell the family home at Allendale. She bought a flat in London. Charleen Miller says:

> The impact of this was devastating in terms of Conway Stewart. Mother always said the other directors cut Kitty out from that day on. Mother said they 'feathered their own nests', and Kitty had very little to do with the firm from that time. It was always a sore point that the widow of the founder should have so quickly afterwards been forced to move to cheaper accommodation, and when she eventually died she didn't leave a single penny.

It took Lionel Crabb some time to get over the sudden loss of Frank Jarvis. Frank had become a second father, a mentor, a companion and a confidant to him. He had sponsored and supported Lionel's education and career through thick and thin. And although Crabb retained a healthy relationship with Kitty and his cousins, he said the 'sparkle had gone out of his life'. He also admitted that the 'family environment' was never quite the same again. General get-togethers became far more infrequent, leaving each member to get on with their own lives. Paradoxically, Crabb was now able to hold his head high after more than a decade of despair, struggles and failures. He found it extremely sad that Frank had not been around to celebrate his success and to see his faith in Lionel justified.

Quite remarkably, Crabb finally became a successful businessman, and could now compete on an equal footing with his friend Maitland and his new French partner de Corlieu. With money in his pocket, boosted by a moderate inheritance from Frank's estate, Crabb surprisingly dissolved the business agreement, claiming he needed a break. He made plans to return to Singapore and the Far East as quickly as he could. He claimed a desire to learn something of the oriental culture and way of life.

Crabb had kept in touch with several people from his previous visit and accepted an offer of accommodation from the son of one of his contacts. He told his family he didn't know how long he would be out there. It now appears this was not entirely true because he had made firm arrangements with people in Singapore and Shanghai, and according to archive notes, he may even have offered some limited financial support in the fight against Communism.

Crabb certainly used the bulk of his inheritance to fund a longer stay in Singapore, and he visited other parts of Asia. He felt this was an ideal opportunity to go while he still had the funds. In addition, he could see that trouble was brewing across Europe, where the Nazi Party was establishing a worrying dominance over a revived Germany. Crabb was well aware of the problems in the Far East. His former contacts had kept him posted; particularly concerning the civil war in China, battles against the warlords, and growing pockets of resistance against the Communist threat. His family have spoken recently of confidential letters and scribbled notes from Singapore, but unfortunately they were all destroyed during the Second World War, when Kitty's flat was bombed.

Chapter 5

Going East

Sometime in 1936, Lionel Crabb set sail for a second time towards the troubled Far East. He told his family he planned to visit Hong Kong, Singapore and the Chinese mainland, and unbeknown to Daisy, Kitty and his family, he later admitted that he expected to find trouble.

He felt his time had come and later claimed that he was determined to experience war at first hand. He told his cousin Kenneth that he had always felt great support and affection for the Chinese nation. He began to develop a strong affiliation with rebel supporters for an independent China, and spoke about the battle against the ever-growing Communist threat. Much of the basic story about Lionel's Far East activities was first reported to Kitty, and then via her daughters Eileen and Audrey to their own children. Lomond, who is Eileen's daughter, recalls some details of Lionel's life as a trainee spy, freedom fighter or mercenary. She says:

The family knew about all his spying activities. He lived with a family in China for just over a year. He was a gunrunner and spy against the Communists. He loved dressing up and, being quite small, he was able to blend in very well. Lionel had dark almond eyes and a dark complexion. He even dyed his hair to look like a Chinaman. He coloured his skin and became a master of disguise, even letting his hair grow. He carried messages on rice paper within his pigtails and on bamboo poles. Mother always said he went out to Singapore and China to fight the Communists.

Ma said Lionel worked as an undertaker in China and carried bodies as well as messages between enemy lines. I gather the bodies were good cover for his work, as no one was ever keen to get too near to a body, which might have died of plague, or some nasty illness, and he was able to come and go throughout all the lines.

So Lionel was able to draw on the training he had had as an embalmer and undertaker in America, shortly after returning from his SS *Bonheur* travels. And as soon as Lionel arrived in Singapore, he later told Kitty, he met up with some former contacts. Many had apparently since been recruited to fight the Communists. He said he was introduced to some political leaders, who gave him a brief insight into the problems. It had been several years since his visit as a chaperon to his alcoholic cousin, but in the years since a bloody civil war had raged out of control on the mainland, and the situation was worsening daily. China was at the mercy of some extreme economic and military policies, with various revolutionary leaders emerging all the time. Lionel told his family that it took him some time to gain their trust. Initially, he remained in Singapore, demonstrating his embalming skills. He first lived with a local family and learned a few useful phrases while looking after the family's young child. Crabb said it provided useful cover until he met representatives of the local resistance movement.

In later years he opened up to Kitty all about his work, and said he had found it easy to make new contacts. He confirmed that, as the war escalated and casualties began to increase, he was told by one leader that his undertaking experience would prove essential. He then met with members of an underground movement, and said that after a brief period of training, he was shipped out to Shanghai under cover of darkness, where he was introduced to another European, who, just like Crabb, had originally come from London. He was a large fiery character who was introduced to Lionel as Morris Abraham Cohen. He was of Polish descent and had previously lived and worked with the Chinese in Canada.

The man also went under the nickname of Morris 'Two Guns' Cohen. Born in the East End of London in 1889, Cohen had endured a difficult and dangerous life after being thrown out of England as a pickpocket. He was a gambler, a hustler, a conman and a womaniser. He and Crabb got along famously, and once each had gained the other's confidence, they worked together fairly often.

Cohen came from a poverty-stricken Polish and Jewish background, and for years 'worked' the streets of Whitechapel. When he was just thirteen and desperate for food, he was caught pickpocketing. He was jailed and committed to the Hayes Industrial Reform School for wayward Jewish boys, an institution designed to teach youngsters the error of their ways.

On completing his sentence, Cohen was shipped out to the Colonies. He ended up travelling across to Canada, visiting the Western Provinces and British Columbia and spending time in Edmonton and Alberta. Cohen also served in the First World War in a Canadian unit, where he first came across Chinese labourers digging trenches for Allied troops. After the war though, and with little hope of ever being allowed back to Britain, or seeing his family again, Cohen began to earn a living in Canada as a gambler and street entertainer.

He was a rough, tough character, who learned to shoot, and to defend himself. He also competed for cash in bare-knuckle fights. In Saskatoon he got to know several Chinese owners of gambling dens. He enjoyed their food, culture and company; and some later hired him as a bodyguard against thieves. One day, his services were needed to defend one of the owners from a notorious gang of robbers. By this time, Cohen had married, settled down and gained the respect of the Chinese community. However the Canadian authorities, knowing his criminal record and reputation, threatened to arrest him for conspiracy. He was forced to flee and, supported by Chinese immigrants, finally arrived in the Far East.

News of Cohen's accomplishments was made known to an emerging young Chinese leader Chiang Kai-Shek, and within a short time he was appointed as his bodyguard. Chiang was a wealthy and well-educated man who was determined to help restore China to its former glory. He too was an experienced fighter who had attended the national military academy, and received military training in the Soviet Union. He had also served with the Japanese Army.

Cohen took to Crabb straight away, and hired him to teach his colleagues about embalming and burial procedures. He also acted as a go-between, negotiating supplies with foreign agents. In addition, archive notes agree that Crabb worked as a messenger, spy and gunrunner. The family also confirmed conversations between Crabb and Kitty and Kenneth, claiming that guns and ammunition were sometimes hidden under bodies, or within makeshift coffins. And due to the nature of his work and the state of some of the casualties, Crabb explained that he was generally given safe passage unopposed. Crabb said he was again billeted with a young family in a Shanghai suburb. And although he could only speak a little Chinese, he rapidly gained a reputation for his bravery, by regularly criss-crossing military lines with information, supplies and war casualties.

As Chiang Kai-Shek rose to power, both he and Cohen had contact with the British Secret Intelligence Service (SIS), later known as MI6, who helped fund part of their campaign against Communism and Japanese militarism. Official documents recently released give Cohen due credit for helping to establish an essential link to the West, and for playing a leading role in ongoing negotiations with the Communists, to counter the threat of a Japanese invasion.

During various skirmishes Cohen was shot in the arm. After that, he always carried the two guns that established his celebrity title. The Chinese marvelled at his ability to fire two guns, if necessary, at the same time. He eventually became a national hero but like Crabb, could also speak little Chinese.

The family claim Crabb spent about eighteen months serving in the Far East. In conversations, he later revealed a close working relationship with Cohen and other rebel militants. Crabb tried to play down his own role, but always spoke highly of Morris Cohen, and said he had once rescued Chiang Kai-Shek from the Communists. Recent papers also acknowledge that Cohen persuaded his leader to call a halt to the civil war, to save lives, and to support a joint campaign against the Japanese invaders. Chiang Kai-Shek and his considerable forces were eventually withdrawn to Taiwan, where they helped secure a strong military base, and played a continuing role in East–West relations. According to Crabb's family, he told his Far East colleagues sometime in 1938 that he needed to return to Britain to fight another war.

His cousin Kenneth Jarvis said Lionel was a patriot and a very brave man for taking such a positive stand against Communism. Crabb also received plaudits from Cohen for his efforts, and as a farewell gift his colleagues presented him with a magnificent piece of jade, two ceramic dogs and a selection of fine silks. He particularly admired the jade and silks but wondered how on earth he would ever get the dogs back home.

Chapter 6

Anthony Blunt and Friends

In time-honoured tradition, Lionel Crabb took the first available passage back to England. He had left the UK as a reasonably wealthy man but after paying his expenses for the best part of two years, and contributing funds towards the rebel cause, he soon found that his bank balance, like his spirit, was drained.

He secured a small but comfortable berth close to the boiler room on a tramp steamer home. It was fairly dirty and smelly but it was cheap and warm. Moreover the mixed nationality crew seemed friendly enough and his recent Chinese connections ensured he ate and drank well. Crabb did not particularly want to return home but his job was done, and as he returned to England in the autumn of 1938 he knew that war in Europe was inevitable. He had written ahead to his old friend Maitland Pendock but had not heard back from him.

Crabb was unable to contact his friend by telephone, and had no idea where he was now living or working. He had just about enough money for a few drinks and thought he would contact Pendock the next day. In London, it was cold, wet and getting dark. As he wandered aimlessly down the street, he came across the Cavendish Hotel on Duke Street. It was a luxury establishment. He went into the bar and a few hours later fell asleep drunk in the main lounge with his head resting on a table. He began snoring loudly. The Cavendish at that time was considered one of London's top hotels and Lionel Crabb was quickly spotted and awoken by a very angry owner, Rosa Lewis. She was short and skinny, and appeared to be in her fifties. She had a sour expression, a wrinkled face and was covered with glittering jewellery.

Rosa did not take kindly to drunks or unwanted visitors, and demanded to know what this long-haired, dirty, dishevelled man was doing in her hotel. Lionel woke with a start. He apologised and said he was searching for his old friend Maitland Pendock, and had tried to make contact without success. 'Can you give me a free room and a job?' he asked Rosa. 'Anything will do!' Rosa looked him up and down. There was something about him despite his appearance, and she had to admire his cheek. 'The Duchess of Duke Street', as Rosa was known, told Crabb he needed a bath, a shave and a haircut. She said she knew Maitland, and claimed he was away, but said he had moved to new premises nearby. 'Tell me,' she demanded. 'Why should I give you a job, even if you are a friend of a friend?'

Crabb asked her for a chance. He said he just needed something temporary. Rosa hesitated for a moment. 'All right,' she said, 'You can have the box room for a few days. You can start work tomorrow, after you have cleaned yourself up! But I suggest you get some rest; you look exhausted.'

Crabb was delighted, though completely wrecked. He remained seated and leaned forward on the table with his head in his hands. Rosa was about to walk away when suddenly she stopped and asked him: 'So why a temporary job?'

Crabb lifted his sleepy head and slowly replied: 'Because I'm a fighter. I want to join the Navy and when this war starts, I want to fight the Germans.'

Rosa smiled: 'A Navy man. Arthur, get the Admiral a better room. He can have one of the rooms on the top floor. He will be quite comfortable there. When was the last time you had anything to eat?'

Crabb groaned and pulled a face. He had no idea.

'A bowl of hot soup and some sandwiches for our guest!' ordered Rosa. 'He can have them in his room.'

Crabb agreed to stay and work for a week but ended up staying for over a year. Whether he ever paid a penny in rent is anyone's guess. Crabb appeared about 10 a.m. the next day, still looking the worse for wear. Rosa joined him for a black coffee and gave him some money and directions to the nearest barber and clothes shops. She asked him to come back for lunch. Despite her hard appearance Rosa didn't have the heart to put Lionel to work on his first full day back. While he was out, she telephoned Maitland's office and left a message with his secretary that a certain Lionel Crabb had returned.

A couple of days later Crabb was sitting at the hotel bar when Rosa and Maitland approached him. He nearly jumped off his stool in surprise at seeing Maitland again, and quickly shook his friend's hand. Lionel felt awkward about the fact that he still hadn't done any work for Rosa. 'I'll start tomorrow, I promise,' he said.

Rosa was relaxed. She smiled at Crabb, saying: 'Don't worry. Talk with your friend. You have plenty to catch up on.'

Maitland insisted that Rosa stay and they chatted until a group of smartly dressed gentlemen entered, whom Maitland duly acknowledged. He shook hands with some of them. They were city art dealers. 'Now about this job,' he said to Lionel. 'You're only in town five minutes and already you're causing trouble with Rosa. She can find you some temporary work, I gather. But now you want to join the war. You'll have to wait, Lionel. It's not started yet!'

Maitland was laughing. He said: 'So, let's look at your CV. Most proper jobs so far have involved working for me. Before that, you had an apprenticeship with the Merchant Navy, which you failed to complete. You worked for a few months as a gas station attendant in America, and then quit. You were a chaperon to a rich alcoholic friend on a Far East cruise, but abandoned him. Now, here's the interesting part – you worked for me in a mortuary as an embalmer. And then you modelled some underwear,' he said, winking at Rosa. 'But didn't you also reject the chance to model some flippers? And eventually, you became a salesman for a foreign textile gentleman – backed by MY money! It's all very interesting – but it's hardly the best CV in the world.

'So, what next? Where have you been?' Maitland asked. 'We missed hearing about all your exciting adventures, isn't that right, Rosa?' Rosa, too, was laughing.

Crabb swallowed the rest of his drink in one gulp, and ordered something stronger. He looked annoyed. 'I've been in China, Singapore and Hong Kong,' he said.

'Doing precisely what?' asked Maitland.

'Working as a spy, a gunrunner, and a messenger. I wore disguise and helped ship supplies out to fight the Chinese Communists. I also had a pop at the Japs.'

Rosa's eyes lit up. 'A spy,' she exclaimed. 'How fascinating. You must tell me more!'

Maitland looked surprised. 'Lionel, if you're after a job, this could be your lucky day,' he suggested. 'These men have come to celebrate the opening of a new art gallery and antique store, I think it's called "Cameo Corner". They are looking for staff, not spies! And they're certainly looking for new customers. What do you think, old chap?'

Lionel wasn't quite sure what to think. He wasn't certain whether his friend and Rosa had planned something. They chatted some more and in between, Lionel kept glancing across to the table where the gentlemen were sitting. About twenty minutes later, Maitland went across to the party. He looked back towards the bar and Lionel saw one of the men hand Maitland a business card. They shook hands and he rejoined Lionel and Rosa. A few minutes later the men left and Maitland handed Crabb the card.

'You are to go to their shop at 2 p.m. tomorrow. Here's the address,' Maitland said, 'Don't let them down, Lionel. Good luck and I'm sorry, Rosa, you might be losing your best worker. It's an interview for a job selling paintings and drawings. Nothing too hazardous.'

They carried on drinking for another ten minutes or so, before Rosa suggested Lionel get some sleep. She agreed that he could keep his room for the time being. Crabb stood up and thanked them both. His thoughts, though, were still fixed on the next war.

Crabb enjoyed working at the exclusive gallery. He had to sell quality landscapes, portraits and drawings, lots of oils and watercolours. The gallery rapidly gained in popularity with London's elite. And Crabb soon felt quite at home chatting with customers. Some of his early visitors included his mother Daisy, all his cousins, and even Aunt Kitty, who lived in a fine apartment close by.

Kitty was always a great supporter of the arts and bought several pictures from the gallery, regularly introducing more new clients. Crabb found the job easy, and although he had not given up on his ambition to join the Navy, he decided his current position would do. He continued to live at the Cavendish and even persuaded the gallery management to hold a few private promotions there. At least that way, he thought, he was helping to repay Rosa's kindness.

Maitland was another regular visitor, as were many military and civil service personnel, who often preferred to talk about potential purchases with more senior staff. Crabb noticed that people kept disappearing into the main office with the manager. Business was brisk despite what was happening in the world, and Crabb felt he didn't have to use much persuasion to sell pictures.

He told Rosa that most customers had plenty of time and money, and just wanted to spend it on something that would be the envy of their friends. The light duties also allowed Lionel much free time to study aircraft recognition and naval gunnery techniques back at the hotel.

Stephen Ward, a notable pastel artist and osteopath to the rich and famous, attended one important social event at the Cavendish. Years later Ward was to introduce Christine Keeler to John Profumo, later killing himself as the 'Profumo Affair' unfolded. Meanwhile, Ward mingled with Maitland, prominent artists and other contemporary stars of the British stage and screen.

Lionel Crabb was talking to some people at the bar when his friend introduced him to his influential employer. 'Mr Crabb, how do you do? I believe you work at my gallery. My name is Anthony Blunt.'

Despite working at the gallery for some time, Crabb was surprised that he had never actually met the senior partner. He smiled and shook Blunt's hand and told him how much he enjoyed the work. Crabb understood the gallery was owned by several partners, and said there were always different people coming and going.

Blunt was tall, stick-thin and slightly hunched. He wore a dress suit and was extremely well spoken, with a cut-glass English accent. He looked, Crabb thought, like a withered camel. Crabb was still watching as Blunt began introducing himself to the other guests. When Rosa tapped him on the shoulder and asked: 'Have you met Anthony?' Crabb replied: 'Oh yes. He seems very pleasant.'

'Well connected too! He is a regular at the Cavendish,' she said. 'He and his friends are always welcome. There are a lot of important men and women here tonight, but he's not interested in the ladies, if you understand my meaning?'

It took Lionel a few seconds for the penny to drop. He looked at Rosa, smiled and nodded. 'I see what you mean.' After downing another drink Crabb disappeared into the crowd. It was some time before he met Blunt again, and then under vastly different circumstances.

Crabb was at the gallery for over a year before war was finally declared in September 1939. He was sitting in his hotel bedroom listening to Prime Minister Neville Chamberlain's wireless speech announcing that Britain was 'now at war with Germany'. His reaction was one of euphoria.

Over the next few days he anxiously quizzed people about where he should go to sign up. Everything seemed very disorganised. People were worried that the Germans would soon bomb London. There was also an invasion scare. The news from the continent was grim. Poland was under threat and troops were being mobilised throughout Europe. Britain had already prepared to make a stand in France with the British Expeditionary Force (BEF), but this was unlikely to deter Hitler.

Lionel was still determined to join the Navy. His first port of call was the Royal Naval Volunteer Reserve offices, where he arrived smartly dressed and ready to sign up. He was disappointed to be told to wait in line. Crabb believed his services would be in demand, and expected to be signed up as an officer. After all, he had Merchant Navy training, and had lived and worked in the Far East. When he reached the main desk, he was stunned when the officer in charge rejected him on the grounds of age. At thirty Lionel Crabb was told he was too old to be recruited. He was devastated. He returned to the hotel and spoke to Rosa and Maitland. He also contacted Daisy, and then Kitty, who was a top civil servant employed at the War Office. Kitty suggested he contact the Merchant Navy – after all, as he admitted, he had gained some valuable South American experience.

As Crabb contemplated his future, he went into central London and had a few too many beers with some old friends at a riverside pub. When he came out it was extremely dark. The blackout was in force and taxis were non-existent, so he decided to join a friend and catch a small launch back across the Thames. However, as he tried to stand to put some change in his pocket he suddenly lost his balance and fell overboard. Fortunately the boat turned around and the skipper pulled him out. Amazingly, Lionel had a broad grin on his face, and was desperately holding his hat out of the water with one hand.

Crabb tried all sorts of ways to join the services but each time was refused because of his age. A few months later, and the Merchant Navy were becoming less fussy. They offered Crabb a near-immediate passage, which would also capitalise on his gunnery and sea-going experience. He was to be appointed as an able seaman, and given a role as gunner on a tanker due to sail out of Thames Haven.

He quickly told his colleagues his good news. It was neither the best position nor a great opportunity, but at least it was the start of his war. The night before his departure Crabb organised a party at the Cavendish for friends and family. Many people, including his cousin Kenneth, had already received their call-up papers, or were already in the services. With so many facing an uncertain future, the mood was subdued, but the next evening Crabb was given a hearty send-off on the quayside. Kitty attended, together with Anthony Blunt, who coincidentally was now her boss at the War Office. They were both involved in counter-espionage duties with Military Intelligence at MI5. Part of Blunt's new brief, Kitty explained after the war, was to keep all neutral embassies and diplomatic missions under surveillance.

Kitty was a very experienced civil servant. She had worked in the Cipher Division in Military Intelligence for years, and was appointed Blunt's personal assistant. Blunt, an Army Intelligence officer, had been evacuated from France just as the Germans invaded. He was attached to the British Expeditionary Force. Kitty later described Blunt to her family as tall, witty and occasionally arrogant. On the whole she thought him charming, and would never have a word said against him.

Blunt was the son of a Church of England chaplain and the grandson of an Anglican bishop, who spent much of his early childhood in Paris. Kitty claimed he adored everything French. He attended Trinity College, Cambridge, where he was said to be a 'brilliant' scholar, later becoming a fellow. He was also heavily involved in the art world and was considered something of an expert on French artefacts.

Before Crabb sailed, Blunt introduced him to three friends. They included Jack 'Oscar' Hewitt – an actor and former boyfriend of Blunt, then appearing in the West End – and two other colleagues, who would soon be working with Kitty. Blunt said they were both extremely bright and had been recruited from his old college at Cambridge to work in British Intelligence. They were Guy Burgess and Donald Maclean.

Burgess was another old friend and former lover of Anthony Blunt. He was a political journalist and had been a member of Blunt's debating group. Burgess was the son of a Royal Navy officer and had attended the Royal Naval Training College at Dartmouth before deciding his talents would be better used elsewhere. He once wrote for *The Times* and produced a weekly series of 'Westminster Reviews' for the BBC. He was also friendly with a number of top politicians of the day – including Winston Churchill. In 1939 Burgess was seconded to the SIS in D-Section and was initially involved with sabotage and operational planning. He later served in Cairo, Paris and Washington.

A third member of the Cambridge Set was Donald Maclean. He was the son of a knighted Liberal MP. Maclean was a diplomat before the war and, just like Blunt, narrowly escaped from France just as the Germans invaded. While working at the British Foreign Office in Paris, he met and married a striking American woman, Melinda Marling. Their wedding took place just as German troops marched into the French capital. It meant a rather hasty and undignified escape to London, where Blunt found him work at the War Office.

As war progressed, others in Lionel Crabb's social circle signed up. They included his cousin Kenneth Jarvis, a keen motor racing enthusiast who joined the Royal Army Service Corps (RASC), and his childhood friend, Stanley North, who fought in the Far East, became a prisoner of war of the Japanese and was incarcerated at the notorious Changi Gaol. He survived and later retired as a major.

Lomond recalls her father Norman Handley's wartime role. She says: 'He was on a Flower class Corvette. He was in the Royal Navy Volunteer Reserve (RNVR) and served on the *Rock Rose* and *Lismore*. He wasn't commissioned until well into the war, and I think he joined the RNVR as a writer. He was brilliant at shorthand and I gather he took down the Captain's messages on the bridge.'

She added that her mother, Eileen, spent part of the war working in Bournemouth as a receptionist for a well-known osteopath called Charles de Coty, known as CD. It was understood that he was later suspected of being a German agent.

Lomond says:

He was certainly pro-German and Burgess and Maclean once went to investigate. To some, he was regarded as a 'quack' but he certainly knew a lot about rheumatism and arthritis. He was also into homeopathy and healthy diets. Ma believed him to be a German sympathiser, and said CD had some very strange visitors at times. She looked in his cellar one day and found all sorts of costumes there, including a nun's outfit. She looked there because he'd told her never to go down there under any circumstances.

She was naturally very 'beaky' and thought he was a spy. She said that his degree credentials, which were framed on the wall, didn't look kosher. She reckoned they'd been forged, or tampered with. There was no doubt that CD knew a lot of people, but Ma said he wasn't English. And I'm assuming that it was mother who told Burgess about her suspicions, through Granny Kitty Jarvis.

Lomond's cousin Charleen spoke about her own parents' involvement. She says:

Mother [Audrey] married my father on the first Saturday of the war. He later commanded a section of the Indian Army on the Khyber Pass – keeping warring tribes apart. He spent the entire war serving away in India. Mother worked in an aircraft factory with Lancaster bombers, and for much of the time lived with Kitty at her Douglas Mansions apartment.

After more than a year working as a gunner, Lionel Crabb applied for and received a transfer. He was offered a position working with the Royal Navy Patrol Service, based at Lowestoft. Unfortunately, it was not quite as exciting as he had hoped for and it meant working with many part-time sailors, fishermen and yachtsmen. Most declined to wear uniforms and hated taking orders from a low-ranking sailor. Crabb considered most of them 'arrogant and ill-disciplined'. And to make matters worse, some younger people were even appointed over his head and made petty officers. Crabb served on a range of ships but mainly worked on trawlers and other small fishing boats on mundane coastal protection duties.

A few months later, when he realised things were never going to improve, he again applied for a transfer, and as the war progressed, he was finally commissioned as a sub-lieutenant. Despite his best intentions, Crabb's lazy eye caused him to fail the RNVR medical. This prevented him from undertaking any sea duties. He was furious. He searched the notice boards for anything else of interest and then saw an advertisement claiming the Navy wanted someone for 'special duties'.

He applied immediately, obtained a quick interview, and was informed that he was to become the new 'Drainage and Passive Duties Officer' for the port of Dover. It meant further heartbreak and disappointment, and again meant working with civilians and part-time soldiers from the newly formed 'Dad's Army'.

With little prospect of action man-style operations or danger, it was not long before Crabb again became frustrated and depressed. As compensation, however, he managed to enjoy trips back to town at every opportunity, where he used to meet Rosa and Maitland. He gained a reputation as someone who enjoyed a good time, and on occasions he met with other service colleagues from Commonwealth countries, and others from Britain's Polish allies.

Certain pubs and clubs were regular haunts for the Poles and among them were RAF support pilots and army personnel. Lionel told his new friends about events at the Cavendish, and with Rosa's permission he occasionally invited large groups back for lively gatherings. At times, some of Kitty's War Office colleagues, especially Burgess and Maclean, attended. And when he could, Crabb joined Kitty for private socials back at her flat. Anthony Blunt was another regular visitor, along with Oscar Hewitt, Ian Fleming and several actors from wartime shows. Lomond Handley explains the background to this exciting period:

My mother and Granny Jarvis knew Oscar from way back. He was an established actor, dancer and occasional singer, who had starred in several top shows including *No, No, Nanette.* He was a former lover of Blunt. He wore an army uniform and used to hang around at the War Office with Blunt and Maclean. Oscar was a charming man who tagged on to Kitty. Mother and Audrey also knew him very well. He used to take Kitty out for meals and to the theatre. He even accompanied her back to Monkswood, our family home. He was a very witty and interesting companion and Granny found him very good and safe company.

Granny also liked a drink. She wasn't a drunk but she could certainly knock back the gin and still stay standing. Granny Jarvis was a great socialite and was very well read. She loved the theatre, the arts and ballet. She also loved good food and during the war used to dine regularly at places like Kettners and The Ivy. Kitty was a great beauty in her time and was still a good-looking woman in her early sixties. She was known as 'Mater' by Blunt, Burgess, Maclean and Oscar, and even lent them her flat at 12 Douglas Mansions, Kilburn, for private meetings. Blunt was her boss and she thought the world of him. I don't think she knew or cared about the sexual angle, because she was too busy enjoying the theatre outings and entertainment and wouldn't have expected them to get up to any hanky-panky or anything at her flat. They spun her a very convincing yarn about needing a safe flat to hold meetings for War Office or Military Intelligence business. Granny believed what she wanted to believe.

Charleen Miller confirms the special relationship between Kitty and Blunt:

> Kitty was a member of the Arts Theatre Club and went nearly every week to the cinema. She loved the theatre and also interior design. Her flat at Douglas Mansions was full of beautiful antiques. Mother [Audrey] lived there with her until the latter part of the war, when they suffered a direct hit and quickly decamped to the Strand Palace Hotel.
>
> During the war years, Kitty worked for Blunt as his personal assistant. She shared the outer office with Burgess and Maclean. I don't know what Kitty actually did at the War Office – she never talked about it. All mother would say was that friends would ask her if their husbands or children in the Forces were OK, and she would get back to them in a few days and just say: 'All I can tell you is that they are safe.'
>
> Many an evening, Burgess and Maclean would take Mother and Kitty out for dinner. Mother always said that if it had not been for this food, they don't know how they would have survived the war. They often wondered why two men took a middle-aged widow and a newly married woman out. I got the impression she didn't even know Burgess was homosexual.
>
> She said that intellectually, she and Kitty weren't in their league, and it was only when the spying came out that it became obvious that to be seen with Mother and Kitty had provided respectability – if anyone had been watching!
>
> At the weekends, Burgess, Maclean and Oscar Hewitt spent much of their time at the flat. Kitty cooked, and Burgess and Maclean brought the alcohol, as Kitty loved a gin and tonic. It usually turned into a party in the evenings. Sometimes other people came. Kitty was a great one for entertaining and used to say she thought B and M just liked to feel part of the family. No doubt Lionel too would have been there if he'd been in the country – along with Kenneth.

These were primarily private parties for family and close friends. In later years the odd disgruntled colleagues of Crabb claimed they were 'Homosexual and Communist parties'. Other occasional guests at both private and public parties included George Blake, who served in the Navy with Lionel, Kim Philby, John Cairncross, Lord Rothschild, Noel Coward and Ian Fleming from Naval Intelligence.

Charleen adds: 'Kitty and Oscar went out to shows together and sometimes left Burgess and Maclean in the flat. I think this only stopped when some trinkets and bits of silver went missing and she thought someone was stealing things.' Lomond, though, thinks the meetings probably ended when Kitty found a suitcase under the bed in the spare room. She said it contained some linen, letterheads and personal items marked with the crest of Lord Rothschild.

Lionel Crabb, meanwhile, had been carrying out a series of boring duties in and around Dover's dockyard. After a few months, he complained again to Navy colleagues at another London party. He hated the monotony of the job. And once, he was so down and depressed that a friend even contacted Kitty at the War Office to express his concern. A few days later, Crabb received a visit from a senior officer. The latter casually mentioned a job that had just been posted on the mess room notice board, one he thought might appeal to Lionel.

The job was voluntary and within a new top secret training unit. The notice suggested it could be dangerous, and mentioned dealing with unexploded bombs, land mines and other explosive devices. Interviews were to be held over the next couple of weeks and successful applicants would be offered a place on a basic training course somewhere in the north of England. Crabb thought that seemed more like it, and was perhaps his best chance to see some real action at last.

Chapter 7

Bomb and Mine Disposal

Within days of submitting his application, Crabb received a handwritten reply. He was to report to an address in London, and to remain on standby. He signed a form agreeing to take part in extensive trials for a new Bomb and Mine Disposal Unit at some secret place in Cumbria called HMS *Volcano*. He thought the name alone sounded fairly interesting. He was given a blank railway warrant and some paperwork, and told to be ready to leave within days. He told his family he had had no idea of what to expect when he signed up for this new course.

Armed with his anonymous railway warrant and a sealed letter, he didn't even know the precise location of his unit until he reached King's Cross and presented his documents. Here, an officer with a superior attitude and a colourful clipboard directed him towards the right platform, and said his train was bound for Barrow-in-Furness, Cumbria. He was told to change there for Drigg and Ravenglass, where someone would meet him. Troop trains, and in fact the majority of service and supply trains, generally moved under cover of darkness to dodge air raids.

The windows were blacked out, and the trains were cold, slow and uncomfortable. Crabb admitted that he didn't look forward to endless hours cramped in a packed compartment, or of sleeping rough in some corridor. He always hated the long haul north. His train left on time at precisely

7.32 p.m. but it simply chugged along, stopping, starting, and waiting in the middle of nowhere. It made several unannounced and unscheduled stops before it finally arrived at its destination.

Crabb said he was always worried about oversleeping, and was thankful when someone carefully pulled back the blinds to reveal the bright daylight of early morning in Barrow. As he prised himself free and stretched out after his long journey, he had to fight his way along the packed platforms in search of news about his connecting train.

The place was full of servicemen and women, and when he saw that his outward connection would be another half-hour or so, he headed straight for the canteen.

This was no less crowded than his compartment on the train. It had been used overnight as a temporary shelter and sleepy bodies still littered the floor and lay slumped in every chair. Crabb managed to obtain a mug of tea and a sandwich from a sympathetic assistant before making his way to another platform.

The second train was equally packed and had steamed along all night from somewhere in the Midlands. After exiting the station at his final stop, Crabb joined a large group which was heading for Holmrook Hall, travelling in several trucks. Holmrook Hall had been the home of the Revd Charles Skeffington Lutwidge, whose nephew Lewis Carroll used to stay there. The buildings and grounds were commandeered as a war training facility. The place was now known as HMS *Volcano*, and as they drove under the grand gates at the entrance Crabb and his fellow passengers were told they would soon learn how to render safe bombs, parachute and magnetic mines, and in fact anything explosive, including underwater devices.

Inside, the party was herded into a large room, where they were introduced to Capt L.E.H. Llewellyn, one of Britain's foremost explosive experts within the Royal Navy, and Lt Cdr Babbington RNVR, who briefed them on their first course. Also attending this remarkable facility with Crabb was Lt Noel Cashford, who not only assisted me in my research and in contacting Navy colleagues of Crabb but also wrote the foreword to this book. Noel explained that he and Crabb happened to be of a similar height and build, had been prohibited from active sea duties due to an eyesight defect and had volunteered for 'special duties'. Noel admitted having mixed opinions about Crabb. He says:

My initial impression of Crabb was that he was definitely not my cup of tea! He seemed dodgy during lectures, and at times seemed to be close to being under the influence. During and after lunch and dinner at *Volcano*, he always had a drink in his hand. He tended to become friendly with other officers in training who also liked a drink. Those of us who didn't had little contact with him. It was also noticeable that when we had turnout, with best uniforms, his always looked slightly grubby. He didn't seem to take much interest in his appearance, and didn't engage in discussions on technical aspects of enemy bombs and fuses.

Noel also gave a brief insight into life at this remote facility. He said course members came from all over the world, including Norway, Canada and New Zealand. He recalls:

HMS *Volcano* had a large wood adjoining the lawn with a factory manufacturing explosives. On the edge of the property was a fast flowing river noted for its salmon and trout. We spent most mornings in the classrooms learning about bombs and fuses. The afternoons were used digging for practice UXBs – some with delayed action and ticking clocks, which I can still hear to this day. HMS *Volcano* also had two large motor launches, used by trainees to do shallow water mine detection. Ravenglass was tidal, and when the tide was ebbing, our commander ordered us to help the local fishermen. We spent a lot of time in the pub waiting for the tide, and at times it was boring. We were either freezing cold or soaking wet. Training included demolitions, the use of explosives under water, dealing with grenades, landmine, anti-tank and personnel, and anything else remotely explosive.

Noel met Crabb twice more for refresher courses and confirmed the dangers and difficulties of the training, particularly at HMS *Excellent*, the Naval Diving School at Whale Island, near Portsmouth, where members were taught how to unscrew several nuts from very long threads – at a depth of at least 60ft.

In family archive notes, Lionel Crabb claimed the instructors at HMS *Volcano* were eccentric. And his papers confirmed Noel Cashford's assessment: that these people generally felt they had failed in their task if any course member was killed while working on unexploded devices. Crabb also told friends and colleagues about constant drills and the making safe of other hidden devices. Noel says:

> The drill was that one party laid booby traps and another party had to locate them and render them safe. We all got extremely cunning at this and even when the day's work was over you could not relax. Pick up a shoe – bang! Flush the toilet – bang! Lie on the bed – bang! They even used delayed reaction charges so that you could open a drawer or a suitcase and nothing would happen, so you relaxed – and then faced an unexpected bang! Our instructors encouraged this activity so that within the week, although the booby traps were laid in increasing numbers, practically all were rendered safe. Your name would be put on the 'Deceased' board if you exploded a booby trap. It all helped to concentrate the mind.

When Crabb left Cumbria he continued his wartime training exercises in Portsmouth Dockyard at HMS *Vernon*, a naval diving school. He spent a week at *Vernon*, followed by another two weeks at HMS *Excellent*. Crabb was only a mediocre swimmer and he had never done any diving before. At Portsmouth, he and other trainees were taken about 300 yards off shore aboard an old sea-going tug, which had been hastily converted into a divers' training vessel. It had no covered accommodation and Crabb said he often stood huddled in the wheelhouse in freezing temperatures amid choppy, grey, rolling seas. The harbour was full of warships, with a host of small launches dashing about from ship to ship. Many of them apparently ignored or misunderstood their red flags, which signalled they were a diving ship and should be given a wide berth.

At Whale Island, Crabb excelled as a diver. He was outstanding, and Noel Cashford, who was with him, admitted: 'He seemed part of the suit. He was a natural diver although he didn't always observe the safety drills.' Divers had to learn to work in a naval pattern diving suit for deep-sea dives. Part of their training involved some very dangerous manoeuvres. The equipment was so heavy that divers needed help putting on their suits. They had to sit on a box while an attendant helped them prepare. A special neck ring was always used to protect their shoulders, aided by a brass corselet and lead weights. These weighed 28lb and were slung on horns on the front and back of the corselet, secured by a light line.

It was the diver's responsibility to ensure the line was secure. In case of an emergency on the seabed, the diver had to make certain he could be released quickly and easily. The next task was to try to stand up, and with a little help, slowly place one leg after the other, over the side and on to the rungs of a narrow iron ladder.

It was exhausting work and quickly burned off any nervous energy. It was also a highly dangerous procedure and both Lionel Crabb and Noel Cashford admitted that descending these steps on an early dive was indeed a frightening experience. The pair told of similar fears on their first dives, and how they learned to control the air intake. Noel says:

With the right amount of air in your suit, you could move around as easily as a dancer. By the end of the course, I was still not thrilled with diving but at least I was confident in what I was doing. And although I had reservations about my ability to render safe bombs and mines under water, as your hands get so cold, and all the feeling goes, I knew it was essential to know what you were doing by touch, as often the harbour waters were murky to say the least.

Noel says that after he bade Crabb farewell:

My impression was that he had few friends. He was a bit of a loner who liked his booze too much. I must add that at no time did I ever see him drunk. And he always seemed to have a cigarette in his hand, when it was allowed. I've since spoken with several officers and men who also worked with Crabb and they all agree he was fearless, but ignored simple safety precautions, and he was not at all interested in knowing how breathing apparatus was maintained. Otherwise, he was quite brilliant underwater.

Another diving associate of Crabb's, and a very distinguished bomb disposal expert, was Cdr Gordon Gutteridge OBE. During a distinguished career Cdr Gutteridge worked with Crabb both under his command and as his senior officer. He knew Crabb from his earliest diving days and, despite a close friendship, retained doubts about Crabb's operational ability. He explained:

> At HMS *Volcano*, Crabb had been an odd choice, as most of his peers were young graduates in engineering and science – but these were desperate times. Crabb was lazy and not prone to making any physical effort, and was remarkably untechnical. Electrical circuits remained a lifelong mystery to him, mechanical complexity was a bore, and tools were for others to use. Nevertheless, he was enthusiastic and determined to make a contribution for his country and only qualified by the skin of his teeth.

Following completion of his basic training, Crabb was posted to Swansea to gain more practical experience working on unexploded bombs and mines. From the word go, he told friends and relatives that he found Swansea duller and more boring than Dover. He soon clashed with the local part-time Bomb Disposal Unit commander, who was a naval padre based within the grounds of the Officers' Club. They disagreed on numerous training proposals and Crabb decided the place was far too quiet for his liking.

With little work to keep him fully occupied, he quickly introduced his own 'rendering safe' exercises on the beaches, or around the town. His mock explosions would occur at any time of the day or night, and soon his unorthodox and irregular workings upset many residents, including senior council officials, who recommended he should be moved to another location. It wasn't too long, therefore, before his superiors agreed to another transfer, this time to far more dangerous waters in war-torn Gibraltar.

Chapter 8

Gibraltar

Crabb had never been to Gibraltar and didn't quite know what to expect. He had often heard some of his shipmates from the SS *Bonheur* talk about the place as a hot and desolate land very close to Spain, which had just ended a very bloody civil war.

He had read up something about Gibraltar in the ship's atlas and in an old history book. He knew it was said that the waters were ideal for diving. It was also the 'Gateway to the Med' and quoted in Greek mythology as the 'Pillars of Hercules'. Gibraltar had been considered a relatively safe haven for seafarers for thousands of years but had endured its fair share of hostilities and invaders, dating back to Roman and Phoenician times.

The body of Admiral Lord Nelson was taken to Rosia Bay following the Battle of Trafalgar, and consequently the local rum was named Nelson's Blood. The British had been heavily involved with the occupation of Gibraltar for nearly 250 years. Admiral Sir George Rooke first captured Gibraltar for Britain with an Anglo-Dutch fleet in 1704 during the War of the Spanish Succession.

Crabb sailed for Gibraltar in November 1942. He was thirty-three years old, and although he had a basic knowledge of the island's history and heritage he knew little about the current situation. At first, he thought it might be just another backwater location where he would probably sit out the war. He certainly hoped it wouldn't be as dull as Dover or Swansea, and told friends he intended to gain a suntan while improving his diving skills. He had no idea that Gibraltar was under almost constant bombardment. The harbour especially faced a host of dangers, with valuable Allied cargo vessels being sunk on a massive scale by Italian frogmen, saboteurs and German U-boats.

As soon as Crabb reached Gibraltar his Commanding Officer, Cdr Ralph Hancock, gave the new arrival a sharp wake-up call. He informed him of the desperate situation, and stressed the importance of his new role. Hancock was a tough, determined character who was in charge of coastal defences and knew all about Crabb's problematic record. Until that moment Crabb had never heard of Italian frogmen, or even realised they were involved in such activities.

It seemed to be a siege-like situation, with packs of German U-boats patrolling the main channels outside, and constant underwater raids from the Italians inside the main harbour areas. Hancock admitted that more than 6 million tons of shipping had been lost during the previous year, and said these losses could not be allowed to continue.

He remained anxious about the expected appearance of further large convoys. And, to make matters worse, he also explained that espionage was rife, with thousands of foreign dockworkers pouring over the borders each day from mainland Spain, which was separated from Gibraltar by a narrow strip of land.

Crabb was surprised at just how close the ships were anchored to the coast of Spain, with one particularly large convoy strung out for miles for all to see, and to attack at will. There seemed little or no place to hide, and knowing both the historical and geographical aspects of Gibraltar, realised that the Spanish, despite appearing neutral, would offer little sympathy, or resistance to further threats.

Lionel Crabb was also introduced to the chief diving officer Lt William (Bill) Bailey, who outlined their defence strategy, and showed him the defensive measures currently in place. Crabb was told that the British had just three small naval protection vessels available. They patrolled ships at anchor and periodically dropped depth charges to deter Italian divers. He said they operated mainly at night to counter expected attacks and used powerful searchlights to skim along the surface of the water. British divers continually checked the underside of ships to search for limpet mines or other explosives, but were told to render them safe on land rather than deal with them while still attached to the hull of ships.

It seemed something of a lottery, and Crabb believed it was primarily down to good luck and guesswork as to which ship would be attacked next. They had so much to do, with so little protection. Bailey said they only had two divers, who were neither technically trained nor qualified in bomb and mine disposal. In addition, he admitted they did not have suitable or sufficient diving gear.

In Gibraltar, Crabb gained the nickname of 'the Admiral', or sometimes 'the Toad'. He remembered the 'Admiral' tag from his first meeting with Rosa Lewis at the Cavendish. Now, however, with constant explosions, air raid sirens blaring out at all hours of the day and night, and pandemonium out in the bay, he wondered just why he had made such a fuss about leaving Dover.

Bill Bailey by comparison was a realist. He even acknowledged that the Italians had far better equipment, far better facilities, and far better training than ever the British could muster. He also explained how defenders had to dive around the clock, wearing only swimming trunks, and any old top they could find for protection against barnacles and other underwater obstacles.

Bailey was very inventive though, and somehow managed to get hold of some sets of Davis Submarine Escape Apparatus (DSEA) that had been employed in crew rescue and practice escapes from submarines. He claimed that although they were not ideal for this type of operation, they were better than nothing at all. The equipment allowed divers to operate more easily, and to breathe freely underwater.

The divers breathed in pure oxygen and exhaled carbon dioxide, which became absorbed by a canister of soda lime. If the breathing became difficult, the diver had to turn a small valve, which allowed more oxygen to flow. They had to be very careful, however, that the maximum oxygen content was available, otherwise they could quickly inhale the CO_2 gas, and could suffer a horribly quick death from toxic fumes. Crabb was introduced to the other two members of the team and examined their basic equipment. No one at that time knew how to service or maintain any of it, and he began to wish he had paid more attention to the vitally instructive lessons back at HMS *Excellent*, at Whale Island.

His first lesson in survival and operational workings was with Lt Bailey and Leading Seaman Bell. Crabb stripped down to his trunks and wore an old shirt and a pair of small weighted plimsolls. He quickly strapped on the DSEA diving set and was shown how to grip the mouthpiece and how to breathe properly. He wore a pair of goggles and a nosepiece, and Bailey tied a short piece of rope around his midriff so that they could maintain contact with the newcomer underwater.

Crabb's first test was simple, and like his earlier training exercise, he was told to descend a ladder carefully into a shallow stretch of water. He climbed up and down several times to gain experience and confidence, working until the rope pulled. He seemed to breathe quite easily. Bailey then took Crabb out in a launch and showed him how to search the underside of a ship. The water was crystal clear and he was told to look for the bottom line of the ship, a regular straight edge that ran along the length of the ship below the waterline.

The divers hauled themselves along until they reached the bilge keel ledge and then the stern. Crabb enjoyed the experience but was surprised at just how powerful a swell there was. They surfaced and returned to shore. After a discussion about previous attacks and probabilities, Bailey then officially welcomed Crabb to the team. Crabb was exhausted but exhilarated. Bill Bailey said he was really an Electrical Officer and had been seconded to these duties because no one else was available. It seemed a thankless task. Bailey also confirmed that the Italians were part of the famed Tenth Light Flotilla, a fearless unit that was constantly creating havoc with Allied shipping. This unit recruited divers from all branches of the services, and included members of the Gamma group, who reputedly trained by walking in ranks for miles along the seabed.

Lt Bailey believed they were operating illegally from interned ships within Spanish harbours, but explained that by attaching a new type of mine, which would not explode until many hours later in deeper waters, the blame was being placed on patrolling U-boats rather than Italian saboteurs.

Lt Bailey and Leading Seaman Bell had gained varied experience of working with delayed action devices, and Bailey admitted that although he was a good swimmer, he had only attended a short course on conventional mines and had learned most defensive techniques from working on the job. Crabb was told about another major attack some months earlier by a large party of Italian divers, who had attached some new mines to ships. Bailey said that rubber rings held the mines up, with the enemy divers using delayed action fuses. Bailey confirmed that many had exploded, and that he had had to use his knife to cut others free.

He likened them to pricking balloons, carefully watching them drop to safety in much deeper waters. Later models, though, had been found secured to bilge keels and, again, they often failed to explode until the ships were well under way. One had become disentangled and was found washed ashore. This later gave Bailey an opportunity to study it. He warned, however, that every single ship arriving from a Spanish port had to be examined.

This demanding routine quickly gave Crabb the confidence and experience to work alone and he began to enjoy the personal challenge and the inherent dangers involved. Within ten days of arrival, he located his first limpet mine and took great pride in releasing it. Later, Lt Bailey received the George Medal for his underwater work prior to Christmas 1942. Many colleagues claimed it was for helping to repel a large armed party of Italian divers during an attack the previous summer.

Cdr Gutteridge also met Lt Lionel Crabb at Gibraltar during 1943. He knew Bailey and understood all the potential dangers. He says:

Whilst Gibraltar saw few bombs – and Crabb saw no unexploded ones – there was a much more serious problem. The port was busy. It was overfull with cargo ships and warships, with most lying in open anchorage. Many were close to the supposed neutral Spanish ports of La Linea and Algeciras. There was much coming and going. Boom defence and security was a constant problem. The Spanish bum boats came and went at will with their supplies, and with ever increasing frequency the ships were subjected to underwater attacks and explosions. Initially, the naval authorities had no knowledge of, and no answer to, these Italian frogmen who were placing limpet mines or steering these two-man human torpedoes called charioteers. Fortunately, Lt Bailey, supported by

Cdr Hancock, began to evolve countermeasures and organised a thorough search of the hulls of ships for explosive devices.

Crabb was co-opted on to Bailey's team. He was willing but apprehensive, as he was a poor swimmer. However, he dived for countless hours with inadequate and dangerous equipment and not only found but dealt with several charges placed by the enemy. Many were relatively simple devices but posed a new and unknown threat. This was the beginning of what was to become his lifelong obsession with diving and all things Italian. Crabb was a good but not outstanding diver but he had a remarkable capacity to endure cold water and discomfort.

Another diving colleague of Crabb's at Gibraltar was Sydney Knowles BEM. He was a First Class Stoker Mechanic, who had risked his life as a gun loader on several warships, taking part in numerous convoy protection duties and attacks against German capital ships before he joined Bailey and Crabb's unit.

An incredibly brave seaman, he had just returned to Gibraltar from Malta after taking part in the daring and memorable convoy, Operation 'Pedestal', when he saw a report on the ship's notice board seeking volunteers for hazardous duties ashore.

After experiencing repeated attacks from the air and from U-boats, he wondered if anything ashore could ever be quite as dangerous. Crabb and Bailey interviewed Knowles in a small dockside office. They hastily explained the problems they were facing, and asked if he could swim, and if he was willing to train as a diver. He said he was, and started immediately.

This was an ideal opportunity for Knowles. He was an excellent swimmer, and like Crabb he later proved to be a natural diver. He was trained within a matter of hours, and was soon introduced to other members of the unit. Other recruits included a Scot called Jock Fraser, Welshman 'Taffy' Thomas and, surprisingly, another man from Knowles's home town of Preston, Joe 'Rattler' Morgan.

A short time later, Crabb took over the unit when Lt Bailey slipped and fell down some stairs, breaking his ankle. He immediately set up a new base at Jumper's Bastion, which dated back to Admiral Rooke's first occupation in 1704. The Bastion was divided into two sections, north and south, and the word 'Jumper' was given to this area in recognition of the first British officer, Capt Jumper, who had first landed on the mole with the Anglo-Dutch force.

Crabb's unit was given a new title. They were called the Underwater Working Party. They occupied this new location, and Crabb soon began collecting a miscellaneous assortment of men with varied service experience – and an equally varied assortment of animals, birds and strays that inhabited this particular part of Gibraltar. His menagerie included an Alsatian bitch called Nina and her six pups, four rock lizards, two cats, some wild birds and a parrot. The lizards belonged to Joe Morgan. Crabb's parrot, though, was a nuisance and kept flying around the ceiling. During meal times, it would perch on a lamp bracket and release its droppings on the dining table.

Noel Cashford recalls an unfortunate incident at Gibraltar just after Lt Bailey's departure, when a friend whom he had first met at HMS *Volcano*, Lt Eric Hood, died while under Crabb's supervision. He explains:

> The officer was a good friend. He had married only a few weeks before being posted to Gibraltar – and for this reason alone, I instinctively disliked Crabb, who had little regard for strangers. Hood reported directly to Crabb's office. He was to be the new Bomb and Mine Safety Officer. He was told that Crabb was out in the harbour checking the keels of moored ships for limpet mines. Lt Hood was taken out to his launch and when Crabb surfaced he greeted his new officer.
>
> Crabb told him to strip to his underwear and gave him a modified DSEA set. He didn't provide much instruction on its use and put the officer in the water with orders to search the ship's bottom. The story ends there, for the officer did not reappear until many days later when the ship was taken to dry dock. The corpse of Lt Hood was later found wedged between the bilge and the main keel.

Noel felt the incident might have been covered up and claimed that surprisingly there was no known memorial to Lt Hood at Gibraltar. Full operational reports from that time are restricted, but more recent recollections by Crabb's ex-diving colleague Sydney Knowles suggests there was no whitewash and it was to all intents and purposes just a most unfortunate accident. Some extracts from wartime reports claim:

When Lt Bailey was posted home, a relieving officer Lt Hood was sent out from England. He was a brave man but unfortunately suffered from asthma and detested diving, however he was determined to do the job. He disappeared under the keel on his very first operational clearance. It was clear water and a good sunny day. A rating went down to starboard but after a few minutes returned to signal that his side was clear. A further few minutes elapsed and it was not considered appropriate to chase an officer on his first dive.

As more time passed, Crabb dived and searched the ship's bottom. He resurfaced and ordered his other divers over the side. They kept searching and he went down again. As each diver returned, they gave a thumbs-down sign. One by one they returned to the launch. Nothing more could be said or done. It was another two weeks before the body was recovered. Lt Hood's goggles and his breathing gear had dragged around his neck in his last struggles for air.

Crabb's diving colleague Sydney Knowles says:

Throughout the whole of my diving time with Cdr Crabb I can report that amazingly – with all that we had been through – only one diver was lost, Lt Hood in Gibraltar. Royal Navy orders claimed that only Mine and Bomb Disposal officers were allowed to handle a mine but due to our workload this was impossible, especially as Lt Crabb was working alone because Lt Bailey had broken his ankle going down a flight of stairs. The first mine that I found was held to the ship's bottom by an inflatable rubber ring. I rose to the surface to inform Lt Crabb but he had gone out in our second launch to another ship half a mile away.

By the time I could have contacted him the mine might have exploded, so I dived again, ignoring orders, and I stabbed the ring with my diving knife and let the mine sink to the bottom. On another ship, I discovered a limpet mine clamped to the bilge keel and heard the clock ticking. I furiously tore it off and let it sink to the seabed – where it exploded some thirty minutes later.

It became obvious to our party that these actions were necessary if we were to save more ships. Before long, another officer Lt Hood, joined our party to replace Lt Bailey. One day, he was diving with me and he went down the port side of the merchant vessel. I went to starboard. Finding nothing at my side, I surfaced and signalled that all was clear and climbed into the diving launch, where we waited for him to appear. Sadly he did not. Lt Crabb and I plunged into the sea and searched the ship's bottom around the area to no avail. Lt Hood's body was not recovered for several days. When it was, it was evident that he had dragged his goggles and breathing gear down around his neck. We presumed that his death was due to oxygen poisoning.

Knowles explained that these basic DSEA breathing sets were wholly unreliable for deeper dives. He said that below 30ft oxygen under pressure became dangerous and affected the body's metabolism. However, he also admitted diving beyond that distance himself at times. He agreed that when he first joined Crabb's unit, he too had learned to dive the 'hard way', with Lt Crabb throwing a Davis set at him to try on.

Within days, Knowles was a duty diver looking after at least six ships each night – and checking every ship that entered harbour from Spain, day or night. Most ships anchored within 400 yards of Spanish shores, close to the small port of Algeciras.

Some convoys stretched for up to three miles. Knowles said he had had no specific bomb disposal training and admitted their clothing and equipment were fairly primitive and inefficient.

Like Crabb's initial experience with Bill Bailey, Knowles and all the other divers were taught to follow a similar pattern of inspection, with a plunge dive by the side of a ship, and to feel their way along to the bilge keel. Many divers ended up with severe cuts and bruises, or faced painful attacks by shoals of stinging jellyfish, resulting in equally painful hospital treatment.

At one time, Crabb and his colleagues located a new type of torpedo mine that had been deliberately locked on to the bilge keel of the 1,200-ton freighter *Willowdale*, which had just arrived via the Spanish port of Huelva. The mine was positioned close to the underside of the engine room. Crabb was unsure when the charge might explode, and hurried aboard the ship to warn the captain and crew.

All hands were ordered forward and the divers received a welcome tot of rum to help keep out the cold. Crabb dived several times to try and free the mine and remained concerned, not only about the timing mechanism, but also about the possibility of booby traps. He didn't want to risk the lives of his ratings and decided to work alone for many hours. He noticed the device had three unusual clamps, and feared for the worst as he slowly struggled with its mechanism.

Gradually two clamps worked free but as he struggled to dislodge the third, Crabb's breathing became laboured. He desperately turned the valve on his back-up oxygen tank to hiss some more life into his airbag. When it emptied, he returned to the surface for more, and continued. The third clamp proved extremely difficult to release, and he was forced to rest. He allowed his powerful colleague Bell to dive, using all his brute strength on the mine. When he returned giving a thumbs-down sign, Crabb dived again. He was near the limit of exhaustion but surprisingly found that it suddenly slackened and thankfully, wasn't booby-trapped.

Crabb knew, though, that if he let the mine drop, it could still explode due to a change in water pressure, and therefore he carefully manoeuvred it back to the surface, where he secured it between some buoys. When he returned to the launch, Crabb towed the mine and the buoys to Rosina Bay and secured it for the night. He hoped it might explode on its own but after reporting back to Cdr Hancock, the senior man became concerned about a risk to other shipping.

He instructed Crabb to take it over to a safe haven to be examined or destroyed and requisitioned a small rowing boat. Crabb pulled hard on the oars and headed for a small deserted area at the edge of the airfield. Here, with the assistance of Hancock, they carefully pulled it ashore by means of a long rope. It was a highly dangerous operation, and incredibly the pair worked within a few hundred yards of a squadron of RAF Spitfires.

They had to work quickly to render safe the 25lb mine. It had a most unusual tail propeller mechanism and Crabb watched anxiously as his colleague carefully stripped and removed the clocks, and all three of its deadly detonators. When it was finally declared safe, Crabb was told to clear up while Hancock dashed off to show the Governor of Gibraltar, Admiral Sir Frederick Edward-Collins, some of the clocks used. Crabb, though, became most concerned when he could only find two of the three detonators, which were extremely sensitive.

He was naturally reluctant to leave his post, despite his fatigue, but as he searched, Crabb also received instructions to attend a celebratory dinner with Hancock and the Admiral. He reluctantly agreed. It was some time later that he discovered Cdr Hancock had inadvertently placed the missing detonator loose in his jacket pocket throughout the entire meal.

Chapter 9

Operation 'Torch'

Lt Lioria Visintini was in charge of the Italian Tenth Light Flotilla at Gibraltar. He was a key member of an elite unit. By the winter of 1942, his small but ultra-efficient advanced group of divers were buoyant, following a series of highly successful raids against Allied shipping.

After a period of frenzy and chaos, when thousands of tons of valuable shipping were lost in a fairly short time, Crabb and his team suddenly became puzzled when the situation calmed. For many nights on end, nothing happened. There were no alerts, and no attacks. And yet, far from being relaxed, Cdr Hancock, in particular, was most concerned. He feared this Italian assault unit might be planning something major. For some time, and initially unknown to the British, the Italian divers had been using the 4,900-ton tanker *Olterra* as an attack base. In addition, they had another valuable observation point at the Villa Carmela, near La Linea, conveniently located just a few hundred yards from the main shipping lane.

The *Olterra* and another similar sister ship had entered the British controlled anchorage in Gibraltar Bay at the declaration of war. Both skippers were initially given orders to scuttle their vessels, but as they considered their options they received new instructions from Lt Visintini, to sail to the nearby port of Algeciras, where they could berth safely in the harbour under the guise of Spanish neutrality.

The *Olterra's* captain claimed extensive mechanical problems prevented any onward departure, and the crew seemed content to sit and wait for spares, or for the war to end. What was not obvious however was that Lt Visintini had helped plan a brilliant strategy, converting the ship into an underwater access torpedo factory. From its hidden location, the divers could attack enemy ships at will. The *Olterra* became a ship of war. Italian engineers and experienced naval officers worked around the clock, and under the very noses of their sleepy Spanish guards, to develop a unique new base for their divers and to introduce some new two-man mini-submarine torpedo units known as charioteers.

A 25ft section was cut into the bulkhead, with a 4ft escape hatch cut into the side of the ship just below the waterline. A door opened inward and was cleverly disguised, allowing divers the freedom to operate without being seen.

The close proximity of the convoys from their other vantage point also allowed for a bird's eye view of all their prospective targets. And working under diplomatic cover, the Italians transported ammunition, diving equipment and supplies to the ship.

On 6 December 1942, three British battleships, *Nelson, Formidable* and *Furious*, arrived at Gibraltar together with a very large convoy of mixed shipping. Crabb and his team were put on full alert. Lt Visintini made a brief study of the defensive operations around Gibraltar, and believed there were several opportunities to breach the protective mole, and to make wholesale attacks on the full convoy. Through powerful binoculars – stolen by an Italian Navy diver from the balcony of the British Embassy – Lt Visintini watched and noted the methods of the British protection patrol boats, and any systematic dropping of depth charges.

These limited precautions, coupled with inadequate security measures at the main entrance to the harbour, led Visintini to believe that his team of saboteurs would be able to enter the target zone in between mortar firings. In addition, and supported by diving colleagues along the Spanish coast, he felt Axis forces could soon execute a deadly series of surprise attacks that would finally cripple the Allied fleet.

Cdr Hancock warned Crabb of the importance of a British defence shield. He also spoke about the prospect of additional shipping arriving as part of the build up for Operation 'Torch', the Allied invasion of French North Africa. Hancock was acutely aware that if the Italians managed to sustain further attacks, the invasion plans could be placed in jeopardy. He was also advised in no uncertain terms – directly from the Admiralty – that heavy losses could even change the course of the war. Gibraltar was nearly always on high alert, and Hancock and Crabb knew the Italians were equally aware of this exceptional build-up of shipping. They realised the Italians must be planning something quite extraordinary, and soon.

Crabb's adrenalin was pumping. He readied his team. He believed the two wide entrances to the harbour posed the major risk and set about producing some extra powerful depth charges. He worked on them back at his base at Jumper's Bastion, but the required additional ammunition caused some obvious concern back at headquarters. The harbour entrances were only protected by some camouflaged wire and a submarine net. Crabb thought a determined two-man mini-sub crew could negotiate them.

Experience had already shown that the harbour entrances were Gibraltar's Achilles heel. Crabb's new explosive idea quickly gained approval, and he continued building his home-made equipment, and assembled some unusual 'projectors' on the north and south moles. They were made from steel tubing and strong wooden supports. They operated like powerful slingshot mortars, firing the explosives some considerable distance, and high into the air, covering a much wider area than before.

Through binoculars, the Italians thought they appeared far more substantial than they actually were. Visintini watched with wonder and apprehension. To the Italian CO, Crabb was a new man, with fresh ideas. Visintini noticed how Crabb seemed to study the British defensive mistakes of the past.

He knew his Axis diving team were heading into the unknown and didn't really know what to expect. Visintini, however, convinced his men that it was simply another barrier to overcome, and spoke clearly and convincingly of their many previous victories, and of operations from their secret base.

The harbour gunners were instructed on how to use these new weapons, which included deploying a series of packed charges in special 'tins' to be fired shortly after patrols had passed. Crabb instructed the men to fire them at irregular intervals throughout the night. He believed it might offer some extra protection across both entrances. As the Italians watched the ongoing defensive preparations and waited for the appointed hour, some concern began to creep into their ranks, and Lt Visintini tried to calm their fears.

He agreed to lead the raid on HMS *Nelson*, and ordered the other pilots to follow him and attack the other two major British battleships. Visintini was an extremely brave officer. He knew his colleagues had completed similar successful operations in the Egyptian port of Alexandria. Up to that stage, the Italians had always been able to employ the element of surprise. They had attacked quickly, and hastily retreated to their secret base under cover of darkness, and completely unscathed. This time, both they and the Allies knew that the stakes were high. They also knew they were expected, and Visintini understood more risks might have to be taken to achieve their objective.

As the clock approached midnight, the *Olterra* suddenly became a hive of activity. Three charioteers armed with deadly torpedoes were lowered carefully into the internal waters of the ship from their cradles and moved towards the underwater exit. Lt Visintini and his diver, Petty Officer Magro, watched as they were made ready. Petty Officer Varini, Midshipman Manisco, Petty Officer Leone and Lt Cella followed them out carefully towards their targets.

All went well until they reached the mole, when suddenly one of Crabb's new inventive charges was fired. It caused an incredible explosion, which severely damaged the first charioteer, and shot a huge spray of water some 30ft or so, upwards and into the cold night air. Visintini and Magro were killed instantly.

The noise and power of the explosion alerted all the harbour guards, and soon another enemy unit was spotted from the detached mole. The British defenders quickly floodlit the area and opened fire. They forced another charioteer to dive and take evasive action. A patrol boat gave chase and threw out a succession of other hand-made explosive devices. The craft submerged for a short while, but about half an hour later it unexpectedly surfaced after suffering a steering fault, and was quickly scuttled by her crew. Manisco and Varini surrendered. They were taken aboard an American ship moored nearby.

Officers were uncertain as to whether they had actually placed their dangerous torpedo charge, and believed they may still have come from an Italian or German submarine. When the third Italian unit heard the explosions and saw the blaze of searchlights and intermittent glare from the patrol boats, it quickly turned and headed back towards its mother ship. Unfortunately, though, its diver Leone lost control, fell into the water and drowned.

With the harbour on full alert, and excitement at fever pitch, and everyone uncertain as to how many other saboteurs might still be out there, Hancock ordered a full-scale assault on this unseen enemy. Chaos returned and depth charges were fired erratically, with ships remaining on full alert for some hours. Crabb and his men still had their jobs to do and began searching the hulls of capital ships, and any important cargo vessels.

He wasn't quite sure what he was looking for as he had not actually worked on one of these new torpedo warheads before and warned all his colleagues to be extra vigilant.

Conditions were bad, with freezing temperatures, but Lt Crabb and his team dived and dived again. They were occasionally warmed by the odd tot of rum but after many hours of examining the hulls and keels of some aircraft carriers, HMS *Nelson* and other capital ships, Crabb finally abandoned the search, believing that if the Italians had planted any mines or torpedoes they would probably by then have exploded.

By morning, it was evident that no mines or warheads had been placed. And when Crabb heard that one of the charioteers had been scuttled, he set about trying to recover it for examination purposes. After several hours of searching, he eventually decided that it was like looking for a needle in a haystack, and aborted the operation.

Back at base, Crabb received a large box containing the Italian divers' equipment. Two bodies were recovered. Their names were listed on their clothing and Crabb insisted that despite being enemy divers, they still deserved a proper burial at sea. He quickly obtained an Italian flag and a wreath, and sailed out with his team into the harbour to complete the necessary arrangements.

Despite this first severe loss, the Italians continued their periodic attacks. It was well-nigh impossible for Crabb and his team to protect every ship, and consequently some were lost. The location of the Italians' base, however, remained a mystery and Crabb agreed that when he was up to full strength he would investigate the matter further. An additional team member, Chief Petty Officer Ralph Thorpe, had joined the Underwater Working Party, alongside ex-stoker Sydney Knowles. Thorpe, too, had been declared medically unfit for sea duties, but proved invaluable at servicing equipment, and training and supervising the other ratings.

The next major incident came on the night of 8 May 1943. Crabb, who had by then been promoted to the rank of lieutenant-commander and awarded the George Medal for bravery and initiative, again studied the weather, tides, and arrivals listings. He informed Cdr Hancock that the signs looked bad. Crabb believed another major attack was imminent.

Intelligence reports confirmed that more than sixty vital Allied ships were assembling in convoy. The Admiralty told Crabb that once again the war effort could hang in the balance. They told him to 'do his best', and acknowledged he had just six divers at his disposal. Crabb demanded a full alert and hastily prepared more home-made explosive slings at the harbour entrance.

He knew that more than half the ships were due to sail by dawn the next day. He spent hours trying to out-think his opposite number, Lt Cdr Ernesto Notari, another very experienced diving officer, by deciding which ships he would attack if roles were reversed. Crabb opted for the early departure vessels and arranged for them all to be searched and cleared.

His team had hardly started their task when a horrendous series of deafening explosions ripped apart the underside of three waiting ships. The 4,875-ton *Camerata* sank immediately, and two other ships, the 7,500-ton *Mahsud* and 7,000-ton American Liberty ship *John Harrison* were very badly damaged. Before the crews abandoned ship, Cdr Hancock raced alongside in his launch, shouting through a large megaphone. He ordered them to steer towards shallower waters, where Crabb found an unexploded warhead on its bilge keel.

Notari and his diver Gianolli, with two additional charioteers, had attacked swiftly and efficiently. In an instant, they had caused havoc. At that early stage the source of the attack remained a mystery, but sentries later found some discarded Italian diving equipment, again suggesting that perhaps they had come from a waiting Axis submarine. Crabb had other ideas though. He thought it a deliberate ploy to distract and confuse. He discounted Hancock's suggestion of parachutists, and suspected the assault force must have come from somewhere much closer to hand, perhaps even from Algeciras, where the converted Italian tanker *Olterra* had been berthed in Spanish waters since the onset of war.

Crabb discussed the probabilities with Hancock and asked if he could check out this possibility. If proved, Crabb argued, the intelligence agencies or commandos could arrange for some sort of surprise. Crabb's request was denied, and he was forbidden personally to inspect any ship in a neutral port. His suspicions remained, and he knew that only a diver could verify the attacking capabilities below the waterline. He also knew that the *Olterra* was berthed at the farthest end of the jetty and was only patrolled by Spanish guards.

Diver Sydney Knowles says that he and 'Rattler' Morgan heard about Crabb's proposal, and his predicament. He says he decided to make his own contribution. Knowles and Morgan admitted that they too had heard rumours about unusual Italian movements on board the *Olterra*, from the crew of a Spanish water boat, which had free and unrestricted access throughout the harbour.

Crabb's team checked the water boats every day, to ensure they were clear, and several members of Crabb's diving team became friendly with their crew. By exchanging bottles of whisky and packets of cigarettes, Knowles and Morgan persuaded the Spaniards to take them under cover across to the mainland. The British divers dressed in casual clothing and headed for a small café close to the Italian tanker. From there, they observed all movements to and from the ship. They also heard many Italian and even German voices in the café, and thought there were far too many deliveries of spares, crew members and coincidences for it to be a supposedly quiet, interned ship. As dusk approached, they quickly returned to Jumper's Bastion, where they informed Crabb of their findings.

Additional dangers were beginning to threaten the Gibraltar convoys, with occasional delayed action mines being planted on board the ships and within deck cargoes, rather than attached as limpet mines or torpedoes. This escalated concerns about the Spanish bum-boats, which regularly ran alongside anchored convoy ships selling fruit, vegetables and mixed goods.

Crabb's home-made charges remained in demand, and he also persuaded most skippers at anchor to drop a barbed wire curtain around the underside of their ships to try to deter any enemy divers. This simple but effective weapon came into its own on the night of 3 August 1943, when once again Lt Notari led another enemy attack, accompanied by three armed charioteers.

Notari, a former salvage operator, always selected his targets with extreme care, first heading for the merchant ship *Stanridge*. As he and Gianolli dived towards the bilge keel, Crabb's unorthodox barbed wire screen caught them out. The pair became completely entangled, damaging their masks and rubber suits. However, Gianolli's charioteer later managed to fix a clamp to the bilge keel, and activated its warhead. He even had time to set his fuse, but then watched in horror as his charioteer lost control. It plunged back into the depths, taking him with it. Somehow he managed to blow its air tank and reversed the process, while hanging on for all he was worth. It suddenly resurfaced within a few yards of the ship. Notari thought it would trigger an alert, but he was relieved when nothing happened.

Notari searched for his diver Gianolli without success, and each presumed the other had drowned. Notari then began to swim away. His colleague, though, was still very much alive but had a badly torn rubber suit. He was therefore unable to escape, so decided to wait and then give himself up. He wanted to allow other members of his unit time to complete their duties.

Gianolli hung on to the bilge keel treading water, while trying to avoid more barbed wire. Two hours later, and dressed in tattered clothing, he finally surrendered. He was taken aboard the *Stanridge*, and the captain sent for Crabb. When he arrived, he agreed to transfer Gianolli to their patrol launch berthed alongside, and which was unknowingly situated just above a live warhead. Crabb ordered his colleague Bell to check the ship's hull, but just as he was about to go overboard, Gianolli's torpedo mine exploded. The blast killed the sentry guarding the Italian, and a sharp splinter also caught Bell full in the face. Crabb pulled his launch away from the stricken vessel, which had been ripped apart by the blast, and they watched in bewilderment as the blazing Norwegian ship quickly broke her back and sank.

Within minutes several other explosions rocked the harbour and, as Crabb headed back to the quayside to hand over his prisoner, another mine exploded under the *Harrison Gray Otis*. Crabb continued working through the night to locate and destroy several other devices, but it became an all-too-familiar story that continued for many more months. Fortunately, Petty Officer Bell survived, but nursed severe facial injuries and a large black eye for many more weeks. Bell was later to share a similar honour to Bailey and Crabb, when he, too, was awarded the George Medal.

As the heavy toll of 'shouts' and clearances continued, Crabb and his team were nearing exhaustion. There seemed no end to the ferocity of attacks, and during September 1943, just as the Italians began planning another series of attacks, intelligence sources reported the arrival of still more charioteers, weapons and ammunition, under the guise of 'spares'. But on 8 September, and on the eve of what was potentially one of the most devastating attacks ever, the Commander-in-Chief of the Tenth Light Flotilla, Cdr Borghese, heard on the radio that his country had negotiated an immediate Armistice with the Allies. Consequently, their war was unexpectedly over – but no one had bothered to tell them. Mussolini's Italy had surprisingly and suddenly capitulated.

The tables turned, the crack team of Italian divers now feared for their own lives. The majority of the unit hated the Nazis, and always had mixed feelings about supporting the war effort, but now they would certainly not be popular with the partisans, nor the Germans, who still occupied a large proportion of their country. After much discussion, several Italians decided they would try to make their own way south, to join the Americans. Meanwhile, on hearing this sensational news, the *Olterra's* crew fled, leaving their skipper Cdr Pierleoni to try to scuttle the ship. He placed some of the diving equipment and torpedo mines together in the hold, and attempted to set the self-destruction charges. He planned to escape via his Spanish contacts but fortunately for both the ship and the harbour, he was hopelessly inexperienced, and the explosives proved ineffective, with little damage caused.

A short time later, as Lionel Crabb watched the bizarre quayside activities with glee through his binoculars, he said it was 'like seeing rats leaving a sinking ship'. Only this time he hoped the ship wouldn't sink. Crabb again informed Cdr Hancock about the prospects of weaponry on board the *Olterra*, and after delicate negotiations with the Spanish port authorities, she was eventually allowed to leave and was towed back into Gibraltar Bay. When she dropped anchor, Crabb was one of the first aboard to examine its haul of piloted torpedoes. Within days, he had trained himself to operate a charioteer, and also shaved off a scruffy beard to test some of the Italians' modern facemasks and diving gear. He was staggered at the amount of ammunition stored. He wondered just how many more lives could have been saved, and ships spared, if the intelligence services had first acted upon his information that the *Olterra* was conducting espionage activities, and operating from within neutral waters.

Examples of Lionel Crabb's wartime exploits were later highlighted in a 1959 British drama, *The Silent Enemy*, a black-and-white feature film based on his wartime experiences in Gibraltar, starring Laurence Harvey, with Michael Craig as Sydney Knowles and a supporting cast including Nigel Stock, Sidney James and John Clements. The publicity material stated: 'Laurence Harvey stars as bomb disposal expert Lionel "Buster" Crabb in this tense action-packed wartime naval drama based on a true story . . . *The Silent Enemy* is a classic British war film especially praised for its authentic underwater action scenes.'

Some scenes in the film were based upon another extraordinary chapter in Crabb's life, when in 1943 he was called upon to help search for survivors from a plane crash that killed eighteen people. Among the casualties was Polish General Wladyslaw Sikorski. Shortly before the general's death, he was informed of the discovery of thousands of murdered Polish officers in the forests of Katyn, near Smolensk in the USSR. They were found by the Nazis, who immediately blamed the Russians for the atrocity.

Chapter 10

James Bond and General Sikorski

Throughout the Second World War Kitty Jarvis was Anthony Blunt's personal assistant in Military Intelligence at the War Office. She was on friendly terms with Ian Fleming, the writer and Naval Intelligence chief who worked close by. Fleming was a frequent visitor to Kitty's outer office, which she usually shared with Guy Burgess and Donald Maclean. Fleming had a dry sense of humour, and according to Crabb's relatives he often joined in with the office banter, observing attempts by Kitty's colleagues to try and throw their homburgs and bowlers on to a tall, highly polished, wooden hat stand in the corner of the room. This action, in times of boredom, always amused Fleming, and was later incorporated into the James Bond books. Fleming's fondness for Kitty became yet another feature of his novels. She was always known as 'Mater' at work, and her friendly, efficient, and almost motherly image became the inspiration for Miss Moneypenny.

Guy Burgess, Ian Fleming and Kim Philby all worked as journalists before the war. Burgess reported for *The Times* and the BBC from 1936 to 1944, while on secondment to the War Office. In 1944 he joined the Foreign Office news team before being sent to Washington as a second secretary at the British Embassy, where he rejoined Philby.

Throughout the war, Blunt had access to the Enigma Ultra codes at Bletchley Park. Kim Philby, on his return from Counter Intelligence missions as head of the Iberian Peninsula, also had access to these highly sensitive files, and later worked with John Cairncross, another regular at Kitty's parties. Cairncross had worked with Kitty before at the Government Cipher School.

Remarkably, very few espionage mysteries from the 1940s and 1950s remain unresolved, but two that do involve Lionel Crabb. Quite apart from his own mysterious disappearance in 1956, he was called upon in 1943 to help with a rescue mission following the crash of a Liberator in the waters just off the runway at Gibraltar airport. The plane had taken off at 11 p.m. on 4 July, carrying the 62-year-old General Sikorski and his daughter, Sofia Lesinowska, several military officials and service colleagues. They were travelling back to London from the Middle East.

Sikorski was the Chief Commander of Poland and Prime Minister of the Polish government in exile. And this extraordinary incident alone is probably worthy of a new independent investigation. Only the pilot Edward 'Max' Prchal survived. He was a Czech, and for some bizarre reason was the only person on board found to be wearing a fully fastened lifejacket. He was rescued from the crashed plane by an RAF launch, while the other eighteen passengers perished. Some bodies were never found, and for decades it has been suggested that the Russians, Germans or even Britain were involved in a daring and highly successful sabotage or assassination plot.

The military leader's body was found floating on the surface; other bodies were trapped inside the plane. Naval divers Lionel Crabb and Bill Bailey were asked to search and recover Sikorski's briefcase. They were also alerted to the prospect of attack or interception by enemy divers.

Crabb and his diving partner had to endure limited visibility and physical risk, due to leaking fuel oil, and contamination from a blue-green dye from cigarette cartons that stained the water, as well as many broken crates of alcohol. Several bodies were later washed ashore on the Spanish coast but the body of Sikorski's daughter was never found. New information now suggests otherwise, together with the possible identification of two saboteurs. Questions remain regarding exactly who boarded the aircraft, whether anyone else survived, and who was responsible for the crash.

The mystery remains the subject of exceptional interest and controversy in Britain, Poland, the USA, Canada and Russia. At that time, the general was involved in crucial negotiations with three of the world's most powerful politicians: Winston Churchill, Joseph Stalin and Franklin Roosevelt.

There was concern from Churchill that the incident could threaten the Alliance. Records now indicate the Russians distrusted Sikorski, as did some of his own countrymen, and that the plane carrying the Polish general was said to have been switched for technical reasons. Sikorski's replacement plane stood relatively unguarded for many hours, and was parked next to a Russian aircraft that had brought Soviet Ambassador Ivan Maisky to Gibraltar. The general's original plane, together with most of his Polish staff, eventually landed safely back in London.

At that time, Soviet spy Kim Philby was responsible for Britain's counter-espionage in that region, and current reports indicate he reported Sikorski as a 'potential danger' to Stalin. In subsequent interrogation notes by Allied intelligence officers with Heinrich Muller, Philby's Nazi intelligence contact within the Abwehr, Muller admitted having had a conversation with him about an assassination. Muller also claimed he knew exactly what Philby had told him about events on that fateful day.

It seems strange that Blunt, Burgess and Maclean from MI5, and Ian Fleming from Naval Intelligence, were all aware of General Sikorski's movements. To add fuel to the fire, Anthony Blunt once claimed he had only one major regret during the war and that was ordering the sabotage of a passenger plane. Could it have been the Sikorski aircraft? It is certainly a most peculiar coincidence that so many of Blunt's associates were actively involved in some way with this incident – including Lionel Crabb.

Also worthy of mention is Ian Fleming. His links with Kitty Jarvis are well known, as was his wartime supervision of the Polish spy, Krystyna Skarbeck, also known as Christine Granville, who worked for the Special Operations Executive (SOE) in occupied Europe. She later became Fleming's lover. Incredibly, a close relative of hers was killed in the crash, and Krystyna was said to have gained access to some very important information.

On 15 June 1952, however, and shortly before Fleming published his very first Bond novel, *Casino Royale*, Krystyna was stabbed to death at the Shelbourne Hotel, Kensington. As a tribute to her beauty and courage,

Fleming created the character of Vesper Lynd. Chillingly, five years later, in May 1957, a friend and confidante of Christine, Teresa Lubienski, a Polish countess, was also found stabbed to death at nearby Gloucester Road Underground station. Press reports of the time claim that she too had spoken about this incident ironically within Crabb's former 'local', the Nag's Head.

There are other links to Lionel Crabb, his relatives and associates. They include Lord Victor Rothschild, whose personal effects were found in a suitcase under a bed in Kitty's spare room following a private meeting with Burgess and Maclean. Rothschild helped investigate the Sikorski crash.

Rothschild interviewed Crabb, and his colleague Lt Bailey, the two main rescue divers. Years afterwards, it was suggested that Rothschild might have been the fifth Cambridge spy. His name was certainly mentioned with suspicion by Crabb's relatives, along with those of the other members of the notorious 'Cambridge Five'.

In 2006, Lord Rothschild's name cropped up again, following the release by The National Archives of some official government papers about the Sikorski incident. Included were copies of letters from the investigative journalist Carlos Thompson to Lord Rothschild, together with his response. Thompson began to investigate the circumstances of the crash in 1969. Here is the letter to Lord Rothschild from the reporter, dated 14 February 1969:

Dear Lord Rothschild,

Through a conversation with one of the many persons who have contributed to the information gathered in the two and half year research I have conducted on the background of the Rolf Hochnuth play, *Soldiers*, it has come to my knowledge that in about July 1943, you visited Gibraltar to investigate sabotage to Allied shipping.

I was also told that following the Sikorski crash, you were again in Gibraltar and had an opportunity to look into the possible causes of the crash.

You may have heard that the end result of my investigation will be a book entitled *The Assassination of Winston Churchill*, which amounts to a strong indictment of the motives and methods of Herr Hochnuth.

I would be deeply grateful should you choose to honour me with whatever recollections you may have of those circumstances. Most respectfully and cordially yours,

Carlos Thompson.

And this, taken from British Intelligence files, is Lord Rothschild's reply:

Dear Mr Thompson,

I had no official connection whatsoever with the Sikorski episode at Gibraltar. It was just a coincidence that I arrived at Gibraltar for other reasons shortly after the tragedy.

However, being interested in such matters, I did have a discussion with two underwater specialists (Crabb and Bailey), whom I believe examined the aircraft wreckage and the corpses in it. I strongly gained the impression from them that there was no question of sabotage.

My memory is somewhat hazy on the following point, but I seem to remember we discussed a known problem affecting Liberators to do with ailerons, but it is a long time ago and I cannot be sure.

Signed,

Lord Rothschild

Other reports and letters in intelligence files clearly implied that Carlos Thompson believed Prime Minister Winston Churchill might have ordered the destruction of General Sikorski's plane. However, two letters, dated 5 May and 12 May 1969, and written at the time of his inquiries, seem to counter the claims of Churchill's interference; from all accounts Churchill wanted Sikorski on his side to help maintain the Alliance. The first letter is from Richard Usborne to Peter Wilkinson. Both were senior British government officials.

Dear Peter,

I write to tell you that I came across a letter from you to me the other day (a file burst open and I spent a rather depressing two hours re-reading correspondence accumulated in the ME [Middle East] years, Cairo, Beirut etc, before strapping the file up again).

I didn't make a note of the date of your letter, but you'd got back to London and were complaining that the girls were all wearing cotton stockings and that a bottle of wine cost 15 shillings. And you said something like, 'I've been trying to get away, and thought I'd be off with General Sikorski. But I got bumped by, of all people, Victor Cazalet.' Would this be the jaunt to Gibraltar and into the drink?

I've been getting an earful of this event not only from the papers but also from Bickham, who is delighted in his mysterious way to have been accused of murder . . .

Yours ever,

Richard Usborne

Wilkinson replied:

Thank you for your letter of 5 May. Your surmise is correct and I very nearly went into the drink. The story is as follows: Sikorski (for purely Polish reasons) wanted a British officer to accompany him to Moscow and I was selected to go (for purely British reasons which I need not go into here but which you can imagine). About a fortnight before the departure, Sikorski learned that Victor Cazalet wanted to join the party. Cazalet was obviously much more use to the Poles than I was, but he was much less to the British.

There was no room for both of us and there followed one of those undignified wrangles which characterised Eden's relations with Dalton. In the end, the dispute went to the Prime Minister who, not surprisingly, decided in favour of Cazalet.

The story has some interest in connection with the present controversy since, if further evidence were needed, it is almost inconceivable that Churchill could have connived at the death of Cazalet (whatever he felt about Sikorski) since Cazalet had been a neighbour, and I think very much a friend during the years in the wilderness, besides being a prominent Conservative MP.

Had I gone instead of Cazalet, I suppose that my special relationship with the Czechs would have deepened the mystery but not even my worst detractors could ever have accused me of a *Todwunsch*.

P.A. Wilkinson

An official report confirms that Rothschild led an inquiry into another plot to kill the Polish leader in 1942 – some sixteen months before the general died. This was said to be just one of three attempts on his life. Secret files confirm that an assassination plot alerted suspicions that either German or Russian agents may have been involved. And even Prime Minister Churchill was questioned about what really happened. Polish pilot Kleczynski at first claimed he had found a smouldering bomb on his plane as VIP passengers boarded for a secret journey across the Atlantic from Prestwick in Scotland to Canada on 21 March 1942.

He told Intelligence Chief Investigator, Lord Rothschild, that he found a burning device hidden under a mattress as he rested before the flight in his B-24 Liberator. Kleczynski said the device then split in two. 'The detached part was so hot that I threw it into the lavatory pan,' he claimed. Rothschild and other officials were highly sceptical about his story, despite the pilot's reputation and experience as a heroic fighter pilot. He said: 'The story is very fishy. I remain somewhat doubtful if this was a real attempt to liquidate the General.'

Investigators later interrogated every single person on the plane and checked out the small incendiary device. Lord Rothschild said: 'There was no evidence of any threat of explosion but some other passengers said they had smelt burning, but this was later traced to a minor electrical fault.' Eventually Kleczynski admitted he had lied. He said the bomb belonged to him and he had kept it in case he was shot down and needed to scuttle his plane. He claimed he had taken it aboard that day in error and said he had panicked at the smell of burning.

Churchill ordered the findings of this inquiry to remain confidential and even wrote to General Sikorski personally, telling him about the pilot, Kleczynski, stating: 'He has been sufficiently punished by the mental anguish that he has passed through. Having told one lie, he was compelled to go on lying.'

A second incident happened a short time later when a plane carrying the general from Canada to America struck the ground immediately upon take-off. Fortunately no one was injured. And within the recently released secret papers are reports that an anonymous telephone call was made in May 1943 claiming General Sikorski had lost his life in an air accident flying from Gibraltar to the Middle East. This was a false alarm that was to become reality just six weeks later.

An inquiry into Sikorski's fatal crash failed to reveal the exact cause of the incident, but at the time, it ruled out sabotage. Another British review however, in 1969, following journalist Carlos Thompson's inquiries, suggested there might have been foul play.

Other recently acquired documents reveal that the surviving Czech pilot Prchal denied wearing his lifejacket at the RAF court of inquiry – despite being rescued from the surface, and even acknowledged by three independent witnesses, that he wore an inflated Mae West life preserver, with all the fastenings secured.

He was said to be the only survivor, and was the only person aboard the plane found wearing a lifejacket. Count Ludwik Lubienski, another important key witness, who was head of the Polish Mission in Gibraltar at the time, said he pulled the pilot out of the sea by his hair. He confirmed the pilot was definitely wearing an inflated life preserver around his neck.

Recent reports say the pilot returned to Czechoslovakia and allegedly told an RAF officer in Prague one evening in 1946, that he had lied to the Court of Inquiry about the circumstances of the crash, because he could only assume that it was his crew's smuggling activities that caused the crash. In letters from Intelligence files released in 2006, it is claimed he said he had had to cover up for them honourably, as they were all either killed or were missing.

And emerging over the past year or so, following the release of some additional government papers and reports from Polish investigators, are strong claims that Lionel Crabb probably met General Sikorski in Gibraltar the day before the crash. They are linked with other credible suggestions that Crabb quite probably met both the general and his daughter some time before in London at one of Rosa's parties for Polish officers, which were often attended by Anthony Blunt and/or his associates.

Newly available documentation from The National Archives gives further mention of Lionel Crabb, and of his 'involvement' in the rescue. The documents state that the pilot was anxious about the delayed take-off, where it waited an unusually long time (some 20 minutes), running up its engines at full because it was tail-heavy. It says that thirty to forty cases of alcohol were loaded into the fuselage and the crew busied themselves repacking them into different bomb bays. This may perhaps explain why a mailbag fell out and was found at the end of the runway after take-off. At this stage, there are also genuine claims that the bullet-ridden body of a former Polish officer was later found at the other end of the runway. The man had allegedly been shot twice in the back of the head. His passport was dry, and yet he was listed as drowned.

Eyewitness accounts of the Sikorski crash confirmed that when the plane reached a certain height shortly after take-off, the dwindling navigation lights of the Liberator stopped climbing. The report says: 'Slowly they began to drop. The plane flew on an even keel and apparently went into the sea intact but at an angle of about 10 degrees. The plane crashed less than a mile from the end of the runway.'

Another vital witness claimed that just before take-off, the general's daughter was handed a large box of chocolates. Her body was supposedly never recovered, and yet it is said that her companion, a woman who sat next to her on the plane, was badly mutilated – perhaps by a bomb blast. More recent reports indicate that the general's daughter was located by local divers, but said they feared bad luck if they were touched by her long flowing hair. They said she looked like a mermaid.

Additional reports suggest there may indeed have been some sort of explosion as the plane crashed into the sea. This claim was given credibility by a Gibraltar air traffic controller who recalled, 'There was a loud bang when the plane hit the water.'

The Polish Ministry of Internal Affairs sent an engineer to examine the crashed plane. He dismissed some of the findings of the Commission and highlighted several other potential factors, including claims that the plane was not properly guarded, and that passengers had not been formally cleared or identified. He had to agree, though, that he also found 'insufficient evidence to confirm sabotage'.

However, a former Polish Minister and Parliamentary Deputy, Karol Popiel, disputed both reports and claimed: 'General Sikorski's death was no accident. It was planned and it was supposed to have happened on his way to the Middle East. The plot failed initially but succeeded a few weeks later.'

The British Investigative Commission said the crash was an accident. The report presented on 27 July said:

> . . . there was no trace of sabotage and that other reasons, which could not be established, were responsible for the catastrophe. The report of the Court of Inquiry, which has been investigating the cause of the Liberator accident at Gibraltar on 4 July 1943, in which General Sikorski lost his life, has now been received.
>
> The findings of the Court and the observations of the officers whose duty it is to review and comment on these findings have been considered and it is apparent that the accident was due to jamming of the elevator controls shortly after take-off, with the result that the aircraft became uncontrollable.
>
> After most careful examination of all the available evidence, including that of the pilot, it has not been possible to determine how the jamming occurred, but it has been established that there was no sabotage.

Lionel Crabb and Bill Bailey dived continuously over several days, helping to recover the bodies and all the documentation. One of Crabb's diving colleagues, Sydney Knowles, recalled the incident. He says:

> We were working out in the bay searching merchant ships at anchor when we heard the roar of engines from an aircraft taking off. But the noise ceased abruptly and the plane crashed into the sea. We of course leapt into a launch and raced towards the accident, hoping to offer assistance, but the plane had sunk just off the edge of the runway. There was only one survivor, the pilot, who was found floating on the surface. We dived, hoping to find other survivors – but in vain. The following day, we dived again to search for the body of General Sikorski, who I believe had in his possession some very secret documents. We retrieved sixteen bodies but were unable to find the body of the General's daughter, Sofia Lesinowska.

A new but undated intelligence file from The National Archives considers other independent investigations at that time. It cast doubt on a possible sabotage attack but did not discount it:

Lt Crabb: the presence in Gibraltar of this figure of daring mystery is almost too good to be true. During the intervening years there have been claims that Crabb was a Russian double agent, not an atom of proof of course. Pure speculation! Crabb, though, if he was a Russian agent could have been the contact for Prchal in Gibraltar, or he might be just a British naval officer, and familiar with many service personnel, could have got close enough to the aircraft to cause some mischief.

If I was writing this as fiction, I would make it the Russians bringing pressure on Prchal, using Crabb as the go-between or paymaster. Perhaps both of them were under the impression that they were working for the British. In reality, though, it could have been a straightforward accident.

According to files from The National Archives and MI6, notes from Crabb and the account of Sydney Knowles, a second plane crashed into the sea off Gibraltar shortly afterwards. This time it was an Albacore with an RAF crew. Unfortunately, all crew were lost and Crabb's team, who were again quickly on the scene, were forced to dive in petrol as the plane had ruptured its fuel tank on impact.

Naval records and the recollections of Sydney Knowles reveal that Crabb and his team once had a lucky escape when a cable-laying ship entered their diving pen by mistake. It completely crushed their only launch, and Crabb had to go cap in hand to the RAF, to borrow one of their boats. The loss caused a tremendous communication problem at a delicate time, and seemed an incredible state of affairs for a team in such demand. Crabb and his men were reduced to attending 'shouts' on borrowed butchers' bikes, with all their gear packed into the front baskets. From their base at Jumper's Bastion, the men had to cycle down the main street to Casemate's Square, and on to the north mole to board their new launch tender.

In the early months of 1944, following the capitulation of the Italian forces and the subsequent downfall of their national leader, the threat of enemy action against important ships in Gibraltar evaporated overnight. Crabb, though, maintained standing orders, insisting that patrols should not become complacent. For a period of time, divers still checked the hulls of convoy and Spanish ships, and even fired a few depth charges. Seeing little or no enemy action, however, contingency plans were put into motion to disband Crabb's Underwater Working Party. The majority of his team returned to England, but Crabb remained and prepared for another new challenge, this time in mainland Italy.

Lt Cdr Crabb was offered a highly prestigious position as a member of the Intelligence Collecting Unit (ICU) operated by the Joint Services. It was a venture comprising representatives from each of the three main services and from both British and American forces. Crabb's mission was to locate, capture or identify important documents, weapons, art treasures and even enemy personnel. He was also put in charge of all anti-sabotage operations, including bomb and mine disposal on the east and west coasts of Italy.

Part of Crabb's brief was also to help locate any remaining charioteers, and to help track down missing members of the notorious Italian Tenth Light Flotilla, which had caused so many problems for Allied shipping.

Despite the end of hostilities in Gibraltar, enemy divers and torpedo mines continued to prove a menace around the Italian coastline. Crabb, in effect, was required to become an investigator, a bomb disposal officer, a liaison officer, and to some extent, a spy. To help with his new role, he needed to travel extensively across Italy and was asked to find a reliable driver from the ranks to accompany him. Crabb quickly selected one of his most loyal divers in Sydney Knowles, a former lorry driver, who seemed reluctant to return home. The pair finally left Gibraltar aboard a Royal Navy landing craft and headed towards Naples.

Chapter 11

The Italian Job

After working under such intense pressure for two years in Gibraltar, Lionel Crabb was at least hoping for a short break in Naples before starting his new job. But as he and his driver Knowles approached the city, they were told that nearby Mount Vesuvius was about to erupt. Crabb could smell sulphur in the air, and the sight of large particles of grey-white ash falling like snow all around reminded him of his early childhood in London. Because of the uncertainty of the situation, he decided to continue to the Allied Headquarters building in Caserta, where he and Knowles collected an American manufactured 6 × 6 lorry. At the base, Crabb quickly loaded new diving gear, tools and supplies, before heading north to Rome along an open highway.

Rome was eerily quiet, and the streets almost deserted, apart from a few military personnel. On arrival at his hotel, the Nationale, Crabb was greeted by Lt Tony Marsloe, a former assistant district attorney from New York, who was the liaison officer in charge of an American Intelligence unit. He was of Italian origin and had a good working knowledge of the language.

Unusually, Crabb rejected Marsloe's offer of drinks and disappeared to the comfort of his own room, to enjoy the rare luxury of a hot bath, clean sheets and pillows. It had been some considerable time since he had slept in a comfortable bed. During this period, Crabb's life had changed almost beyond recognition. He had also become a Roman Catholic, much to some obvious concern back home, and the following day he took the opportunity to visit St Peter's. Sydney Knowles recalls: 'Commander Crabb was a devout Catholic. He organised a visit to St Peter's and ask me to accompany him. We were probably the only tourists in Rome, and I remember he kept referring to the priests as "God's Butlers".'

Crabb later wrote to his mother Daisy with an update of his movements and told her that the war had changed his attitude to life – and death. He explained that he first converted to Catholicism during his stay in Gibraltar. His family believe it was the shock of losing comrades and witnessing the death of enemy divers that sparked his religious conversion. This decision caused another temporary rift in the Crabb and Jarvis families, and it was only later that Lionel was able to return home and explain his reasons face to face with his mother. Lomond Handley says:

> I don't quite know what Lionel told Daisy, but she went absolutely ape! She was wailing and weeping on the phone to my mother. My mother finally soothed her and commented how wonderful it was that Lionel had found such comfort at last. I don't really know what sparked this conversion, but I imagine his time in Gibraltar and Italy, and his good relationship with the Italian POWs, and the widows of those brave men probably had something to do with it.
>
> There was a lot of mutual respect, and I can believe that Lionel would have insisted on honouring those dead Italians, whom he may well have had a hand in killing.

Crabb and Knowles left Rome a day or two later, with orders to head first to Leghorn (Livorno) and on to Florence. They carried a distinctive white Navy ensign on the roof of their lorry and found many roads badly shell-holed. They drove into Leghorn with the American Fifth Army, and were announced as the official clearance team for the British Navy. Part of their task involved checking and clearing the port areas surrounded by rubble from the bombing. Crabb then received urgent instructions to report to ICU headquarters, but as they entered Florence they came under heavy sniper fire.

Florence was supposed to have been a safe and open city, but at this time no one had told the Germans and problems continued, as Crabb's stopover at the city's popular Excelsior Hotel was disrupted by shelling from another division of Nazi stragglers. Despite much of the country being declared open, life was still full of danger, with numerous small towns and villages constantly changing hands; and although Crabb and his driver were both fully armed, they had no intention of taking on the whole of the retreating German army.

Throughout much of Italy at that time Crabb was prevented from reaching certain areas to help clear mines, because they were still occupied. At his new headquarters, Crabb was handed a variety of assignments including an important mission to transport a high-ranking Allied officer, and to take him across the river near the Ponte Vecchio. The officer was required for an urgent meeting with the partisans at Porta Rossa, but the only way to ensure his safety, according to Sydney Knowles, was to deliver him at dead of night. He said they had to 'half carry and drag the man across the river', and later faced mortar and sniper attacks.

On their return Crabb was contacted again by American Intelligence chief Lt Marsloe, who said he was holding a young Italian sailor sent on from the Intelligence Collecting Unit (ICU). He admitted the man spoke little English and was claiming to be a certain Sub-Lt Venturini, a twenty-year-old former member of the Italian Tenth Flotilla. Although Marsloe spoke some Italian, he and Crabb had great difficulty in understanding Sub-Lt Venturini until he started making a sketch of a delayed action limpet mine on the back of an envelope. Venturini also outlined a proposed plan of attack against Allied shipping at Leghorn and described how to secure a torpedo mine against the bilge keel of a freighter or warship. They knew his information was vital and arranged for him to be taken under guard to the British Naval HQ at Caserta to be formally interrogated.

Knowles recalled his first meeting with this young Italian diver and spoke about the harsh realities of those days. He says:

When Lt Venturini first appeared, I was ordered to take him to Naval headquarters in my jeep under escort, followed by a vehicle carrying two Royal Marines. It was over a track that I had driven many times before.

But all at once there was a tremendous explosion behind me. The escort vehicle had driven over a land mine. By sheer good fortune, I had passed over it between my wheels. The explosion threw the vehicle and the men high into the air. Both Marines were killed instantly. It certainly left a lasting impression on me.

Venturini, however, provided essential information about proposed raids, together with names and details of enemy attackers. He also provided facts about a number of German surface units protecting coastal convoys, and claimed that some former members of the Tenth Light Flotilla might even be persuaded to support the Allies. He added, though, that many other Italian divers and saboteurs, who had refused to surrender when Italy sued for peace, still posed a serious danger.

Crabb didn't really know how much, if any, of this was true. He also knew that it could have been a trap. And Venturini explained that the Italian Cdr Borghese, who had previously helped organise such devastating attacks at Gibraltar, had since formed a new land division with remaining members of his unit. He was reported to be hiding out somewhere near La Spezia.

Naval HQ believed the story and agreed to release Crabb from his other duties, requesting he organise an urgent anti-sabotage unit. Venturini was also released into Crabb's custody. Within just three weeks, Crabb had had three very different roles, and each one had been more dangerous.

As he opened his forwarded mail at the Unit's HQ at Caserta, Lionel Crabb was amused to see a signal from his old training school at HMS *Volcano* in Cumberland. It had been passed on from his Commander-in-Chief. It claimed he had not attended a refresher course since 1942, and stated he could no longer be considered a competent bomb safety officer.

Crabb was ordered back to Leghorn, where he quickly reported to the harbour commander, who greeted him warmly. Crabb had been there before to help clear mines from the quayside while under constant sniper fire, and as he looked around the war-torn area, he thought it resembled Gibraltar all over again, with Italian divers threatening to attack Allied shipping.

In addition, the American Fifth Army and remnants of the German Army were still engaged in fierce battles close by. Despite this continual chaos,

Crabb was still trying to locate and assemble his new diving team. So far, it consisted of just Crabb, Knowles and the young Italian diver Venturini. The harbourmaster said he might be able to find another volunteer, and claimed a local boatman had already applied. He said the name was Vago Giari, and claimed he was another former Gibraltar raider.

Sydney Knowles says: 'One morning, we opened the door to Giari. He asked for a diving job and to my amazement, he said that he too had been a member of the Tenth Flotilla which had attacked our shipping in Gibraltar. When Italy surrendered, he returned home to Leghorn. He had already been cleared by Navy HQ, so we welcomed him with open arms.'

Giari told Crabb that he had been awarded a gold medal for his successful operations against the Allies. He willingly volunteered for this new Underwater Working Party, and was awarded the rank equivalent to that of a petty officer. He happily showed everyone his Italian swim flippers and modern Italian diving suit and equipment, but was told by Crabb that unfortunately the British did not have any similar kit available; he said they would have to make do with old-fashioned DSEA sets as before.

A few more weeks passed. The fighting around town stopped, and Crabb and his colleagues were able to complete some basic training. He reorganised security patrols and prepared more 'home-made' depth charges, and again installed barbed wire curtains around the hulls of all capital ships.

One day, another former Italian diver arrived at Naval HQ. This was Cdr Ernesto Notari, another diving colleague of Venturini and Giari, who asked to see Crabb. He shook Crabb's hand and thanked him for taking the trouble to bury the dead from his unit back in Gibraltar. Notari had taken over command of the Tenth Light Flotilla following Lioria Visintini's death. He said he had often travelled close to Crabb aboard one of the Spanish bum-boats. The pair later dined together and spoke about the time a guard had died, and both Crabb and Petty Officer Bell were almost killed, when Notan's warhead exploded under their launch, sinking the merchant ship.

At Leghorn Crabb collected another painful war wound. He and Knowles were diving under an American freighter when Crabb caught his leg on a roll of barbed wire, which, ironically, had been dropped on his orders by the ship's captain to deter enemy frogmen. Knowles had to dress the wound when they returned to the surface. It left a deep and permanent scar on Crabb's knee.

As he was being treated, Crabb received new intelligence reports that the Republican officer Borghese was preparing to lead a small group of pro-German divers against Allied shipping at Leghorn. They were warned that the attack was imminent. The harbour at that time was packed with varied shipping, including several American Liberty and capital ships. Giari, Venturini and Knowles were advised. They were instructed to examine many hulls, and to keep vigilant.

A round-the-clock watch was implemented, and as darkness fell and sentries patrolled, there was an acute sense of nervousness in the air. Suddenly the crack of a single shot rang out as a warning, followed by the start-up of sirens, and searchlights bathed the moles and jetties with bright lights, soon revealing two very bewildered-looking enemy frogmen. They were dressed in lightweight Italian diving suits and had arrived in a motorboat towing a number of booby-trapped mines.

The men were later identified as Italian Republican divers Lt Malacarne and Sgt Sorgetti. Surprised and surrounded by numerous sentries, they surrendered. A short time later another diver, Lt Bertoncin, was also located and captured.

The only injury that night was to one of Crabb's working party. Patrols had been instructed not to throw any depth charges into the water without permission, as Allied divers were still working underwater. It seemed one man disregarded this order, and the subsequent explosion caught Giari as he surfaced.

He was badly injured, but dare not call out in his native Italian for help. Later he was rescued, but first had to surrender to the guards for his own safety. He was taken to a military hospital and soon recovered. The next morning, a fourth prisoner, Lt Pavone, was captured trying to escape through the dock gates. When the prisoners were finally interrogated, the identity of other potential raiders was also established.

Intelligence sources confirmed that if this series of attacks had proved successful, the renegade group would have continued further attempts on Allied shipping at many other ports. However, it was the beginning of the end of hostilities at Leghorn. Crabb's defensive strategy had worked again, and he was relieved to report back to the ICU team that no mines had been placed, and all enemy divers had been captured.

Despite several moderate successes, it was a difficult period for Crabb. At times he was very ill. He was exhausted from the stress and strain of dangerous operations. Colleagues agree he developed a short fuse and that his behaviour became somewhat erratic. He completed some difficult tasks at La Spezia, and a particularly challenging job in the south of France, before he finally ended up in hospital.

Crabb was on call twenty-four hours a day, seven days a week, working as a much-needed shallow diver, in addition to his other duties. He said that at times he felt most unwell. He was drained but claimed it was almost impossible to take any rest. He began packing his kit, and said he needed a short Christmas break in Leghorn. Just as he was about to depart, he received urgent instructions to go to the military airport and catch a small plane to the south of France, to render safe some troublesome German mines.

Reluctantly, he and Knowles took up the challenge. When they arrived at a place called Port Sete, they were put into a temporary billet in part of a bombed-out hotel. The arduous journey and discussions about rendering safe one particular mine took its toll on Crabb, who was clearly very ill. He kept complaining about the taste of his drinks and started sweating and shaking. Knowles says:

He [Crabb] became very moody, and looked a very strange colour. We had taken a flight on an American Dakota from Pisa to Marseilles to clear some mines in southern ports. We arrived in Port Sete in a battered old taxi to find the whole fishing community pleading with us to remove a German mine that was blocking the entrance to their harbour. We wanted to blow it up *in situ* but the Mayor protested because it was only a few yards from a statue of the Virgin Mary. After discussion we dived and attached heavy ropes and cables to an old steamroller. We were watched by a couple of hundred bystanders. We wanted to drag it into the centre of the basin. At last it began to move. We dived again and removed all the ropes and placed an explosive charge just under the mine. We connected the charge but the result was just a dull thud.

It remained delicate and dangerous but Crabb dived again. He placed another charge and we detonated it. This time, the basin erupted into a tremendous roar, and the entire crowd raced forward to collect the resulting dead fish floating on the surface. The same evening, Cdr Crabb was admitted to a French hospital. He was suffering from yellow jaundice and complete exhaustion. This was towards the end of December 1944, and he remained there for about two months.

A new disposal officer, Sub-Lt Bull, joined Knowles, and they continued working on other mines. They were billeted in Marseilles and were first told to check the harbour areas while waiting for Crabb's discharge. Crabb's recovery, though, took much longer than expected. Eventually Knowles was ordered back to Leghorn, where he met up again with Vago Giari, who presented him with a new Italian two-piece diving suit, complete with underwear.

One of Knowles's future dives almost ended in tragedy when, searching for mines in the Port of Genoa, he was rendered unconscious from oxygen poisoning. Fortunately, he was spotted on the surface, and was quickly dragged back aboard a patrol boat. When he recovered, he travelled across to the island of Elba and then back to Leghorn, finally teaming up again with his Commanding Officer, Crabb, at a local villa.

Friends could tell when Crabb was close to recovery: he clashed with a 'sergeant major' of a matron at the hospital, who argued with him about pinning up some original Picasso prints that he had found. Crabb's colleagues wanted to send Crabb back home, but he resisted, and said he wanted to be with the army when they entered La Spezia. He also said he wanted to meet the Italian divers, who were mainly POWs, and to visit the headquarters of the Tenth Light Flotilla in Venice.

Crabb stayed at the Villa Banti to recuperate, but just as he waited for news of a move to La Spezia, he was unexpectedly ordered to go to Ancona, and then Venice, to become their new bomb safety officer. Regrettably for Crabb, while he was away, his team was split up and sent to different places.

Knowles also travelled towards Venice from Caserta. He reached Savona before meeting up with Crabb again, and driving him back in the same old truck they had started with, complete with Navy ensign. Crabb then flew on to Ancona to join a new token naval force that was rapidly being assembled.

As for Knowles, his war was over. His father, a widower, had remarried. Knowles senior had moved to a new address with his new wife, and wrote directly to Lord Mountbatten, the operational commander, complaining that as the war had nearly ended, he wanted his son back home. He said he had neither seen nor heard from him for over three years. Knowles says:

> I was ordered to return to my depot in Plymouth, and I received the news with a heavy heart, as I was enjoying the work and the adrenalin rush. I really had no wish to return. So Cdr Crabb and I exchanged farewells, and I boarded a train that took three days and nights to reach Dieppe. I then crossed the Channel. It was several years before I was reunited with Crabb. He was a man I held in high esteem, and with whom I felt a mutual bond.

Crabb's new CO was Cdr Backhouse. The senior man greeted Crabb as a war hero. He was aware of Crabb's record, and said he had just received new orders directly from Mountbatten's HQ. He asked Crabb if he would lead the party into Venice at the head of a large convoy of Allied trucks that were being driven by Cypriots. Backhouse claimed he had other duties to attend to, and told Crabb to 'look smart'. Everyone was issued with new uniforms, and Crabb later explained that it had been 'the proudest day of my life'. Lt Cdr Crabb finally entered Venice on 29 April 1945, accompanied by members of the 56th London Division.

It was a gala occasion, and within minutes of arriving Crabb was asked to accept the surrender of a five-man crew from an Italian mini-sub. Shortly afterwards, he was joined by his former colleague, Lt Tony Marsloe, and then his CO, Cdr Backhouse, for a celebratory drink. As they chatted, Crabb asked Marsloe what he was doing there, as he understood he had been chasing the remnants of the Tenth Light Flotilla, and wondered why he was in Venice rather than La Spezia.

The reply had to wait because Crabb was pulled away to examine a series of deadly booby traps found along the Grand Canal. As he began his work several captured Italian divers appeared and offered to help him with his search. Almost to a man, the rebel divers saluted Crabb and agreed to make Venice safe again.

Crabb welcomed their assistance and removed two particularly difficult torpedo bombs placed by the Nazis under the Bridge of Sighs, before retiring to his new billet at the Danieli Hotel. There, and obviously tired from the day's exertions, he began to argue furiously with the hotel waiters. They were still speaking German to their new guests and Crabb had forgotten that until just a few hours earlier the city had been under enemy occupation.

The island of La Vignole, situated north-east of the Lido, was the home base for the Tenth Light Flotilla. The island had also been a major training camp for German and Italian divers, and a delighted Crabb finally achieved his ambition and visited their workshops and laboratories. Shortly before, Crabb had again willingly accepted the surrender of some very able and experienced divers. They included Sgt Fraguglia and Sgt Berni. Crabb had travelled to the island with the American, Lt Marsloe, who had spent most of the morning negotiating with the local partisan leaders for the release of some other Italian naval prisoners held at the Naval Academy. The Italians demanded a formal surrender to Crabb, as a matter of honour to a formidable opponent.

The Italians proudly gave Lionel Crabb and his men a guided tour of the island, and heard them admit that they had been prepared to defend themselves to the death against the partisans. Crabb marvelled at the Italians' modern facilities and extensive weaponry. He was then advised that Cdr Angelo Belloni, a First World War submariner and inventor who was the real brains behind the success of the Tenth Light Flotilla, had fled the island just as the Germans retreated. His Italian colleagues were concerned for his welfare.

Crabb agreed to make inquiries and told the sergeants that although they were officially prisoners of war, they could stay on the island to look after the equipment until other arrangements could be made. He even considered whether their experimental laboratory could continue under Allied supervision. As he pondered on this thought, Crabb met the partisan leader and asked him whether he knew of Belloni's whereabouts. It was still a very precarious time, and any captured Italian divers could face repercussions or retribution.

The chief laughed out loud, and explained that despite his army surrounding the Naval Academy, Cdr Belloni, who was now safely locked away in the local jail, had calmly tried to walk away dressed in casual clothing. He said his men had arrested him and claimed he was lucky not to have been shot as a spy. Crabb was horrified and claimed Belloni was perhaps one of the country's most important POWs.

Chapter 12

The Restoration of Venice

As Crabb and his party of Allied officers departed from La Vignole, they were bombarded with requests to search bridges in many parts of Venice. Warnings of booby traps and other unexploded devices were rife. And with few experienced officers at his disposal, Crabb had to attend many incidents himself before either dealing with them or delegating the task to willing POWs.

All the time he was driving back and forth across the city, Crabb's mind remained fixed on the fact that the Italian inventor, Cdr Angelo Belloni, was still detained in prison. Crabb later met up again with Lt Marsloe – the former American attorney – and demanded he accompany him to the main jail. Crabb thought his legal skills might come in useful, and so it proved, for Cdr Belloni had indeed been locked away, along with his teenage son, Julio.

The young man, who had been told about his father's detention, had dashed down to the jail to try to secure his release. However, fearing reprisals against either one or both of them, the prison chief decided to put Julio in jail alongside his father pending intervention by the new authorities. Venice was still a hotbed of violence and uncertainty however; the two Allied officers eventually persuaded the jailers to release the commander and his son into their custody.

Thinking quickly, and realising the potential of having the Tenth Light Flotilla on their side, or at least not battling against them, the jailers released Belloni into the care of a new Navy Experimental Station which Crabb called 'Sant'Andrea' – the name of the Italian fort on La Vignole.

Because of the ugly mood within the city, Crabb transferred the prisoner and his son immediately. When they had cleared the city limits, however, they persuaded the sixteen-year-old to go home and wait. They explained that they had no authority to detail the youngster and felt he would be safer with his family than in temporary confinement. Belloni was a tough old campaigner. He was in his mid-sixties and quite deaf. He had learned to lip-read in English. And amazingly, during discussions, he said he was disappointed not to have had the opportunity to try out some of his new weaponry against the Allies, both in Gibraltar and in Italy!

Belloni was critical of the kit used by British divers, and couldn't understand why they failed to use modern suits. Back at the small island, the commander was soon reunited with the two Italian sergeants Fraguglia and Berni, who showed Crabb and Marsloe some other experimental gear. They also met up with Belloni's eighteen-year-old daughter, Minella. She had arrived without warning and declared that she disliked both the British and Americans. She spoke with obvious pride about her sisters, who had fought against the Allies.

As they were talking, Crabb's boss, Cdr Backhouse, arrived. He had heard about the prison rescue and greeted Belloni before repeating the dangers of returning to central Venice at that time, and agreeing that interrogation should continue at La Vignole. He deployed a contingent of Polish soldiers to keep watch and urged his party to remain on the island.

Just as Crabb and Marsloe were finalising arrangements to make their own quarters there, they received a cable advising that Trieste was no longer considered a safe supply port, due to the volatile situation in Yugoslavia. Therefore Crabb, as Venice's bomb safety officer, was instructed to clear all remaining explosives in the city dock areas, and to provide an alternative and safe supply route. Surprisingly, the two Italian sergeants immediately offered their services. Crabb already had several other former members of the Tenth Light Flotilla working for him around the clock on similar duties, but readily accepted their help. Cdr Belloni also volunteered but Crabb decided he could best serve the clearance of Venice by advising where any other remaining divers were hiding.

If they agreed to help Crabb, they were told they would have protection from the partisans, and knew their bomb disposal work would be for a good cause. Belloni gave the newly promoted Lt Cdr Marsloe full co-operation and mentioned several names that were already familiar to Crabb from previous attacks in Gibraltar. Once agreed, the deal had to be approved by the leader of the partisans. At first he was reticent, but finally accepted, believing it better to risk the lives of Italian divers than those of his own men.

Cdr Backhouse ensured that all the outstanding unit members were located and detained. Incredibly, some remained hostile, blaming Crabb for the loss of former comrades. Many were reluctant prisoners, believing rumours that some Italian prisoners had been forced to walk through minefields, paying the penalty for their traitorous actions. Eventually, after much negotiation, they all agreed to work for Crabb. Soon a formidable diving team was established and former enemies became friends, determined to champion a just cause. The team now included Cdr Belloni, senior Italian naval surgeon Dr Moscatelli, Tadini, Fraguglia, Berni, and many other notable POWs. In total, Crabb could now boast eight experienced Italian divers.

Mine clearance proved an immense task. One particularly difficult assignment related to an Italian tanker which the Germans had used as a freshwater reservoir. The tanker was sitting in the mud in shallow waters waiting for the tide. Reports suggested a magnetic acoustic mine had been attached and Crabb feared that if this were true, it could explode as soon as the ship lifted or started her engines. He warned the Italians that only non-magnetic equipment should be used. The Italians didn't quite understand and watched as Crabb prepared to dive. Rather than be humiliated by an Englishman, the Italians felt they could do equally well, and agreed to help him search the hull.

Crabb located the mine and re-surfaced. He told the ship's captain not to use any machinery. He noticed a tail fin sticking out of the thick mud. It looked like a new type of mine. There seemed no obvious way of dealing with this device without risking destroying the tanker and probably half the dockyard too.

Crabb discussed the problem with Belloni. He wondered if they could blow the tail without triggering the mine. He agreed to find a similar recovered mine and return it to the base at La Vignole for a controlled explosion.

The experiment worked and Crabb dashed back to the ship and attached a charge to the tail and repeated the exercise. Again it worked, but as he prepared a second charge, he decided to clear the whole area, and to evacuate the ship. It had been more than four hours since he had first located the mine and the skipper was anxious to move away from the danger zone. He also realised that he could re-float his ship, as Crabb had requested, without using any machinery, and began preparations to sail. It meant blowing his ballast and opening the seacocks to drain out the fresh water.

The mine, however, was firmly lodged in the mud directly between the vessel and the quayside, and as the water poured out, the ship slowly lifted and consequently the mine exploded. Surprisingly, the ship continued to rise and to everyone's surprise there seemed little or no damage to the quayside or the ship. The mine had become deeply embedded, and the heavy silt absorbed much of the blast. As the dust clouds settled, Crabb and his men dived to inspect her hull. There was only minor damage with just a severe dent in one of the plates.

Back at La Vignole, Crabb introduced some urgent house rules. He found a cache of weapons that the Italians had hidden in case of attack, and was aware that at least one member of the Italian team, Tadini, was returning home most nights to visit his girlfriend. Crabb was keen to instil discipline, and yet wanted to allow the men a certain amount of freedom. He called them together and explained that although he was technically in charge, they were responsible for their own actions. He said he knew about all the hidden weapons and absentees, and said that any weaponry must be declared, with permission sought for city visits.

It was a bold gamble on his part. He left them alone to consider their actions, but within an hour a senior officer returned with a large collection of arms and ammunition. Tadini also agreed to ask permission before absconding again.

Crabb believed this was a major turning point in accepting Allied rules, finally acknowledging that they were all ready to play a key role in the rebuilding of Venice.

When Trieste was eventually cleared, Crabb was delighted to hear that more British officers would be arriving to help with his clear-up. New arrivals included Lt Joe Howard and Lt Gerald Shirley, both members of the RNVR. Thankfully for Crabb, they were also fully trained divers, and their assistance came in extremely useful, although Howard had a narrow escape when a lone sniper once took a few pot shots at him.

At one stage Lt Howard thought a torpedo mine too dangerous to work on and suggested detonation, which would undoubtedly have destroyed an historic bridge, and much else around. Crabb, as determined as ever, pushed him aside, and within an hour or so defused the mine. He later explained to the young officer that he had become rather fond of the bridges in Venice. It soon became obvious to all new arrivals why their senior officer was so popular with all Italians.

While the end of hostilities was approaching in Europe war still raged in the Far East, and Belloni gave details of an innovative two-man submarine that he had designed a couple of years earlier to attack American ships. He was in his element. He seconded all sorts of equipment and heavy-duty machinery from the Allies, including some captured Italian gear.

La Vignole was becoming a busy Allied Naval Experimental Station, and to cater for Belloni's demands, officials even allowed one of his former rebel daughters, an ex-medical student, to join him as his secretary.

Lord Mountbatten followed the progress of this new unit with interest and pride before taking on his new role in the Far East. A few months earlier, he had welcomed news of a successful Anglo-Italian assault on German shipping in Genoa harbour. Crabb's combined Underwater Working Party eventually transferred most of its duties from searching for mines to locating or salvaging piloted torpedoes, and testing some re-designed models.

A few weeks later, another former rebel Italian officer, Lt Eugenio Wolk, asked to see Crabb. He mentioned that Maria, the widow of Lt Lioria Visintini, who had been killed in Gibraltar, wanted to meet him. She had written a letter to Crabb and wanted to know the full circumstances of her husband's death, and asked if he would come to her home near the Grand Canal. Crabb went and talked to her. She spoke fluent English and had previously worked as a secretary. She was living with her husband's mother in cramped accommodation, was virtually penniless and terribly unhappy. When Crabb returned to La Vignole, the POWs asked about the possibility of her coming to work with them. The idea was discussed with Lt Cdr Marsloe and fellow officers, and within a few days Maria joined them.

With life in Venice gradually returning to normal, Crabb felt quite at home. He even accepted an invitation to attend Lt Shirley's wedding as best man, and incredibly, at a war crimes tribunal in Venice, even gave evidence on behalf of several former members of the Tenth Light Flotilla. They had been accused of siding with the Germans against the Allies after Italy's capitulation. With Crabb's extraordinary support, however, and their voluntary minesweeping duties taken into consideration, the charges against Lt Wolk, Dr Moscatelli, Tadini and Cdr Belloni were dropped, and they were all permitted to continue working at the base. All went well until one day, when a large contingent of American military personnel arrived unannounced to take Berni, Fraguglia and Tadini under armed escort to the United States.

They explained they were required to work on other similar charioteer experiments. Crabb knew a heavy-handed approach would only lead to trouble. And after discussion with Marsloe, Crabb persuaded his colleague to speak with the senior arresting officer, to suggest a compromise whereby the men could volunteer for this assignment. That way, there was no need to arrest or handcuff them, and they could travel freely to America. Tony Marsloe also confirmed he would be returning to the States. He said he was preparing for his wedding, and would be taking his new bride back home with him. His wife, he told his friend Crabb, was Cdr Belloni's other ex-rebel daughter Minella.

By September 1945, Crabb received orders that his services were urgently required elsewhere, this time in Haifa, Israel. A farewell party was arranged at La Vignole to thank everyone for their support; and Crabb was totally staggered when his Italian team crowned him the 'King of Sant'Andrea', awarding him a metallic crown specially made in their workshops.

Before everyone departed for pastures new, Crabb was informed that he had been awarded an OBE for his high-risk operations in Italy, to add to his George Medal from Gibraltar. He arranged for a grand firework party, which would also destroy the piloted torpedo warheads. When set alight, they burned so fiercely in the darkness that the white-hot glow lit up the whole area. To the amusement of all, the spectacle even summoned surprised Venice fireboats.

As the drink flowed, Lionel Crabb ceremoniously handed over La Vignole to the care of some Italian officials. One of them, a former enemy diver and now a trusted friend and colleague, was Cdr Ernesto Notari. He had dined with Crabb in Leghorn but was also the man who had almost killed Crabb and others back in Gibraltar. All was now forgiven, and proudly dressed in his new naval uniform, Notari stood to attention and saluted Crabb for the final handover. Notari had been appointed the island's new commandant.

Chapter 13

Friends in High Places

Lionel Crabb had met his Commander-in-Chief, Lord Louis Mountbatten, shortly after arriving in Italy. Mountbatten had a passion for diving and spear fishing and had been taught to dive by some of Crabb's former colleagues. Mountbatten said diving was his second hobby after polo and it is understood that he and Crabb dived together during Mountbatten's tour of duty.

Crabb's heroic exploits and family connections were already well known to Mountbatten, who was keen to meet another daring adventurer. From October 1941, Mountbatten had been Head of Combined Operations Command. He had studied Crabb's operational files and was also aware of his cousin Kitty's vital role with another of his royal relatives, Anthony Blunt at the War Office.

Crabb's colleagues have suggested that Mountbatten and some of his trusted contacts had encouraged Crabb to attend some of Kitty's private parties at her flat and the Cavendish Hotel to share information on known Communists. Indeed, it had been Mountbatten who had recommended Crabb's promotion, and his later transfer from Gibraltar to Italy. Mountbatten realised that a new role within the Joint Services Intelligence Collecting Unit, would give Crabb more of a roving brief in his search for art treasures, weaponry and key personnel.

Archive notes indicate Crabb also met Lord Mountbatten in Gibraltar, probably just after the announcement of his George Medal. According to Crabb's friend Gordon Gutteridge, the pair got along remarkably well. Crabb's latest appointment with the ICU was part of a secondment to a newly created 'special branch' of the Admiralty, where his personal reports were seen directly by Mountbatten. It was at a later meeting in Italy that Mountbatten first heard about Crabb's 1936 involvement with the Chinese anti-Communist leader Chiang Kai-Shek, and Morris Cohen. It proved a most useful link and provided some rich dividends, and a new base in Taiwan. Crabb's unique relationship with Lord Mountbatten remained confidential for decades.

Only a small number of Crabb's associates knew much about his secret missions, or his unusual war work in Italy and beyond. During this period, Crabb accepted commissions for several risky assignments in Israel, the Far East, Russia, Malta and Egypt, before redirecting his skills homewards for diving operations around British waters.

Lord Mountbatten was a controversial military leader. He was the Queen's cousin, and an uncle to Prince Philip. As he was great-uncle to Prince Charles, it is said that Mountbatten had a strong influence on the young prince's upbringing. They were undoubtedly very fond of each other, calling themselves 'honorary grandfather' and 'honorary grandson'. Louis Francis Albert Victor Nicholas – His Serene Highness Prince Louis of Battenberg, to give him his full title – was born at Frogmore House, Windsor, on 25 June 1900. He was the son of Prince Louis of Battenberg but due to ill feeling towards the family during the First World War, the surname was changed to Mountbatten. Lord Louis attended Osborne and then Dartmouth Naval College 1913–16, before joining the Royal Navy. He enjoyed active service and served on both HMS *Lion* and HMS *Elizabeth*.

During his childhood, Lord Louis was invited to attend the Imperial Court of Russia at St Petersburg, where his parents remained close to the royal imperial family. Fondly known by his family and close friends as 'Dickie', he married the Hon. Edwina Cynthia Annette Ashley in June 1922.

The Mountbattens were *the* celebrity couple of the day, enjoying a spectacular and glamorous honeymoon in America. They were even invited to Hollywood, where they were introduced to many famous British actors and film stars including Douglas Fairbanks, Mary Pickford and Charlie Chaplin. In 1922 Mountbatten accompanied Edward, Prince of Wales on a grand tour of India. He continued in the Navy and at the start of the Second World War served as captain of HMS *Kelly*. He was known as an outspoken, fearless and resolute leader. He became a war hero for his role in the Norwegian campaign, helping to evacuate hundreds of soldiers. However, his ship was later attacked and sunk by the Germans during a fierce battle for the Greek island of Crete on 23 May 1941, with the loss of 130 men.

Mountbatten was a close friend of Winston Churchill, and deemed a 'fine naval officer' and a very 'gifted diplomat'. He was a bold, brash figure, who delighted in upstaging the establishment, and yet enjoyed a succession of highly prestigious promotions during a notable wartime career: Commander of the 5th Destroyer Flotilla, Vice-Admiral, Lieutenant-General and Air Marshal.

Mountbatten gained notoriety as well as plaudits. He is probably best remembered, unfortunately, for his role at the Nazi-occupied port of Dieppe in August 1942, when a difficult and dangerous commando raid ended in disaster. The losses were heavy, many of them among brave Canadian troops.

In October 1943, Churchill appointed Mountbatten Supreme Allied Commander in South East Asia, working with General Slim. It was an important position, which Mountbatten held until 1946. During that period he was involved in negotiations for the Japanese surrender of Burma and Singapore. And, as he later acknowledged, it was a remarkable period of change, where his diplomatic skills were tested to the full. Mountbatten also met rebel and anti-Communist leaders, including Lionel Crabb's former boss Chiang Kai-Shek, the leader of the Chinese Nationalist Forces, and his bodyguard and deputy, Morris Cohen.

The day after the handover to the Italian authorities at La Vignole, Crabb flew to Naples to meet Sir John Cunningham, Commander-in-Chief in the Mediterranean, who was acting on behalf of Lord Mountbatten. Cunningham gave Crabb his orders, confirming immediate arrangements for a special posting to the port of Haifa in Israel, where the British Navy was experiencing repeated attacks from a Jewish terrorist organisation among others. For Crabb, it seemed a constant merry-go-round of overseas assignments: Gibraltar, Leghorn, Venice, and a host of other equally dangerous situations. Cunningham said that militant Jewish groups and rebel divers had attacked British warships and freighters at will. Crabb was told a private plane was on standby and was asked to form another Underwater Working Party as a matter of urgency.

Chapter 14

International Operations

When Lionel Crabb arrived in Haifa over Christmas 1945, he must have wondered what sort of hellhole he had landed in. Sent again by special appointment, this was to prove one of the toughest challenges of his life. He remained in Haifa for just over a year and had great difficulty understanding the completely bizarre and contrasting situation. Ships, people, premises, service personnel and vital equipment were constantly being bombed and destroyed by a range of terrorist groups, all claiming that they were operating 'in the name of peace'.

Initially Crabb was billeted in a city centre hotel, where, from his balcony window, he was able to watch thousands of Jewish settlers arrive. He also witnessed occasional sheikhs selling dubious plots of land to desperate families. In stark contrast to Europe, where the populations were relieved to see Allied troops drive out the Nazis and restore normality, here the British were the enemy.

The area was dominated by various extremely hostile organisations, all determined to drive the British and Americans out. Service personnel became obvious targets and there were numerous reports of shootings and bombings at military establishments.

Crabb was briefed on a glut of new Soviet-made limpet mines which were being attached to anything that floated in Haifa harbour. He was told about a successful underwater sabotage attack on some large British police launches. By the time Crabb returned to his hotel, he found the area had been cordoned off, and the premises declared 'out of bounds'. A car bomb had triggered a series of smaller explosions and sporadic gunfire. Murder and mayhem were commonplace: an important sheikh whom Crabb met on his very first day was found hacked to death. The man had been accused of breaking strict Arab laws that encouraged segregation between Arab and Jew, laws designed to prevent Arabs from selling their land to Jews. Each punishment attracted highly excitable crowds.

Crabb was responsible for all bomb and mine disposal operations throughout the region. The defence of all dockyards and harbour areas was to be given priority. Intelligence reports claimed a major attack on British and other shipping was highly likely, therefore Crabb, together with other trusted officers, inspected what were loosely considered to be harbour defences. Crabb spoke with sentries and checked on floodlighting and patrol routines. He also visited a British destroyer, HMS *Chequers*. She was under the command of Capt J.H. Ruck Keene, and was berthed in the main harbour. She was obviously a prime target. The skipper was unconventional, and although Crabb had a few difficult moments with him, they soon became friends. Ruck Keene shared his concern over potential attacks and after a preliminary dive in the harbour waters, Crabb returned to discuss the probability of new remote-controlled bombs. The captain said he was ready to refuel at a nearby oiling wharf that he believed was extremely vulnerable to attack.

Crabb was also warned that raiders might hide somewhere near an old wreck. A large amount of cable had recently been stolen, and to the skipper the theft seemed more than a coincidence. Naturally, he didn't want to move on to the wharf until the area had been checked and cleared. Crabb realised that any explosion would not only sink or severely damage HMS *Chequers*, but would also probably destroy most of the surrounding area. He agreed to investigate.

Crabb returned to his new headquarters and met the Haifa diving team. He had six men under his control. They were all petty officers. They were all bright, young and enthusiastic but had limited experience. He repeated the captain's concerns and called for an immediate search around the oiling jetty and ship's hull. They went out in the motor launch and Crabb, as usual, was one of the first men over the side.

At the wharf, he quickly located a mine. It had been clamped to one of the supports of the quay structure. It was also attached to numerous cables and, to his horror, he realised that it could still be attached to a remote control. He knew terrorists could be watching his every move, and might decide to detonate it at any time. Crabb quickly returned to his launch for some wire cutters and severed the connections, again hoping this would not trigger the device.

It was certainly very dangerous territory in more ways than one for the veteran war hero. The long cable was traced back to its source, and proved the skipper was correct in his assumptions. It led directly back to the wreck, but fortunately there was no sign of anyone on duty.

During this search Crabb received another wound, more severe than the barbed wire at Leghorn. He was attacked by a suckerfish, which left its barbed spikes in his thigh. After having the wound dressed, Crabb visited Capt Keene and presented him with a section of cable as a souvenir. Crabb was asked how many of his team had dived and when he said all of them, the team was invited aboard for celebration drinks.

Crabb realised that he was up against a new type of enemy. They were faceless terrorists to him and yet many of these organisations knew of Crabb. Various militants were well aware of his photograph and war record, and one extreme Jewish group was understood to have put a price on his head.

As the weeks and months passed, Crabb watched as a steady stream of European Jews entered Haifa with nothing more than hope and a few battered suitcases. He saw them struggle through the dirty streets searching for jobs, food and accommodation. Mothers and fathers carrying babies and grubby children crowded into the city, with the accompanying sound of infant cries, bombs, sirens and the call to prayer. Other newcomers reminded Crabb of the American Wild West – men armed to the teeth with pistols, rifles or sub-machine guns, making them look the epitome of mercenaries.

The Royal Navy, like Crabb, faced an immense, if not an impossible task. Any ship deemed unworthy of a berth, or appearing threatening, was turned away. Others, abandoned or thought likely to cause problems, were either boarded or sunk.

One or two ships also included booby traps, and Crabb and his team were in constant demand day and night. Just like his previous assignments, there was no respite and at times Crabb longed for the challenge of Gibraltar, where at least you knew who your enemies were.

When he began defensive operations in the port of Haifa, Crabb was forced to use the standard DSEA diving equipment but gradually he persuaded his seniors to stock his preferred Italian diving suits and breathing equipment.

A Bomb and Mine Disposal officer who later joined Lionel Crabb in Haifa was David Shane, another friend of Noel Cashford. Shane had gained extensive wartime experience rendering safe a host of explosive devices, ranging from inside the war-torn port of Bremen to unexploded bombs in the Manchester Ship Canal. He had been sent by the Admiralty to help with Crabb's search team, inspecting jetties, cargo boats and refugee ships. At Haifa Lt Shane lost an eardrum when, as a gesture of solidarity with Jewish refugees, a hand grenade was dropped over the side of an American ship. Noel Cashford recalls other incidents in Haifa:

> Several bloody battles took place between naval parties and desperate people aboard the 'coffin' ships, and David Shane was in St Andrew's hostel when it was attacked and blown up by a terrorist bomb.
>
> The actions of the Jewish Stern gangs Haganah and Irgun were reported daily. Haifa was an unhappy place in those days, although one plus for David was his new diving suit [a mixture of British and Italian], which he confirmed was superb. David said, though, that it was a relief when he was finally sent to Malta to locate UXBs [unexploded bombs] in Valetta harbour.

Towards the end of his first twelve months in Haifa, a rather weary-looking Crabb was met by his old comrade Gordon Gutteridge, who had been sent to assess the overall situation and to give Lionel a welcome break from the constant pressure of mine clearing. Gutteridge arrived with a fresh 'P' Party of fellow divers to hold the fort. It was February 1947, however, before Lionel Crabb received his orders to return home. He and his team had either been on call, or diving continuously, for the majority of his time in Israel. And when Lt W. Jackson eventually relieved him, Crabb was a very ill man, suffering from a range of complaints, caused by heat, humidity, dehydration and depression – the most constant of which was haemorrhoids.

Crabb, now 38, had given little thought to his future prospects. About fifteen months earlier he had had conversations with the Commander-in-Chief of the Mediterranean, Sir John Cunningham, as well as brief chats with Lord Louis Mountbatten about other occasional specialist services. He had not heard from either of them for a while but as he left Israel, he was advised by Sir John Cunningham to get fit and to stay fit just in case. He was given a pass for three months' leave. The senior officer, who shook his hand, said the Navy would need him again. When he arrived back in London, it came as no great surprise to find the weather cold, wet and windy. It had been nearly four years since he had been able to rest and relax in a London bar. He couldn't even recall the last time he had felt that distinctive cold bite of winter, or the chill blast of sleet and snow on his suntanned face. The wartime street furniture of London had long since gone, and he found it dull and dismal compared to the brightness of the Mediterranean.

Crabb longed to watch the slow pulling of a pint of beer, and to hear the constant chatter of an English pub, without fear of air raids, or the heart-stopping dash amid shouting in the small hours of the morning. He returned to the Cavendish Hotel, where everyone was pleased but surprised to see 'the Admiral'. Several friends and former staff hardly recognised him. Others casually asked if he had been on holiday. Little seemed to have changed. Crabb smiled. He didn't have the energy or inclination to tell them the whole story. He discovered that some other friends were still away and were unlikely to return – presumed to be among the casualties of war. 'But which war?' Crabb asked. 'German? Japanese? Israeli?' Many didn't know about other wars, focusing instead on the war in Europe, which had ended two years before, in 1945. Unsurprisingly, Crabb's bar tab was still unpaid, as attested to by the white chitty in the glass. He might have been a war hero but he couldn't escape an unpaid debt.

The barman stared at Lionel. He kept wiping the same glass with the same cloth and Crabb watched him with fascination until he finally snapped out of his trance. 'The usual is it, Mr Crabb?' he asked.

Lionel smiled, thinking what a hell of a long time it had been since anyone had called him that. He felt comfortable in his civvies. He sank a few shorts, then began to relax. He suddenly felt at home: a stranger again among other strangers.

Shortly after Crabb's return from Israel, he enjoyed an emotional reunion with his cousin Kenneth in London. Crabb was never a great, or even a regular, letter-writer and his commitments in Gibraltar, Italy and most recently in Haifa had made severe demands on his time. Most letters to and from his cousins therefore went via Kenneth's mother, Kitty, at her London flat.

Lionel and Kenneth spent a couple of days catching up on all the gossip. Kenneth served in the RASC during the Second World War. His own activities were almost as exciting as Lionel's. He too had seen extensive action in North Africa and Italy, and as a captain, he also took part in D-Day operations. He had been attached to the 51st Highland Division, and had been Mentioned in Despatches, which earned him an oak leaf on his breast pocket. Kenneth had been part of the Army of Liberation in Belgium, and told Lionel he had gone back to working for Conway Stewart, the family firm selling imported American pens. He was also enjoying weekend stints as a racing car driver.

Kenneth gave Lionel some news about a mutual family friend, Mr Kintz, a wealthy Belgian gold agent, and one of Conway Stewart's major nib suppliers. Kenneth explained that he had travelled out to see Kintz just before the start of the war and had tried to persuade him to leave. He had refused and nothing had been heard from him since, until Kenneth arrived as part of the Liberation Force. Lomond says:

When Belgium fell to the Germans, Kenneth naturally feared the worst. Mr Kintz had two children, with the elder boy serving in the Belgian Army. The younger one, Max, was only small and frail and lived at home. Kenneth knew where he lived and soon located him. Kintz wept with joy when he saw Ken. Unfortunately, Max had died from a poor diet and lack of medical care. It broke Mr Kintz's heart.

His elder son was still away either fighting, or as a POW. Throughout the war, Mr Kintz stored all his gold safely under the floor of his barn. It remained there for years and the Germans never found it. When Kenneth arrived, he took him to the barn and showed him the trapdoor under all the straw. If the Germans had found it, Kintz would almost certainly have been shot! He was a great friend of my grandfather Frank Jarvis, and to all his family.

Back on the world stage, during 1947 Lord Louis Mountbatten was awarded the rather grand title of Viceroy of India by Prime Minister Clement Attlee. He became heavily involved with helping to create and control the new independent states of India and Pakistan. He was to be the last Viceroy and the first Governor General of India, but his controversial and at times unorthodox handling of India's independence was said to have caused some disagreement with Winston Churchill.

It was the best part of five years before he officially returned to England, where he resumed his extraordinary life of fame and notoriety. In 1952, Lord Louis returned to sea duties as Commander-in-Chief of the Mediterranean Fleet. It was a proud position that he held until 1955. He was appointed First Sea Lord 1955–9, and in later years Mountbatten also held the post of Chief of the Defence Staff.

It must have been at least two months after meeting Kenneth that Lionel was contacted by the Admiralty. He was asked to go to a government building in London, where a senior naval officer greeted him. He was then taken into a private room and handed a white envelope. Crabb's name had been handwritten very neatly in fountain pen on the front. For a moment, he wondered if they had used a Conway Stewart pen. As he opened the envelope, he noticed that it was headed 'For Your Eyes Only'. It contained a travel warrant to Singapore, with instructions to stay at a certain hotel. Crabb was asked if he fully understood the message. He replied that he did, and as he stood up to leave, an officer counted out several large bank notes and handed him some sealed documents.

Crabb decided to take a taxi back to his hotel. He knew little about this new assignment, and wasn't quite sure what this adventure might involve. The original letter had been taken back from him and destroyed in his presence. He tried to recall its precise wording. Years later, he admitted that it had mentioned something about a request to attend a special British Trade Mission as a diplomat and contained orders not to discuss the matter with anyone. He said it had a bright red Royal Seal, and was just signed 'Dickie'.

Crabb had three days to buy some new lightweight clothes. For the first time in months he felt more like his old self, and free from illness. There was hardly time for a drink before he returned to visit his mother Daisy, cousin Kitty and family. And in between, he had even considered asking an attractive young woman, Pat Rose, to marry him. It was a flying visit and after being away for so long, few of them could understand his urgency to disappear so soon.

When his boat arrived in Singapore, Crabb went directly to the Raffles Hotel. Much had changed from his pre-war visit, and just like London the whole area seemed much shabbier and dirtier than he remembered. He thought the place looked vastly different and claimed it wasn't quite so luxurious. Moreover, he thought, there was less bowing and scraping to Europeans.

He arrived in civvies and signed the register. A message was waiting for him. He was to report to the British Embassy at noon the next day. He arrived in good time and was shown through into a reception room. Crabb could hear muffled voices in the distance and even recognised some former navy colleagues. After a few minutes he was shown into another room where several rather austere faces stared back at him.

Mountbatten's name was casually mentioned and there was some talk about Crabb's association with Chiang Kai-Shek and Morris Cohen. After about an hour's discussion he was asked to attend another meeting the following day at the same venue, when all would be revealed.

Crabb met a member of the Embassy staff for dinner that night, and felt the man was probably some sort of security minder. Within a couple of days, he met up with some old friends from his visit nearly ten years earlier. They too had been seconded to work for this trade delegation. Crabb was eventually shipped out to a secret location where he caught up once more with a much older-looking, yet more smartly attired, Morris Cohen.

Lionel then spent a couple of months travelling between Singapore, Hong Kong, Taiwan and China. He met representatives of the British and American governments, where funding and equipment were being considered in exchange for pressure, both military and economic, against Communist China. The Americans explained the urgency of establishing a military base in Taiwan. There were many conditions to consider, and people kept referring to Lionel Crabb as a diplomat.

It was a most unfamiliar position for Crabb and, in private, Cohen confided that he was now working in a similar role himself. Cohen was officially listed as a 'cultural liaison officer' operating between the British and American delegations. Cohen, though, was now hunched and walked with a slight limp. He said that he had been held captive in a Japanese POW camp. He had travelled to Hong Kong from Singapore in 1943 to help rescue Madame Sun-Yat Sen from the Japanese invaders. He told Lionel that he had been arrested, tortured, starved and detained for two years in a concentration camp, and had been most fortunate to survive. Since his release in early 1945, Cohen said he had been working for British Intelligence and the American CIA. In return, he claimed, he was now a wealthy man.

Chapter 15

Salvaging a Career

As Lionel returned to London in the autumn of 1947, he knew he faced an uncertain future in the services. He was thirty-eight years old, unfit and relatively ill equipped for civilian life. Back on Civvie Street, like countless other war heroes, Crabb found England in peacetime a harsh economic environment. The George Medal and his OBE, awarded for wartime bravery, offered no guarantee of employment.

The family said they believed that on the same day he received his war medal, Lionel also became engaged to war widow and former society beauty Pat Rose. Born in Dunster, Somerset, she had first met and married an RAF fighter pilot who had flown for Coastal Command. Tragically, he was shot down in the Channel during the latter days of the war, and his body was never found. Pat later became friendly with Peter Aitken, the son of Lord Beaverbrook, but he drowned in a tragic sailing accident. Crabb told his family that when he first met her in London at his local, the Nag's Head, Pat had been on the brink of suicide. Lomond Handley remembers Pat Rose as a very pretty, strong and assertive lady.

Pat was a real character. She was blonde, very well spoken and had a reasonably good figure. She was also very well dressed. She could take her drink and was a well-educated lady. She regularly visited France where her brother, James, a badly burned Second World War pilot, lived. James had married Naomi, the woman who nursed him after he was wounded – and I gather his injuries were pretty bad, and he was scarred for life.

Aunt Daisy didn't approve of Pat, who was a very modern and glamorous woman. Daisy considered her 'fast' and said Pat wasn't the weeping willow type. She didn't approve of any women who were 'modern'. Pat was tough. She was a survivor and she would question authority and speak her mind. I liked her, but I think she could be pretty formidable if crossed. Daisy was very old fashioned. Pat liked her gin but I never saw her any the worse for wear – but she could certainly drink, and so could Lionel.

Lionel and Pat celebrated their engagement at the Cavendish Hotel. Their engagement party was organised by Crabb's friends Rosa Lewis and Maitland Pendock. Within six months, however, Lionel's fears about his future were confirmed. Despite a massive mopping-up exercise nationwide to rid the country of any remaining mines and unexploded bombs, Lionel finally received his marching orders, and in the spring of 1948 he left his chums at Portsmouth with all his worldly goods packed into an old cardboard box. It was a heartbreaking moment for him, and something of a betrayal. Wearing his new demob suit, and with just a few pounds in his pocket, he caught the first train back to town and got completely smashed with many of his old mates back at the Cavendish Hotel.

Some time later, Pat broke off her engagement to Lionel, due largely to his irregular working hours, and left for France, where she later married. It was not too long before Crabb found himself in an old and familiar story: no job and no money. Yet far from feeling sorry for himself, he set about promoting his underwater expertise. He tried to obtain work as a diver and consultant. He was still on the reserve list for the Navy, and Maitland Pendock provided a few casual jobs. He obtained some work briefly as a consultant on a few small film projects, providing diving reality advice to actors playing the roles of Second World War heroes.

A chance conversation in the Cavendish Hotel bar provided a few more months' work, in the form of a temporary contract to act as a go-between for a printer and a client who was trying to publish a sports book. The deal was later extended to include some other print work, and he rented a small office on Fleet Street in the heart of the newspaper world. The hours were flexible and it suited Crabb to be tasked with lots of wheeling, dealing and deliveries. While handling one particular order, Crabb's attention was caught by an unusual article in a London evening paper. The article was a send-up of the eccentric plans of a small fishing fleet owner, who believed electronic echo sounding could be the answer to his business prayers. He believed that echo-sounding equipment could save him time and money by identifying where the big shoals of fish were, so that he could take his boats to them and fill his nets.

Crabb thought the businessman would need a diver and phoned him to offer his services. The owner was puzzled but invited him to his home near Great Yarmouth. Lionel suggested using a special underwater camera to study the movements of fish, and convinced the owner that he could use his echo-sounding equipment like radar, spotting the fish, as the RAF had done with Luftwaffe raids.

In October 1948, Crabb sailed with a small fleet of fishing ships. He watched the blips and beeps of the sounder and, remarkably, he was able to identify some large shoals. He also made a number of shallow dives with the camera whenever the nets were thrown, to show the owner how the fish reacted. The filming was not great, the equipment and undersea lighting being poor and the weather rough, but the owner was more than satisfied. After several trips, he decided he could probably find Crabb more work. This was just as well, as Crabb's print jobs gradually dried up because of a national paper shortage, and he was again facing financial difficulties, even pawning whatever valuables he had left, including the precious piece of jade given to him by his Chinese friends in Singapore.

In respect of Lionel Crabb's wartime and postwar career and the events leading up to his death, I am indebted to Rear Admiral Edmund Nicholas Poland CB, CBE, a former Director of Undersea Warfare, and torpedo and submarine expert. Despite failing health, Rear Admiral Poland – known to his friends as Nicho – generously supported my investigations, allowing me unrestricted access to his unedited notes and files on the Crabb affair, following his own review of matters in 1988–9.

Poland was educated at the Royal Naval College, Dartmouth, and retired from the Navy in 1968 after holding key positions including staff officer to the Naval Force Commander in Burma, commander with the Air Warfare Division of the Admiralty and the British Naval staff in Washington, a member of the NATO standing group, Director of Undersea Warfare at the Ministry of Defence, and Commander-in-Chief of the Home Fleet. He was awarded the CBE in 1962 and the CB in 1967.

Some forty-three years after Cdr Crabb's death in April 1956, Rear Admiral Poland wrote *The Torpedomen – HMS* Vernon's *Story 1872–1968*. While researching his book, which recorded the fascinating history of HMS *Vernon*, Poland commissioned several former Navy colleagues to help him review the circumstances surrounding Crabb's mysterious disappearance. Among his sources was Noel Cashford's friend and colleague, Cdr Gordon Gutteridge. Rear Admiral Poland says:

> It may seem strange but it was necessary to examine the facts surrounding the Crabb affair – even though it goes back a long way into HMS *Vernon*'s history – because *Vernon* was involved and has had to endure many years of unwelcome notoriety. It is fitting that former members of the Torpedo Anti Submarine and Diving branches, who were serving at the time, are able to provide a balanced analysis of the facts.

In the foreword to Rear Admiral Poland's book, HRH Prince Charles recalls his time as Commanding Officer of the minehunter HMS *Bronington*, and his knowledge of the Torpedo Branch. He confirms that in rendering the story of *Vernon*, Nicho Poland is 'well qualified to tell it'.

With Rear Admiral Poland's help I was able to trace former contacts and to interview key personnel with first-hand knowledge of events concerning Lionel Crabb's final dive. Poland confirmed that when the last 'P' Party returned from mine clearance at Dunkirk harbour during 1946, the majority of the team were either RNVR or 'hostilities only' personnel, therefore most, like Cdr Crabb, were demobilised. Rear Admiral Poland recalls:

All that remained from the Naval Party was Lt Cdr Gordon Gutteridge, together with one leading seaman and three able seamen. They were transferred to the Minesweeping and Countermeasures base at Lochinvar, Port Edgar on the Firth of Forth. Gutteridge received a five-year Royal Naval short service commission. During the next few years he received a few additional ratings who were trained in postwar development and mine countermeasures. There was now a clear division between the deep diving team at *Vernon* and the Clearance Divers at Lochinvar.

Some five years after the war, and throughout the early 1950s, a major mine-hunting project, led by a former Post Office scientist, D.G. Tucker, began at Portland to develop an improved version of search apparatus known as Asdic Type 179. The apparatus had been installed in many British mine countermeasure vessels after the war. At HMS *Vernon* other deep sea diving trials and the testing of new and varied equipment continued, while at Admiralty Research Laboratory (ARL), Teddington, scientists were busily developing a much more sophisticated system of detection.

Despite his constant lack of money, Lionel remained a popular man at the Cavendish, entertaining guests with his war exploits and tales of pre-war adventure. He told everyone that he still wanted to dive and when the news reached some of his former colleagues, it was suggested he should contact Lt Jimmy Hodges, who was then involved with secret work at the ARL. Crabb spoke with Hodges, visited the unit, and watched some of his underwater films, where Hodges enthusiastically told him about some new developments with experimental work.

Crabb expressed a keen interest and was asked to meet his supervisor, the director of Boom Defence and Marine Salvage. Lionel gave a brief resumé of his outstanding war and postwar career and mentioned the charioteers, his recent use of basic Asdic equipment, and of his limited knowledge of undersea filming. To Crabb's surprise, the man was 'hooked' and Crabb was hired as a temporary technical advisor. He was asked to write a script, and to help Jimmy produce a film promoting the benefits of underwater experimental work.

It had always taken Crabb hours to write a letter home. Now he had to find a typewriter to set about writing the reasons for his existence. He had already paid out the rent on his Fleet Street premises so it seemed fitting that he should return to that location to write the story. Incredibly, the result of his labours, written just a few weeks later, was highly acclaimed, and Crabb became producer and scriptwriter for a successful short film, *Wonders of the Deep*.

In June 1948, a new Admiralty ship, HMS *Reclaim*, was introduced into service. She was developed into a deep diving and submarine rescue ship. She had a top speed of 12 knots and a crew of ninety-two, including a team of twelve divers. One of her most distinctive features was her sail. *Reclaim* was commissioned to help increase the diving limits and capacity of this specialist vessel and fittingly, within a couple of months of her introduction, Petty Officer W. Bollard achieved a world deep-sea diving record of 535ft.

The ship was frequently used in the Mediterranean for a series of successful trials, one of which was to support a recommendation to increase the limit for Royal Navy divers to 360ft. In the spring of 1949, Crabb was called into the director's office at ARL in Teddington and offered a three-year naval contract to work as an underwater diver and photographer. Commissions included additional secret work for the government and the Intelligence services. Many of Crabb's new tasks were completed with Jimmy Hodges. They involved diving at various locations around the British coastline, specifically at ports and harbours, inspecting and filming underwater wrecks for potential salvage. Crabb also tested and reported on the use of revolutionary underwater weapons.

Rear Admiral Nicho Poland claims that during this period Crabb returned very briefly to the Far East. Most of the papers are still on the Official Secrets list but what we can say for certain is that Crabb took part in specific missions with *Reclaim* in Malta and elsewhere, in the autumn of 1949. It was highly dangerous clearance work, and in Malta he filmed his colleagues operating underwater as they removed and made safe a number of unexploded bombs from HMS *Breconshire*, sunk during air raids in the Second World War. Coincidentally, this site was also a favourite diving spot of Lord Mountbatten. Crabb's numerous overseas commitments unfortunately coincided with another family tragedy. It was at this time that Crabb received the shattering news that his cousin and best friend

Kenneth Jarvis had been killed in a motor racing accident. The death of Kenneth probably had more of an impact on Crabb than any other event in his life. It also marked a third major emotional milestone, following Kitty's affair and the sudden death of his guardian, Frank Jarvis. Crabb's grief was compounded by the fact that, working overseas, he couldn't even attend Kenneth's funeral.

Lionel and Kenneth had grown up together and were practically the same age. Kenneth was just an amateur driver, who always claimed he didn't race for money, merely for the love of the sport; however, during the 1930s and 1940s, he distinguished himself as a racing driver, winning prizes at top blue riband events. After the war Crabb and Kenneth had renewed their friendship and Lionel had joined his cousin at a few race meetings as a spectator without sharing Kenneth's enthusiasm for the sport.

Initially, as a member of the Berkhamstead Car and Motorcycle Club Kenneth attended many sprint and hill races before finally gaining experience at more major events. He was fondly known as 'KCJ', and owned about four racing cars over the years – mostly Austin 7s – all built for him by top mechanic Bill Williams.

In the course of my reasearch I came across Stuart Ulph from Lincoln, a vintage sports car club member. Stuart was himself doing research on the life of Bill Williams and revealed that he still owned one of Kenneth's vintage cars. Stuart was also able to provide a detailed record of Kenneth's racing achievements before and after the Second World War, including the crash which cost him his life. Stuart says:

Kenneth was killed during a practice race at Luton Hoo in 1949, when he drove his car into a tree. The course was the best sprint venue in the country. The road was about three-quarters of a mile long with beautiful parkland and lined with big trees. Reports said that when he entered the bend, the car didn't do as he expected and he skidded sideways.

Lomond Handley recalls the incident: 'Ma said Lionel was working away at the time. He went away on missions and used to disappear for weeks or months on end and then he'd suddenly turn up. The family were in

a terrible state. I remember Mother learning the news via a phone call
– possibly from Audrey. Granny Kitty insisted on seeing Ken after he'd
been killed, and my dad went with her.' Remarkably, Lomond added that a
medium had had a premonition of the crash, and had tried to stop Kenneth
from racing that day. Lomond goes on:

> Ma or Audrey once said that one of the nuts or screws was too tight
> and this caused the accident. Mother had a phone call from one of
> her medium friends a few days before Kenneth was due to race. She
> warned her that Kenneth shouldn't go. Ma phoned Kenneth and tried
> to persuade him, but he thought that if he didn't take part people
> would think he had 'bottled out'. Ma said that at around the same
> time Kenneth lost his St Christopher, which should have warned him
> of danger, as to lose it was a bad omen. Anyway, he promised Ma that
> he was only going around the track once. He said to Aunt Margot (his
> second wife), 'Hold my cigarette for me,' and off he went. But he didn't
> stop after the first lap. Next, they heard a crash and then saw that he'd
> hit a tree. I understand the steering wheel locked.

Crabb, meanwhile, had begun to receive increasingly hazardous commissions, some involving work with *Reclaim*. The missions helped Crabb re-
focus his life after the loss of Kenneth, and he loved working with his friend
Jimmy Hodges. They joined *Reclaim* on several more occasions, sometimes
to test the operational workings of a new underwater camera developed at
the ARL. Rear Admiral Poland says:

> Their mission in 1949 was to photograph the workings of a British
> cruiser's propellers at various speeds to ascertain the extent and effect
> of cavitations – the bubbles formed by fast-moving propellers. A special
> lane was hastily prepared between some radar-reflecting Dan buoys
> – through which the cruiser would steam at ever increasing speeds.
> The senior diving officer, Lt Cdr W.B. – Bill – Filer, who was a very brave
> and experienced diver himself, considered this to be a 'highly dangerous'
> task but Crabb was keen to continue and eventually completed
> his mission.

Crabb appeared in shallow water diving dress and took up his position by one of the mooring buoy wires, and at a depth he considered suitable to achieve the required result. In spite of Filer's misgivings, the project was completed without incident.

Chapter 16

The *Truculent* Disaster

In 1950, Crabb and Jimmy Hodges were to experience one of the most dramatic incidents of their careers. *Reclaim* was being refitted and Lionel was resting in his billet on Thursday 12 January 1950, listening to the ten o'clock news, when he heard details of a collision in the Thames Estuary between a 600-ton Swedish tanker, SS *Divina*, and the navy submarine HMS *Truculent*.

The report said that a Dutch vessel *Almdijk* had rescued five survivors including the skipper of the *Truculent* but confirmed the submarine had sunk. It asserted that the *Divina* had rescued another eight men and pulled two bodies from the water. Two men were reported to have escaped when the submarine settled on the seabed.

Crabb listened intently. Fifteen men had been saved but he realised that normally a submarine would carry a crew of seventy to eighty men. He thought that the submarine had probably settled within about 60ft of water, a depth accessible to shallow water divers.

He contacted Jimmy Hodges, and the senior duty officer at the Admiralty. He outlined the possibility of rescue and was calmly told to stand by. Within an hour, his offer had been accepted, and Crabb and Hodges went to the stores at the ARL in Teddington to collect their diving gear before starting out on the long drive to Sheerness.

At the scene there was panic and confusion. It was very cold, dark and wet and the rescue services informed them that they had been unable to locate the submarine's automatic distress buoy. Without this information, they could not locate the wreck. As they waited, they saw some survivors being discharged on to the quayside from the *Divina*. The crew were clearly in a state of shock and suffering from exposure. Crabb also noticed that the colliding ship had been very badly damaged just above the water line and he and Hodges jumped aboard a tug to try and locate the exact site of impact.

As Crabb departed, they were misinformed that a special team of Navy rescue divers, dispatched from Scotland in an old Lancaster bomber, had crashed en route. At first it was said that Crabb's friend and colleague Gordon Gutteridge was among the casualties, but fortunately this turned out to be false. Rear Admiral Poland explains the error:

> The accident happened on a dark Saturday night and the intention was for Gutteridge and his team in Scotland to be tracked down to help at the scene. In the event, they were unable to help, as most of the submarine crew were already dead by then. Gutteridge's crew of ten divers and two officers based at Rosyth were sent for, and a converted Lancaster was dispatched to RAF Kinloss, to fly them down to Biggin Hill. Unfortunately, the Lancaster crashed on its way to Kinloss and consequently his team were never collected. The BBC reported the crash, claiming that the rescue team were on board, and said there were no survivors. It proved most upsetting for all concerned.

Eventually, a searchlight picked out the distress buoy and Crabb and Hodges were instructed to transfer to a fast patrol boat. As they arrived for the exchange, however, they found the boat packed with Press reporters and photographers, all reluctant to make way for the rescue divers.

A Naval frigate marked the approximate site of the sinking and on board Crabb met up with some surviving officers from *Truculent* and obtained a brief about the collision. The survivors were in a bad way and were covered in oil. They explained they were diving to avoid a ship when it hit them. It had flooded fast. They said the skipper had been thrown clear but insisted that many men were still trapped in watertight compartments.

An officer believed all the men in the aft compartments had managed to escape but said a lack of opportunity and equipment had restricted other attempts. Tragically, though many men had escaped from this hatch, all but ten died awaiting rescue in the estuary. Most were swept out to sea by the strong ebb tide, where they either drowned from exhaustion, or died from exposure on the mud banks.

Crabb and Hodges made several attempts to reach the stricken submarine in the fast flowing tide using a trailing anchor line, which then hooked on to the periscope tower. The divers had to descend slowly and carefully in thick silt and darkness, using just a small lamp run by a line from a portable generator. As the tide slackened, they finally reached the conning tower and began to search the boat.

Working from opposite sides, they tapped their way around without response, but soon Crabb's cable links became entangled and he realised he was running low on oxygen. It almost became the end of his exploits too, for as he stretched to open a valve on his other air tank, his grease-covered hands kept slipping and he failed to gain any purchase on the valve. Fortunately, as he desperately struggled towards the surface, the valve finally turned, releasing some fresh air into his lungs, but he was only just able to make it back to the ship.

When both divers returned, they reluctantly agreed that all hope of finding other survivors had gone. After they had changed and rested, they were asked to re-examine *Truculent* for a more detailed report for the Admiralty. The tragedy was made even worse by the fact that *Truculent* also carried a party of Chatham dockyard officers. The submarine was returning to Sheerness after a refit at Chatham and was undergoing sea trials. Just fifteen men survived.

The SS *Divina* had had specially strengthened bows for Arctic conditions, and the submarine suffered from enormous impact damage on her starboard side and sank very quickly. The ship was salvaged just two days later, then beached and moved inshore where another ten bodies were recovered. HMS

Truculent had had a formidable war record. She was responsible for the sinking of the German U-308 in Norwegian seas during the war. She later took part in successful attacks on Japanese shipping.

Some years later, one of the few remaining survivors gave his account of the tragedy. Frederick Henley had served for over fifteen years in the Royal Navy, including at least four on submarines. In 1954 he received an honourable discharge and later worked as an electrician.

Henley said it had been a miracle that he had escaped the *Truculent* disaster. He explained that the submarine had left Sheerness at 8.30 a.m. for engine and snorkel trials. They submerged off Margate and again later off Ramsgate before surfacing in the late afternoon. He claimed it had been an uneventful day and said they had had eighteen civilians aboard from the Naval Dockyard, totalling seventy-nine men. Henley was ordered to take the *Manual of Seamanship* to the bridge, where a young sub-lieutenant leafed through the pages. It was a cold, dark night, and he didn't see the tanker ploughing towards them. He had hardly reached the ladder before his captain, Lt Charles Bowers, began issuing a stream of urgent orders. Henley explained that there was an almighty crash and said he was pinned to the side of the conning tower. The submarine lurched at a crazy angle and sank like a stone. The conning tower flooded and he had to squirm around the periscope standards and only escaped by remembering his escape drill, before swimming to the surface.

Henley said it was icy cold and that although he could hear others shouting and calling for help, he couldn't see them. He said he was in the water for over an hour and admitted the ebb tide was quickly dragging him out before a Dutch freighter finally rescued him. Only later, when told that sixty-four of his shipmates had perished, did he remember the unusual order to find this seamanship manual that almost certainly saved his life. Had he not gone aloft with the manual, undoubtedly he too would have drowned.

Chapter 17

Admiralty Business and the *Affray*

Not long after the *Truculent* disaster Rear Admiral Poland said they heard further tragic news about the death of Crabb's diving partner, Jimmy Hodges. It was yet another massive blow to Crabb, and came a short time after losing his cousin Kenneth. They were close friends. Rear Admiral Poland says: 'We heard that Jimmy had lost his life while filming with the underwater photographer, Hans Hass.'

Surgeon Vice-Admiral Sir John Rawlins recalled the days of Crabb and Hodges. He says:

It was Jimmy Hodges who first started me on diving. He visited Malta in 1948 to film a torpedo being fired from a submarine, presumably for ARL [Admiralty Research Laboratories], and to study the drag pattern. I was one of the few successful spear fishers on the island at that time and Jimmy came to watch me in action. I also knew Hans and Lottie Hass, whose diving exploits among sharks in the Red Sea – all on oxygen – were truly amazing. And I know what happened to Jimmy when he was working with them. But diving, as we know so well, is a risky business and we all make mistakes. I have had my fair share of near misses but as the old Navy adage goes: 'If you can't take a joke, you shouldn't have joined.'

In early 1950, Crabb received another call from the Admiralty for another unusual job, this time in Scotland. He was requested to lead a Royal Navy clearance team, but not to find any unexploded mines. This time, his mission had intimations of buried treasure: helping locate an old Spanish galleon that had sunk during storms about five hundred years before in Tobermory Bay on the Isle of Mull. The Duke of Argyll had requested the commission. Lionel received a grid reference, some background details and a brief that the galleon was probably buried in several tons of ancient silt. He was issued with a railway travel warrant and details of his new team. Crabb thought it was a peculiar assignment, but nevertheless accepted it and hastily set out for his new base at HMS *Lochinvar*. On the train north, Crabb met several members of his team including Sydney Knowles, who had been his diving colleague in Gibraltar and Italy.

Recalling the meeting, Knowles says: 'During the journey, I left my compartment to visit the toilet. As I glanced into another compartment, I saw a person sitting there with three gold stripes on his sleeve. I was overjoyed to see that it was my old boss and diving companion, Cdr Crabb.'

The exercise, however, proved very difficult and time consuming. There were constant delays due to adverse weather conditions, and in more than two months the team was able to dive on just seventeen occasions. Crabb, on the other hand, was constantly diving and observing his younger divers in action as they sought to locate and identify the wreck – a survivor from the Spanish Armada.

Finally the ship was located 80ft down and in two halves, buried in 20ft of heavy silt. Many centuries of thick mud had semi-preserved the timbers. Using high pressure suction probes, the divers were gradually able to expose the ship's timber frame, together with a Spanish dagger and several planks of African oak. There was no treasure, and when they had done as much as they could, Crabb was recalled to the Admiralty Research Laboratories at Teddington, for other experimental work. Rear Admiral Poland confirmed:

Cdr Crabb continued working with a range of other innovative, secret test equipment, including the development of the first-ever underwater television camera, which beamed real-time black and white pictures back to a surface support vessel. This provided a unique breakthrough in technology and allowed experts immediately to examine wrecks or underwater obstructions. The system came in particularly useful in April 1951, more than a year after the Scottish expedition. This was when Crabb and several ARL colleagues were instructed to attend the crash site of another submarine disaster, the *Affray*, to help rescue workers locate its position, and determine the extent and cause of damage.

Crabb rejoined the specialist diving ship, *Reclaim*. This time he was to act as a liaison officer, working with the ship's crew, scientists and divers. His experience, however, was deemed essential in the search for survivors. *Affray* had been reported overdue from a planned surface. And the operation became even more poignant for Crabb and his colleagues when they realised that the son of the captain of HMS *Vernon*, Sub Lt R.G. Howard-Johnston, was on board the stricken submarine as part of a training class of sub-lieutenants.

Finding the submarine proved a very difficult task. The 6th Frigate Squadron led the search but *Affray*'s last known point of reference remained a mystery and consequently it meant a rigorous and painfully slow grid search from the originally known datum point some 10 miles south of the Nab Tower.

The team investigated numerous echo soundings relating to old wrecks and obstructions, diving continuously, day and night, before they finally found her resting on the seabed. She was on the very edge of the Hurd Deep in 287ft of water. She was more than 37 miles south-west of her previously reported position, but close to an area where an oil slick had occurred.

HMS *Affray* was the last Royal Navy submarine to be lost at sea. Rear Admiral Poland confirms that it was an extremely difficult search and find operation for the *Reclaim* and her crew, who were recalled from annual leave to carry it out. The ship had to be moored in the open channel while her divers inspected every possible contact. Rear Admiral Poland says it took many weeks before *Affray* was located, and said it followed a bizarre story, confirmed by the Admiralty. On 16 April, the wife of a rear admiral, alone at her house in Guernsey, reported that she had been confronted by the figure of a man she recognised as the engineer from the *Affray*. The figure told her: 'Tell your husband we are at the bottom of the north end of Hurd Deep, nearly 70 miles from St Catherine's Point. It happened very suddenly and none of us expected it.'

Poland says the rear admiral's wife was so shaken by the incident that she immediately telephoned her husband at the Admiralty and reported the matter. 'At that time however, no submarine had been reported missing and it was some hours before *Affray* failed to surface. It was not until 14 June that the Admiralty agreed to search that particular location.'

Bill Filer, who was head of the search team, confirmed the contact and sent Able Seaman Middleton to inspect the site. Middleton was a former submarine rating and was carefully lowered in an observation chamber where he reported extensive damage to the snort mast. Filer wanted to make a further inspection to see whether the snort induction valve was open or closed. He had developed a unique system whereby a diver could be lowered over the conning tower hatch of *Affray*.

His daring plan, however, was thwarted by the Commander-in-Chief, who said it was too risky and so Crabb and his colleagues were asked to step in. Lionel Crabb had arrived with his own underwater television equipment and crew. Officials hoped this would aid rescue attempts, yet his appearance and intentions seemed to upset certain individuals, who felt the workings of his party might even hinder their work. Poland says:

Their anxiety was justified when a diver's descent was delayed by the use of the TV camera. When the time came for his ascent, the tide had turned and *Reclaim* had yawned across the wreck causing the diver to rise at an oblique angle. His air hose and communication cable became entangled and he was turned upside down. He managed to pass a message back to the surface before he became unconscious. There was no time to send down a relief diver and it was decided to take the drastic step of heaving away on the diver's lines. They were wrenched free and the diver was projected like a missile to the surface. He was rescued and placed in the decompression chamber and fortunately suffered from no ill effects but it was a lucky escape.

Poland explained that the television camera proved a valuable aid to the search but said it had been hurriedly mounted on scaffolding, which was unwieldy and had few directional properties. And without a compass, or reference point, Poland said it was difficult to manoeuvre within viewing distance until a member of *Reclaim*'s crew supplied a rudder. He continues:

> After Filer first identified *Affray*, he was able to reposition the ship, so that the submarine's name plate appeared on the television monitor screen in the Captain's cabin. This was the first time that underwater television had been used to identify a wreck. The image on the screen was photographed and made great use of by the media. The cause of the accident still remained to be established.
>
> Using the underwater camera it was confirmed that the snort mast was broken and lying over the side of the submarine. The snort mast was recovered by divers and sent to HM Dockyard at Portsmouth where metal fatigue was diagnosed.

Following this tragedy and the loss of seventy-five brave men, awards were made to seven officers and twenty-four ratings, duly acknowledging the outstanding attempts of the rescue team, and all the divers.

Crabb continued with extensive operational duties, often in much warmer climes, particularly around Malta, which was said to be the most bombed place on earth. It was here that he met Lord Mountbatten again on dives in the Mediterranean. One of Crabb's colleagues, Lt P. White, admitted he was frequently called upon to organise some underwater fishing trips for the Commander-in-Chief, and for the area governor. He says: 'Mountbatten was also interested in personally testing some new diving and breathing equipment.'

In 1952, just after Crabb failed to reach a reconciliation with Pat Rose, he met and married Margaret Elaine Player (née Williamson). It had been a whirlwind romance and it did not last. Margaret had had a child from her previous relationship and for a time they lived together in a caravan in a small field practically opposite his place of work. They separated in April 1953. There were many reasons offered for the sudden collapse of the marriage. Crabb's family blame Margaret's alleged adulterous affairs due to Crabb's long periods working away from home. Others, including his friend Cdr Gutteridge, suggest Crabb had a bizarre fetish for rubber, which his wife was unable to accommodate. He said:

> During our two years together, I got to know Lionel very well – seeing him through his marriage and his divorce. He and his wife became firm friends of mine. Crabb married for the only time to Margaret Player. She was a successful commercial artist. They married on the strength of his new appointment as commander to the UCWE [Underwater Countermeasures & Weapons Establishment] and a regular pay cheque. She was able to divorce him just over a year later – within the normal three years – on grounds of perversion. His oddity was rubber. He liked shiny blue rubber bed sheets and a wide variety of mostly domestic rubber items . . . he also wore a cut-down, pink ladies' mackintosh underneath his uniform and Margaret once said, 'He rustled like a Christmas tree.' It is for consideration that his long standing addiction to dreadful Pirelli dry suits, and indeed all things rubber, had at least some bearing on his career and the pattern of his diving.

All these claims, however, are strongly denied by the Jarvis family. His cousin Charleen Miller explains:

> It was the thing that really upset Mother, and that she mentioned often, every time we used to ask what Lionel was like. It was the fact that after his disappearance there was a rumour that he had a fetish for rubber. And that he even went to bed wearing his rubber diving suit, and had 'kinky sex'. Ma said people kept saying this but it was absolutely untrue. She knew this wasn't what he was like. Whether it was his lifestyle or not, obviously something had prompted this fact to stick in Mother's mind to the extent that she repeated it over and over again. Mother wasn't the kind of person who would have known about this type of

thing, or even thought of it, unless she had read it, or been told about it by someone.

Her cousin Lomond Handley also denies the allegations. She says:

Margaret had had a number of adulterous affairs, and Lionel could stand it no longer. She said he was always away and just couldn't cope. He said it was a shame, as he loved her child as his own.

They lived in a small caravan in a field. It posed several problems and he eventually decided to allow her to divorce him. He was now a Catholic and a very honourable man and didn't want her to have to admit to any relationships, so he arranged for a prostitute to come to his hotel room. Nothing happened. They just played cards all night but it allowed Margaret to divorce him quickly and without too much fuss. Eventually, when he returned, the caravan had gone and all his belongings were left dumped in the middle of this field. It was a shameful way to treat him.

Shortly after this trauma, sometime in 1953, Crabb received another special request to do a 'little job' for the admiral (Louis Mountbatten) in the Canal Zone in Egypt. He returned again the following year to test some new underwater camera equipment for the ARL. Rear Admiral Poland confirms Crabb's involvement, saying: 'Lewis, the Chief Staff Officer to the Flag Officer Middle East at Fayid, recalled Crabb's visit to Egypt in 1954. He said he had been informed by the Admiralty that Cdr Crabb was arriving to do some secret diving trials in the vicinity of the five decaying merchant ships interned by the Egyptian authorities in Lake Timsah.'

In naval reports Lewis says: 'To preserve secrecy, and because I knew him, I arranged for Lionel Crabb to stay with me. He carried out his trial, presumably satisfactorily, and left for England after about a fortnight.'

Rear Admiral Poland agrees that various reorganisations took place during this period to keep pace with worldwide demand. He said that following the creation of the Clearance Diving branch, an experimental clearance diving team was attached to the Underwater Countermeasures and Weapons Establishment at Havant. He recalls:

Additional scientific support was made available. Gordon Gutteridge served as Commanding Officer of the team and as Mine Investigations Officer to the service. In addition he was appointed the naval application officer and a liaison officer between all the scientists and the Royal Navy.

It was a demanding role and with continuous sea trials and regular testing of new and secret equipment, it became an impossible task. Consequently Cdr Crabb was seconded from the ARL unit at Teddington and given a new three-year short service contract back in the Navy and placed in charge of the Experimental Clearance Trials team. Initially, he worked under Gutteridge, but within a short time, their roles were reversed, with Crabb put in command. This allowed Gutteridge to concentrate on the Underwater Countermeasures and Weapons Establishment, where his experience proved most helpful in dealing with scientists and new developments. Meanwhile, Lionel was put in charge of an experimental trials team leading the way in new technological achievements.

It was to prove something of a 'foreign' role for Crabb, who for years had always been the most 'non-technical' officer within the service. Gutteridge wasn't too happy about the arrangement either, and said:

Crabb happily served under me but with typical unpredictability, their Lordships almost immediately promoted him to commander rank. This gave rise to monumental celebration but Crabb, realising his own technical ignorance and suspicion of boffins, willingly allowed our working relationship to continue. He was non-technical and was neither interested in innovation, nor in dealing with the adventure and frustration of breaking new frontiers.

He secured the loyalty of his team but often regarded scientists as 'nut cases'. He was a diver of enormous experience, with a singular ability to endure discomfort, and his lack of fear was unquestioned. But his assessment of experimental equipment and techniques bordered on the bizarre.

Crabb also became a familiar figure in and around the mess rooms of HMS *Vernon* at Portsmouth, and with his lively personality, manner and dress he became something of a legendary figure. Many described him as 'small, dapper and eccentric'. And one of the ratings, R. Hartley, who worked with Crabb on several underwater trials, recalls:

Back in *Vernon*, Buster was a very quiet sort of person. He always seemed to be on his own, but was very distinct with the bright green stripes he wore between his gold rings, and the large tufts of hair on his cheeks. We were told, or rather understood, that his coloured stripes were 'Special Branch'. What he was like in the wardroom, of course, would be for officers to answer, but we ratings found him very likeable.

Chapter 18

Scotland Again and the *Sverdlov*

In August 1954, Crabb made a return visit to Scotland to continue where he had left off four years earlier, working under contract once more for the Duke of Argyll. A naval clearance diving team had been approved to search for the wreck of the *St Jean Le Baptiste*. Crabb also employed several civilian divers, including his old pal, Sydney Knowles, who had since left the service and taken unpaid leave from his job as a lorry driver to help out.

Knowles continued to follow Crabb's progress and had even called upon him at times at his new flat in Hans Road, London. He also helped to form the team of ex-Navy divers to work on the wreck. It was to be another treasure hunt. This time it was claimed the ship had been the paymaster to the Spanish Armada. Again, the wreck was identified, buried under thick layers of silt. Crabb used similar underwater suction ejectors to try to reveal her secrets. The assignment proved both dangerous and fruitless, and nearly cost Knowles his life. Knowles says:

We were working in shifts, 80–100ft below the surface of the bay, controlling an airlift that functioned like a giant vacuum cleaner sucking sand, clay and stones from the seabed. We were hampered by the amount of rubbish that had accumulated in the area and over the wreck, and directly in line with the flow of water that roared over a large waterfall nearby.

I was working 87ft below in a deep hole facing a solid wall of clay when a boulder slid from the wall behind me and held my body and diving helmet down on the seabed. I was buried and held down for more than an hour before my standby diver, Terry Yetton, was sent down and struggled to remove the boulder. I was not injured but the following day, hearing about the accident, the Duke and Duchess of Argyll, together with young Ian, the Marquis of Lorne, came down to the dive boat. They were concerned for my wellbeing but were surprised when they heard I was back down again, working on the seabed.

The team worked for several weeks on the wreck but were again hampered by long spells of bad weather, which also affected the nearby waterfall, producing a tremendous amount of debris over the wreck each time it rained. Eventually the mission was abandoned.

On Crabb's return to Portsmouth he was told that his time in the Navy was coming to an end. He was again at a loss to know what he would do on Civvy Street, and once again started to make representations for other diving work. He had talks about becoming an advisor to the Iraqi Navy and even considered joining the Canadian Navy with a colleague, Lt Cdr Bathurst, who worked with him on the *Affray* rescue attempt. This role, however, would have meant a probable demotion, and at that stage in his life Crabb felt he didn't need to prove himself again, especially to a foreign power.

Fortunately Crabb did not have to wait long for another call from the Admiralty. In the summer of 1955 he was asked to meet Lord Mountbatten and some senior colleagues from the Admiralty and Naval Intelligence, to discuss the imminent arrival of a modern Russian cruiser, the *Sverdlov*.

Some additional facts have been confirmed in secret paperwork recently released from MI6 and files from The National Archives. Crabb's work with the ARL and their associated units had developed to such an extent that the Admiralty now wanted to test some underwater camera equipment under a foreign vessel. They had many questions requiring urgent answers.

In October 1955, *Sverdlov* took part in a special Coronation Review in Portsmouth. Crabb's orders were clear. He had to examine her hull, screws and rudder. He was also to try and determine the reasons for her unique manoeuvrability in narrow waters. Crabb needed someone else to help him prepare for this mission and spent the next day or two phoning around several experienced colleagues to ask for their assistance. Gordon Gutteridge was one of many who turned him down flat. Crabb said it was an 'unofficial' mission for the Intelligence Services.

Finally, he telephoned Sydney Knowles. Crabb said he had a small job for a large fee. He explained that it was in Portsmouth but was obviously reluctant to tell him any more at that stage, especially over the telephone. By then, Lionel was also back working part-time for his old friend Maitland Pendock in London.

Crabb had begun selling bits and pieces of self-assembly furniture, mainly to increasingly fashionable Italian coffee bars. He was also in touch with Pat Rose. Both had had disastrous marriages, and they soon became an item again. Crabb arranged to meet Knowles in a London bar, where he briefly outlined the mission.

Knowles was working as a lorry driver and making regular visits to the Fleet Street premises of major national newspapers with reels of newsprint from the Starr Paper Works in Blackburn. At the meeting, Crabb introduced him to Matthew Smith, an American CIA agent. Smith claimed it was an important mission for a 'special branch' of the Joint Intelligence Services. Knowles says:

I was told Smith was a member of the CIA, who were organising the mission to look under the Soviet cruiser, *Sverdlov*. I must admit that I was very excited at the prospect of being on a secret service mission. I was told about the purpose of our dive and informed that the Americans and the Admiralty wanted to know what made the *Sverdlov* so manoeuvrable. My ERF wagon also became an integral part of the plot. I had left Preston as usual and delivered my cargo of newsprint to Fleet Street.

I then picked up Cdr Crabb at his flat and we proceeded to drive down to Portsmouth, arriving in the late evening. The weather was overcast with a cold, strong wind. My wagon was parked up on the seafront and not too far from the Railway Jetty where the *Sverdlov* was berthed. We used the wagon tarpaulin as cover and dressed in our Italian made diving gear. We had kept some of this gear from our wartime exploits. Smith joined us for a final briefing. We donned our suits and breathing sets and entered the water. We wore skullcaps with black netting over our hands and face. This was to break up our silhouettes on the surface. We approached at no more than drifting speed and finally reached the *Sverdlov*. My entire body was tingling with adrenalin.

We swam gently to examine the two rudders and four propellers but found nothing unusual. We then moved along the bilge keel where I was to wait until he had searched forward. It was total blackness except for a faint dockside light. My oxygen bottle clanged against the side of the ship but I wasn't too concerned for the activity in the ship above my head was very noisy, with the constant roar of fans and generators. I saw the shadowy figure of the commander approaching with his thumb up as a gesture of success. He signalled for me to follow where I found myself on the edge of a large circular opening in the bottom of the hull. We went up inside and examined a propeller that could be raised, lowered or directed to produce more thrust from the bow. We were overjoyed and swam back to keep our secret rendezvous and reported this to Smith. Without changing, we crept back under the tarpaulin and cracked open a bottle of single malt whisky to celebrate.

On returning to base the next day, Crabb had a huge grin on his face and called into the wardroom of HMS *Vernon* for a chat, and to deny with a twinkle in his eye any coincidence between the Russian warship's visit and his own. Several colleagues asked if anything was happening but he simply gave his standard reply: 'Just popped down for a haircut and a shave.'

The Coronation Review was perhaps one of the best times to carry out such a daring inspection. Portsmouth Docks and HMS *Vernon* were packed. More than 1,000 VIP guests had been invited, together with the royal families of three nations, every ambassador to Britain and many other notable public figures. The main training rooms were temporarily converted into waiting rooms, lounges or bars, and the car park was extended to accommodate more than 500 cars – including nine Rolls-Royces. Rear Admiral Poland remembers *Sverdlov*:

At the time of the Coronation Review, Crabb briefly appeared in the Portsmouth area, where he met Gutteridge and suggested that he might join him in a dive, which he later guessed would be under the Russian cruiser then at anchor off Portsmouth. Crabb also talked to the Commanding Officer of the Experimental Clearance diving team and asked to borrow an old Italian diving set. Since it was not naval stores and was of no use to the team, it was given to Crabb. Crabb did a test dive in Horsea Lake and left. Gutteridge indicates that Crabb was working for British Intelligence but not Naval Intelligence. Gutteridge believed Crabb was later intercepted by the authorities and sent back to London.

What Crabb and Knowles did not know at that stage was that Naval Intelligence had also arranged for a separate diving operation. They sent a party of four Navy divers, via HMS *Vernon*, to complete a similar inspection. This was said to have taken place later, while the ship was still at anchor. Both parties were apparently wholly unaware of each other but when the facts were revealed some interesting conversations took place back at the Admiralty.

Crabb continued with life 'as normal' back with Maitland and his furniture business. He worked long hours. He even welcomed visits from former members of the Italian Tenth Light Flotilla, and their offspring. They often travelled to London for long weekends. Crabb was also visited by Pat Rose, and on occasions by Anthony Blunt and some of his friends. Blunt by then was Keeper of the Queen's Pictures, and had become a director of the Courtauld Institute. He deliberately retained a generous association with Lionel – his former gallery salesman – and Crabb's cousin, Kitty Jarvis, who had been his wartime PA.

Burgess and Maclean, Blunt's former wartime colleagues, had by then been exposed as Russian spies and had fled from London in 1951 to enjoy respectability and acclaim in Moscow. Kim Philby also retained a close friendship with Blunt and was about to follow a similar path.

Pat Rose met many of Lionel's friends and former colleagues and heard something about his wartime experiences. In addition, she met the American agent, Matthew Smith, but told Crabb's family that she didn't trust him.

Chapter 19

The Final Dive

In March 1956 Lionel received an urgent message to meet privately with Lord Mountbatten. He was offered another secret Admiralty mission, run in conjunction with the Intelligence Services. Cdr Gutteridge was one of several officers who recalled the date. He said: 'In the spring of that year, Lionel had gone down from London to Portsmouth for a few drinks with his chums, and on the last day, the Saturday, he turned up at my house for drinks and lunch. He said he was on his way to meet Lord Mountbatten at Cowdray Park at 4 p.m. Unusually, he didn't tell me why, either before or after the event – and I didn't ask him. But what reason did Mountbatten have for wanting to see Crabb then, or at any other time?'

Other senior naval officers noted Mountbatten and Crabb's unusual association. It was a few more weeks before Crabb received any more information. He was advised it was another 'His Eyes Only' mission, and that he would be working under Lord Mountbatten's personal supervision. By then, Mountbatten was First Sea Lord, but this time Crabb was told the results were to be shared with MI6, in addition to the CIA.

CIA agent Matthew Smith became a constant visitor to Crabb's London works. And within a day or two Crabb asked Maitland if he could borrow his car as he had a 'little job to do down in Portsmouth'. This next mission obviously worried Lionel. Although it was similar to previous requests to inspect the hull of a visiting Russian warship, this time it would be without the razzamatazz of the Coronation Review. Mountbatten also warned Crabb that the Soviet authorities had noted both earlier dives on the *Sverdlov*, including the one sanctioned by Naval Intelligence. It therefore seemed highly likely that some contingency plans would be put into effect to prevent such a dive from happening again.

Before the mission, Crabb began visiting his relatives and friends, many of whom he had not seen for some time. A few days before the dive, he even wrote a brief note to his mother Daisy. And, strangely, he asked her to destroy the letter once she had read it. His family were fully aware that he was 'on call' and working for the Intelligence services, and Mountbatten's name was mentioned several times by them, and by other close friends. The precise nature of his mission, however, remained secret.

The following information has been obtained from many people directly involved or associated with Crabb's 'final dive', and lately corroborated by official records recently released by the Cabinet Office, National Archives, MI6 and other Intelligence agencies. It is also based upon several interviews. Some additional information was obtained from Rear Admiral Poland, and former members of his research team, who reviewed the incident in 1989. I have recorded the facts in chronological order.

Tuesday 17 April: Lionel Crabb advised Maitland that he probably wouldn't be back at work until the weekend. He had another 'little job to attend to first in Portsmouth'. His colleague knew better than to ask what it was all about and wished him well. Crabb said he would telephone Maitland sometime during the visit. During the day, he met up with his fiancée, Pat Rose. They had finally agreed to marry. Pat knew he was tasked with something of immense importance this time, and agreed to accompany him on the train from London Victoria to Portsmouth. It would give them a chance to talk. Pat knew that Smith was also involved and demanded to know what was happening – she even threatened to call off the engagement if he didn't tell her. Crabb then asked Smith to travel down in a separate compartment and to keep out of the way. In the official intelligence notes, Pat says:

I was first engaged to Lionel in 1948. We became engaged on the same day he received his George Medal. After that, we split up and we each married. It didn't work out and we were both divorced about the same time. We met once more and at the time he disappeared, we had been engaged for about four months.

On 16 April, Lionel came around to my flat and we went out to a pub. We had lunch together but he was terribly jittery. He normally drank quite heavily, but he only had half a pint of beer and just picked at his food. I asked him what was wrong and he said he was going to Portsmouth the next day to test some equipment. Although I didn't want to go he persuaded me. On the journey down I threatened to break off our engagement if he didn't tell me what was really going on. I said he was always testing new gear, so there was nothing new in that. Finally, he admitted he was going to look at the bottom of the Russian cruiser. I said he had already done a mission like that before, but this time he said the Admiralty were sending him. I had met Matthew Smith a few weeks before. He talked like an American, and I didn't like him one bit. At Portsmouth, Crabbie said we could not stay in the same hotel because he had to leave and meet Smith. He said that if he didn't phone tomorrow, he would call in the evening. That was the last I saw of him.

Pat Rose was put on a train back home and outside Portsmouth station Crabb met Smith, a relatively junior member of the liaison team between SIS and the CIA. The pair made their way to the Sallyport Hotel, a small and convenient hotel, where Crabb booked in under his real name. However, it is said that Smith phoned ahead and reserved two single rooms. The American had a number of aliases but was always known to Crabb as Smith. They accepted the keys for rooms 17 and 21, with Smith agreeing to take the slightly smaller attic room, No. 17. When Crabb telephoned Pat later he told her he had a view over the cranes and Naval Dockyard.

In his luggage was his favourite Heinke dry suit and diving gear. Once they had unpacked, Crabb and Smith travelled to a secret rendezvous to meet the Chief Constable, Mr A.C. West, who introduced his senior colleague Superintendent Jack Lamport. He was to be their liaison officer. Lamport was an old hand, vastly experienced in intelligence operations.

Ironically the Chief Constable had also met with General Serov, the head of the Soviet Security Service in the UK, shortly beforehand, to reassure him about local security measures during the visit.

Arrangements were made to meet Lamport again the following morning. During the evening Lionel Crabb also made contact with his friend and colleague, Lt George Albert 'Frankie' Franklin. He was an expert diver and worked as a senior clearance diver at HMS *Vernon* under the command of John Grant, captain of *Vernon*, and executive officer Cdr Charles Emmerson.

Franklin first met Lionel Crabb in 1949, when they were both serving in the Navy. They had become good friends and Crabbie used to call at Franklin's house when he visited Portsmouth. During the course of their friendship, they were at times both engaged in similar diving operations and underwater swimming.

Franklin recalls: 'Some time in 1955, Crabbie returned to civilian life. He was engaged in the furniture trade but still kept up his interest in diving. On the evening of 17 April, he phoned me at home and invited me for a drink. When we were together, he asked me whether I would help him in a dive, as he needed someone to assist getting him into his underwater clothing.'

Wednesday 18 April: Later that morning, Crabb appeared in the wardroom at HMS *Vernon*. Whenever he stayed over in Portsmouth, Crabb normally occupied cabin No. 11, which nearly always contained his swordstick and a framed photograph of Pat Rose. He also met John Emm, a wardroom steward. Crabb had spoken to him in advance and asked if he could borrow his car to transport some heavy diving gear after drawing it from the *Vernon* diving stores. Emm agreed. Crabb also used to store a few odds and ends in an old air raid shelter close to the quayside, and when he finished, he returned the car to its allocated bay.

Vernon's former executive officer, Cdr Charles Emmerson, confirms that Crabb's arrival coincided with that of three Russian warships, and this is corroborated by friends of Crabb, who say he watched the warships arrive through binoculars. The principal ship was a very modern cruiser, the *Ordzhonikidze* (roughly pronounced 'Our Johnny Kids You'), accompanied by her sister ships, the destroyers *Sovershenny* and *Smotryashchi*. The vessels had brought Soviet Premier Nikolai Alexandrovich Bulganin and Communist Party chief Nikita Sergeyevich Khrushchev to England for a unique goodwill visit.

Emmerson said they had been delayed due to fog and that the two Russian leaders had entered the harbour by launch. When visibility improved the *Ordzhonikidze* and her escort ships berthed at the Southern Railway Jetty in Portsmouth Dockyard. The Russian leaders then travelled by special train to London, where they were met and welcomed by British Prime Minister Anthony Eden and his Cabinet colleagues. Ironically, the *Ordzhonikidze* was a sister ship to the *Sverdlov*, another powerful Soviet cruiser that had visited British waters less than a year before. Cdr Emmerson says:

Later that afternoon, Crabb sat down to tea with me. I took the opportunity to thank him for a pair of Jade Laer dogs that he had presented to *Vernon*. Without actually giving me a reason for his visit, he said that the jade dogs had never brought him anything but bad luck, and said he was glad to get rid of them. I hadn't seen him for ages. I knew all about him but didn't know anything about this current adventure. He said he had come down to buy some furniture. He also told me that he'd brought me a small memento, a small brass monkey!

He was a very non-committal chap. He kept himself to himself, especially on that occasion. Crabb was a very popular chap but he never really had that much to say. I knew of his reputation and his war record but he always kept quiet about that. He came to see me in the afternoon. Instead of taking tea in the wardroom, we went into my cabin. There were just the two of us and I was under the impression that he'd travelled here (to Portsmouth) alone. He certainly didn't mention his girlfriend or anyone else.

I hadn't seen him for such a long time, and if he stayed at *Vernon* that was something I knew little about. Nobody at that stage, though, thought to question his presence. But why *was* he there?

It seems that someone wanted a diver to make a dive under the Russian cruiser on this delicate political occasion, to look at, or to do something. It is known that Crabb did attempt a mission at 17.30hrs but became entangled in the pilings of the jetty and aborted.

Lt Franklin, however, disputes that there were any problems. He says:

> I agreed to help Crabbie and on the afternoon of 18 April I helped him
> into his underwater clothing and assisted him over the side of a boat in
> the Portsmouth area. He dived and was underwater for about half an
> hour. I helped him on board and he then said he would like to make
> another dive with a little additional equipment. We decided that early the
> next morning would be a good opportunity for this because the tide was
> favourable.

After his preliminary dive, Crabb returned to his hotel and phoned Maitland
back at the office. He told him he was 'not as old as he thought'. It seems
Crabb had originally planned to dive that morning but had changed his
mind due to extreme security precautions and the delay with the arrival of
the Soviet ships.

Crabb also phoned Pat Rose. She knew it was a dangerous mission and
that it was only loosely connected with the Admiralty. She had wanted to
know who else was involved but all Crabb would say was that it was an
'important mission'. He then had a meal before arranging to meet a fellow
officer and his wife at another bar a short distance away. During much of
his time at the hotel, Crabb was alone and saw very little of his travelling
companion Smith.

Thursday 19 April, 06.10hrs: Crabb and Smith left the Sallyport Hotel
at the crack of dawn. They intended to return later, enjoy a late breakfast,
perhaps, and check out. The men made their way to the approach to
the Naval Dockyard, where they were met and accompanied through
the security cordon by Supt Lamport and another CID officer. Inside
the gates, Franklin joined them. They then travelled a short distance
in a car across the dockyard to the edge of the quay. Crabb, Smith and
Franklin walked towards some stone steps known as the King's Stairs.
A launch had been secured from the Boat Pound. Crabb collected his
pre-stowed gear from his private store and the group carried the equipment
a few more yards to the edge of the water, where the police officers bade
them farewell.

Smith then ran through a final briefing. It was practically a repeat of Crabb's previous mission. This time, however, he had the latest Admiralty Research cine camera in his possession. Crabb was concerned, though, about poor surface visibility and estimated the task would take about an hour. They synchronised their watches. It was 06.45hrs. The weather was relatively fine. It was a cool and rather damp morning. And just as the previous day, there was a touch of fog in the Channel.

Initially, the mission went well. Crabb dived on time, but returned slightly breathless about 20 minutes later, complaining about limited underwater visibility and the cold. Franklin checked out all Crabb's gear before Lionel dived again, but he never returned. Franklin waited until 09.15hrs, and despite a frantic search of the area in the launch, was forced to abandon the mission and report the incident to the authorities. Franklin confirmed the events of that day:

This next morning I again helped him into his equipment, which included some additional weights for which he had asked. I assisted him to go over the side of the boat. This was shortly before 7 a.m. He was then wearing a cotton vest, bathing trunks, rayon combinations, stockinet combinations, and socks beneath the two-piece Heinke diving suit. Crabb also wore rubber flippers on his feet, breathing apparatus, and on his head he had a little woolly balaclava with the bathing cap on top. The breathing apparatus would have enabled him to breathe comfortably for about 90 minutes. I turned the boat about but I was unable to find him. I went ashore and reported that he was missing.

In a statement he later gave to the authorities Franklin explained:

Crabb had asked me, as an expert diver, if I was prepared to assist him entirely unofficially and in a strictly private capacity. Cdr Crabb told me that on no account was I to inform the naval authority. I agreed on my own responsibility and I accompanied him on the morning of 19 April.

The exact position of the dive was from a boat moored in the Boat Pound immediately south of the Southern Railway Jetty. I assisted Crabb to put on and adjust his equipment. He entered the water from the boat at 7 a.m. I am satisfied that his equipment at that time was correctly adjusted and in proper working order. He appeared fit and well. The weather was fine and the sea calm, with a slight ebb tide.

He carried sufficient oxygen for nearly two hours and the conditions for diving were good. The weight and nature of the apparatus were such that, if through maladjustment subsequent to entering the water, or through some physical failure on the part of the wearer, he became unconscious, it is most unlikely that the body would have risen to the surface – as long as the apparatus remained in place.

Smith and Franklin quickly gathered all Crabb's clothing, together with all the spare gear. Some were returned to the shelter and secured. Smith contacted the Chief Constable's office and informed him of the problem. He was told to wait for Lamport. Smith was anxious to disappear and he telephoned his own security chief at the CIA from the police station. They in turn notified MI6 and Naval Intelligence.

Smith was ordered immediately to clear everything from the Sallyport Hotel and to return to London. He called at the hotel reception, settled the account and collected his and Crabb's luggage before dashing to the station and catching the first express back to London. Within hours he was safely back in his protective security bubble. Franklin was ordered to return to *Vernon* and to take no further part in the affair.

This 'mishap' as the government first called Crabb's final dive, was quickly reported to Naval Intelligence. They ordered another launch to search the area but without any real prospect of success. A Naval Intelligence chief quoted in official papers then informed his colleagues that a full search with all available facilities could be arranged, but was not advisable since it would reveal the whole story without there being any hope of saving Cdr Crabb (who was weighted).

Later another secret intelligence report confirmed that 'The officer who had been helping (Lt Cdr Franklin), reported the occurrence to the captain of *Vernon*, John Grant, who immediately acquainted the Commander-in-Chief, Portsmouth (Rear Admiral P.W. Burnett).'

All these facts, however, were quickly buried. Clear evidence of a cover-up begins to unfold in a note from the Director of Naval Intelligence, Rear Admiral John Inglis, copied to Admiral of the Fleet Sir George Creasey. Inglis considered it essential to try to avoid implicating the Commander-in-Chief, Portsmouth, and his staff, and other naval executives, as the following extract from Inglis shows:

> If it had been a *bona fide* naval diving operation, then immediate and extensive rescue operations would have been ordered by the Commander-in-Chief, accompanied by warnings to all naval and police authorities in the area. This would have been done for humanitarian reasons, even if there had been no hope of Cdr Crabb's survival. Franklin was ordered back to his ship and asked to take no further part. In consequence, any cover story purporting to show that this was a *bona fide* naval operation would only have exposed John Grant and the C-in-C to charges of negligence, lack of humanity and an error of judgement. Even as a last resort, this was considered unacceptable.

A further note from Naval Intelligence to Creasey added: 'Careful consideration will therefore have to be given in the Admiralty on how the situation is handled, but this can only be done when the exact nature of the legal proceedings is known – as well as the part that Lt Franklin will be called upon to play in them.' Cdr Gordon Gutteridge recalls the dive:

> At approximately 7 a.m., first light, Crabb entered the water. He had some difficulty with his equipment. After a breather, he returned to the water and was never seen alive again – except briefly on the surface about 7.35 a.m. between two of the Russian ships. The choice of first light for the start of this dive is odd, if not inept, since it posed a high risk of discovery if the slightest thing went wrong. Subsurface visibility in Portsmouth harbour was nil and the dive could just as easily and safely have been carried out in the middle of the night – and with little risk of disclosure.

Cdr Emmerson from HMS *Vernon* adds:

When Crabb's disappearance was noted, there was not too much fuss at the time. I was not questioned about his visit – and I was never questioned about what he was doing, or what was said. It was immediately apparent that no one at the Admiralty would want to be engaged in what was obviously a hazardous and unnecessary operation. Therefore that 'someone' had to find an experienced diver – and not in the Royal Navy – to make a dive involving a long swim, in cold water, in tidal conditions and nil visibility, to a depth of about 30ft. It was a depth which is dangerous using equipment which would not produce telltale bubbles at the surface. In Crabb, they found an unfit, heavy drinking, heavy smoking 47-year-old, using equipment which was dangerous. There was little prospect of success. Whoever employed Crabb for that mission was woefully ignorant of the magnitude and risk of the task and seemingly had no good reason for doing it.

It is also known that again, and contrary to earlier claims, many members of the HMS *Vernon* diving team were also ordered into the water. Surgeon Vice-Admiral Sir John Rawlins says:

I happened to be on what was termed an 'Acquaint Course' at *Vernon* at that time. During the week before he disappeared, I met Crabb, dressed in that green two-piece Pirelli suit, and subsequently in uniform, wearing green wavy-navy commander's stripes. In the following week, Petty Officer Rogers lined up all the trainee divers and told us to get into the water and to search under the jetties. When we asked what for, he just said, 'Anything unusual.' We were booted and there was zero visibility, and as I blundered around in the mud, I thought that if the water suddenly vanished, all that would be seen of us would be bumps in the liquid mud representing the tops of our heads. We brought up various bits of rubbish, which Rogers threw back into the water. And one lad got a hell of a fright when he somehow got into an ancient boiler. He thought he must have entered a sewer and didn't seem to be able to find his way out. Fortunately, he did manage to do so before his gas ran out.

1. Lt Lionel Crabb, officer in charge of the Underwater Working Party, in Gibraltar during 1944. *(Imperial War Museum A 23270)*

2. Frank Jarvis, one of the
founders of the Conway
Stewart pen company.
(Jarvis Family Archive)

3. Kitty Jarvis (right) with
Lionel Crabb's mother,
Beatrice (Daisy) Crabb.
(Jarvis Family Archive)

4. A traditional family portrait. Frank and Kitty Jarvis with their children Eileen (left), Audrey and Kenneth. *(Jarvis Family Archive)*

5. Kitty Jarvis (centre) with her two daughters, Audrey (left) and Eileen, during the Second World War. *(Jarvis Family Archive)*

6. Kenneth Jarvis pictured in action during his motor-racing days. *(Jarvis Family Archive)*

7. Kenneth Jarvis with racing support colleagues at the Brighton Speed Trials in September 1947. *(Jarvis Family Archive)*

8. Lt Noel Cashford (centre) and his Bomb and Mine Disposal Team working on a wartime mine. *(Noel Cashford Archive)*

9. A wartime photograph of members of Lt Noel Cashford's team helping to secure a mine ashore in readiness for being made safe. Pictured (left to right) are Able Seaman Fisher, Lt Noel Cashford MBE, RNR, and Lt Cdr Ned Smith OBE, RNVR. *(Noel Cashford Archive)*

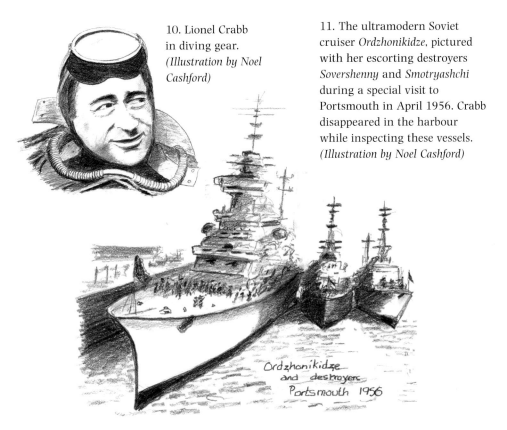

10. Lionel Crabb in diving gear. *(Illustration by Noel Cashford)*

11. The ultramodern Soviet cruiser *Ordzhonikidze*, pictured with her escorting destroyers *Sovershenny* and *Smotryashchi* during a special visit to Portsmouth in April 1956. Crabb disappeared in the harbour while inspecting these vessels. *(Illustration by Noel Cashford)*

Ordzhonikidze and destroyers Portsmouth 1956

12. The sinking of Crabb's first ship, SS *Bonheur*, off the Butt of Lewis by U-138, commanded by Lt Wolfgang Luth, on 15 October 1940. *(Illustration by Noel Cashford)*

THE LONDON GAZETTE,

TUESDAY, 25 JANUARY, 1944

CENTRAL CHANCERY OF THE ORDERS OF KNIGHTHOOD.

St. James's Palace, S.W.1.

25th January, 1944.

The KING has been graciously pleased to approve the award of the George Medal to:

Temporary Lieutenant Lionel Kenneth Crabb, R.N.V.R.,

Acting Petty Officer David Morrison Bell, P/JX. 144608,

for gallantry and undaunted devotion to duty.

13. The citation for Temporary Lieutenant Lionel Crabb RNVR upon receiving the George Medal on 25 January 1944. The description is taken from a clipping in the *London Gazette* for Lt Crabb and colleague Acting Petty Officer David Morrison Bell 'for gallantry and undaunted devotion to duty'. *(Royal Naval Museum)*

14. The Soviet cruiser *Ordzhonikidze*, which arrived in Portsmouth in April 1956, carrying Soviet officials on a state visit to Great Britain. *(Royal Naval Museum)*

15. Lt Lionel Crabb (left) and a Spanish civilian diver. In April 1944, they sometimes found themselves working together. *(Imperial War Museum A 23267)*

16. Lt Crabb wearing his diving gear. *(Imperial War Museum A 23261)*

17. Three members of the Underwater Working Party wearing their breathing apparatus. Left to right: Petty Officer Amey from Southampton, Crabb and Able Seaman Thomas from Swansea. *(Imperial War Museum A 23268)*

18. HMS *Affray*, the last Royal Navy submarine lost at sea, pictured during October 1946. The *Affray* failed to surface during an exercise in the English Channel in April 1951 resulting in the loss of its crew of seventy-five men. Cdr Crabb, working from the specialist diving vessel HMS *Reclaim*, took part in the attempted rescue operation and utilised his innovative underwater television equipment, beaming back exclusive pictures of the stricken submarine to the bridge of the *Reclaim*. (*Wright & Logan Collection, Royal Navy Submarine Museum. Picture courtesy of Alan Gallop and the Royal Naval Museum*)

19. HMS *Reclaim*, the specialist diving ship used by Crabb on numerous occasions in various parts of the world during hazardous underwater commissions, including the attempted rescue of the submarine HMS *Affray*. (*Photograph courtesy of Alan Gallop*)

20. Royal Navy diver Lionel 'Buster' Crabb prepares for a dive in Tobermory Bay, on the island of Mull, during a search for treasure believed to lie in a 300-year-old shipwreck, 11 April 1950. (*Getty Images*)

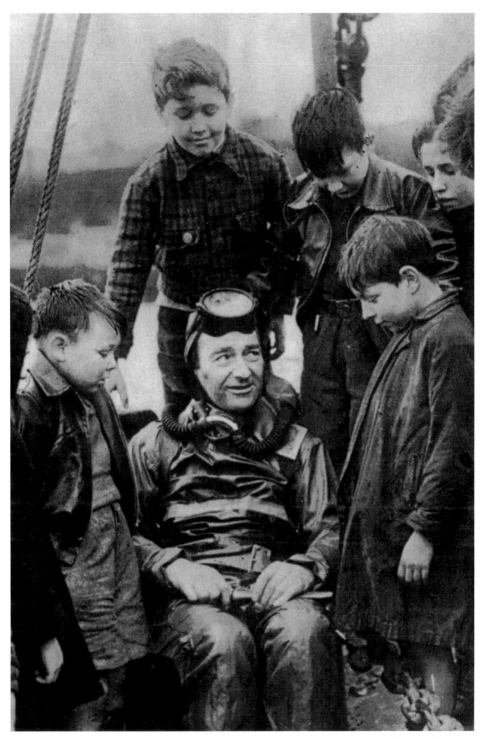

21. Crabb relates some of his experiences to an attentive audience of schoolchildren in Tobermory, 13 April 1950. *(Getty Images)*

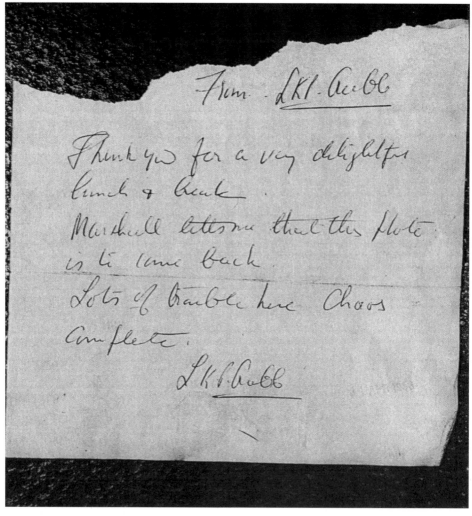

22. One of Crabb's last letters to his publisher in 1956, relating to his forthcoming biography. *(Time & Life Pictures/Getty Images)*

	REGISTRATION DISTRICT				Chichester				

1957...DEATH in the Sub-district of .Chichester North....................................in the ..County of West Sussex.

Columns:–	1	2	3	4	5	6	7	8	9
No.	When and where died	Name and surname	Sex	Age	Occupation	Cause of death	Signature, description and residence of informant	When registered	Signature of registrar
258	Ninth June 1957 Found Dead in Chichester Harbour &c.	Lionel Kenneth Philip CRABB	Male	48 Years	of 29 Hans Road London S.W.3. a Retired Commander Royal Naval Volunteer Reserve	Not Ascertainable P.M.	Certificate Received from G.H.L Bridgman Coroner for West Sussex Chichester Inquest held Eleventh June 1957 and adjournment on Twelfth June	Twenty Eighth June 1957	J.A Setton Registrar

CERTIFIED to be a true copy of an entry in the certified copy of a Register of Deaths in the District above mentioned.

Given at the GENERAL REGISTER OFFICE, under the Seal of the said Office, the ....17th........................day of ....March............... ...2006

DYA 963348

See note overleaf

039895 10103 06/05 SPSL 012027

23. Lionel Crabb's death certificate. *(General Record Office)*

24. Commander Crabb's medals (left to right): OBE (Order of the British Empire); George Medal; 1939–45 Star; Atlantic Star; Italy Star; Defence Medal 1939–45; War Medal 1939–45. *(Royal Naval Museum)*

25. Lionel Crabb pictured trying to keep warm in a woollen hat and duffel coat in between dives.

The next day, the story of Crabb's disappearance hit the headlines. The clearance divers took many pints off the press in the Still and West by hinting that they'd been with Crabb. John Grant, the captain of *Vernon*, gave his explanation, which differed slightly in the timing claimed by other officers, and reported later in official documents. He explains:

My senior clearance diver Franklin came and reported to me that he had been asked by Crabb to help him to dress for an important dive, and to take him by car to the waterside in the dockyard somewhere near to the Russian cruisers. This was done without reference to anyone else, at the request of Cdr Crabb. Having seen him into the water, Franklin waited for his return. My senior clearance officer then continued that, owing to the time which had elapsed since he last saw Crabb, he had cause for alarm. As I myself had received no information whatsoever on this operation – which apparently involved a member of my own *Vernon* staff – I was, somewhat naturally, extremely annoyed. Accordingly, I took the officer with me in a car to see the Chief of Staff to the Commander-in-Chief, Portsmouth (Rear Admiral Burnett), and asked him to report the matter to the C in C as a matter of great urgency.

As was expected, the C in C went through the roof and the wires to the Admiralty must have nearly fused. The Director of Naval Intelligence (Rear Admiral Inglis) visited, and then, in my opinion, a stupid statement was given to the press by the Admiralty to the effect that Crabb had been lost in Stokes Bay. As that was the *Vernon* Exercise Area I was consequently bothered by pressmen – but they only got a 'no comment' out of me.

The intense secrecy of Crabb's dive, and his supervision by Lord Mountbatten, was such that the operation was known to only a handful of trusted officers. In fact two of Mountbatten's close aides had been embarrassingly unaware of his precise instructions and involvement on that day. They admitted, however, that Mountbatten was quite capable of planning this mission.

Rear Admiral Poland confirmed that on the day of Crabb's final dive he was serving in the Ship Requirements Section of the Naval Staff. He says:

Shortly thereafter, I moved to the Plans Division as temporary relief for Michael Pollock (later First Sea Lord). I can vouch for the fact that no one in Ships Requirements section had any knowledge of clandestine operations on the Soviet Cruisers. It was widely known that the Prime Minister had issued strict instructions that no intelligence operations were to be carried out. It was my duty as Assistant Planner to brief the First Sea Lord, Lord Mountbatten, on world trouble spots and the naval involvement. Had the dive been officially sanctioned, I believe the Ships Requirements Section and the Captain of *Vernon* would have known about it. I conclude therefore that the dive came about as the result of an 'off the cuff' discussion between members of the Intelligence Department and naïve members of the naval staff. All were quite unaware of the likelihood of a major technical failure with Crabb's diving equipment.

I suppose it will go on and on without any logical conclusion except for some mistake by a fairly junior member of the intelligence staff. I can only repeat that in my area of naval staff responsibilities, nothing was known about Crabb and his activities.

Admiral of the Fleet Lord Hill Norton, says:

Mountbatten was First Sea Lord at the relevant time. I knew him very well. We were on Christian name terms. He must have been quite capable of setting the whole operation up, unacknowledged, but I don't think he did. He was too proud of the Navy to risk us getting the blame (which we did) when it all went wrong and his own conceit would have been seriously damaged.

I was Captain of the *Decoy* and chairman of the Defence Research Policy Staff, from which seat I should certainly have known if the Admiralty and the fledgling MOD had been the sponsors. I am as sure as I can be that the Navy was not involved before the event. I can therefore assert with confidence that the Admiralty was not in any 'official' sense aware in advance that this absurd venture was planned. I do not believe that any members of the Board would have broken the formal undertaking, which had been given to the Russians.

Remarkably, at the time of Crabb's disappearance the First Sea Lord, Lord Louis Mountbatten, the Director of Naval Intelligence, Rear Admiral John Inglis and even the MI6 chief Sir John Sinclair were all said to be out of the country. In later notes about the incident, Lord Mountbatten stated: 'I returned from a long tour of South East Asia to find myself at the centre of a squall over the activities of Cdr Crabb.'

Mountbatten claimed he knew nothing about this mission until he was told by the Admiralty on his return. By that time, he said the press had got hold of the story, and it was clear that a scandal was about to break. He insisted he should have been told at once. The accuracy of some of his claims, however, has often been disputed and was certainly at variance with his own Vice-Chief of Naval Staff, Admiral Sir William Davis.

In his autobiography, Mountbatten asserted that he had instructed Davis before he left on his tour, that 'no such operation was to be undertaken'. He was justifying 'what seemed superfluous precautions on the grounds that it seems irresistible for spies to look at ships' bottoms'. Admiral Davis, though, claimed to have no knowledge of this instruction. And he said that Mountbatten agreed not to tell the First Lord of the Admiralty when it seemed likely that the story would never become public. He demurred only when Davis asked him to wait a few minutes until Cabinet Minister John Lang joined them.

Mountbatten's position regarding the Crabb incident came under scrutiny following attacks in the House of Commons, when the Labour MP, Lord Wigg, called out: 'The man responsible is the First Sea Lord; he should be thrown out!' Wigg, who also knew that Lord Mountbatten was abroad at the time of the incident, added: 'Nothing in the Navy happens unless you want it to . . . they wouldn't have dared do it if they thought you would disapprove.' And both the *Daily Mirror* and *Daily Express* vigorously attacked Mountbatten, with the First Sea Lord retorting by asking the *Daily Mirror*'s Hugh Cudlipp: 'Hugh, are you trying to get me sacked?'

Certain aspects of this embarrassing incident were later debated in Parliament. It caused mayhem within the establishment, and led to a massive breakdown in Anglo-Soviet relations. Not surprisingly, it had an effect on Franklin's naval career, and led to the removal of some senior naval personnel, top politicians and key civil servants. For several months heads rolled left, right and centre. It also triggered a quite extraordinary and unprecedented shake-up of the Intelligence Services.

The extent of the panic which ensued within the establishment and its attempts first to ignore and then cover up Crabb's final dive are shown in the following summary.

Friday 20 April: At the time of his disappearance, only a few people knew of Crabb's movements. They included his boss, Maitland Pendock, his fiancée, Pat Rose, some close family members, Lt Franklin, and a journalist, Marshall Pugh, who was writing an account of Crabb's war service.

Matthew Smith, of course, was Crabb's liaison officer between the Intelligence Services and the CIA, and the senior officer, whom Crabb met the night before his mission; Gordon Gutteridge had an idea that something was happening, as Crabb had hinted that he was working on a very important mission connected with Mountbatten. And the arrival of the Russian ships was probably too big an opportunity to miss.

When news of Crabb's 'accident' reached HMS *Vernon*, the lid came down hard. There were severe restrictions placed on any discussion of the matter and Franklin was sworn to secrecy. At this stage, Cabinet members claimed they were still unaware of the full circumstances of Crabb's disappearance, and understood it was still being kept 'in house' with only limited details released by the Admiralty.

Perhaps Cabinet Ministers and politicians were awaiting a decision or a response from either the First Sea Lord or from the Director of Naval Intelligence. There was also an obvious reluctance to reveal a political scandal. The Soviet delegation, however, was already aware of the incident. The Russians had been notified by the captain of the cruiser. At a dinner in London that evening, hosted by Prime Minister Anthony Eden, and the majority of his ministers, and members of the royal family, Khrushchev made a humorous reference to the *Ordzhonikidze*. The point may have been lost in translation but he asked about 'missing or lost property'.

The British party claimed to be ignorant of any details, and couldn't quite understand the joke. It was the following morning before Eden received a brief report from his MI6 security chief Sir John Alexander Sinclair.

The Prime Minister was acutely embarrassed. The air was full of choice expletives in Downing Street, as the operation had been carried out against Eden's instructions. Because the Prime Minister had given a personal undertaking to the Soviets that nothing untoward would happen, he was furious with his MI6 intelligence chief Sinclair, and relations were never the same again. He admitted that the SIS had authorised an inspection, and that it had even been given a code name of Operation 'Claret'. He said it was a joint operation with the American Intelligence services.

What was not divulged for another fifty years was the fact that Crabb's mission was probably a decoy run, as Naval Intelligence had again organised their own spying mission – similar to the search of the *Sverdlov* the previous year, using four naval divers. And regrettably, something that was either unknown or undisclosed at that time is that one of Naval Intelligence's men also went missing.

The Operation 'Claret' tag almost certainly related to the Naval Intelligence mission rather than Crabb's attempt. Certainly Mountbatten claimed to have had no immediate knowledge of the Naval Intelligence dive and was said to be more angry about that omission than the fact it may well have jeopardised Crabb's attempt, and cost him his life. There was another major concern at the time, which remained unreported: that Crabb was carrying some new and highly sensitive underwater camera equipment for the Admiralty Research Laboratories. The government stopped a decision for any further search until after the Russian ships had departed.

Saturday 21 April: Admiral Burnett, Chief of Staff to the Commander-in-Chief, Portsmouth, spent much of the next day with his Soviet counterpart, Rear Admiral V.F. Kotov. No doubt both parties were still trying to find out what had happened, and why. It was during coffee and after dinner that evening that Kotov delicately raised the matter with Burnett. It was a light-hearted inquiry but he said that three Russian sailors had spotted a diver in the water near the ships at about 8 a.m. on Thursday 19 April. Kotov asked Burnett if everything was OK. He said he was not proposing to make a fuss, or make any formal complaint. Burnett, who had obviously been aware of most of the facts for the past two days, offered his apologies but claimed to know nothing. He said he would make further inquiries. The Russians were angered by his unhelpful and non-committal response.

That evening, Crabb's commercial boss, Maitland Pendock, phoned the Sallyport Hotel at Portsmouth. He had not heard from Lionel since Wednesday night and was concerned for his welfare. He had also spoken to Pat Rose, who was also worried. The hotel owner, Edward Richman, confirmed that Crabb and a Mr Smith had checked out on Thursday morning. This Mr Smith had settled the bill for both rooms. He had also removed the luggage and left for London.

During that day, Maitland received a telephone call from the naval commander and his wife, who had shared a few drinks with Crabb the night before his final dive. They had arranged to meet Lionel on Friday night but said he didn't turn up. Maitland said he would make inquiries at his end, and asked the officer if he would check with HMS *Vernon* to see if anyone there knew anything.

The officer made several calls around Portsmouth, and contacted some members of Crabb's family, but Lionel had not returned home. Shortly afterwards, the officer contacted the hotel proprietor, without any real update. The officer then phoned Maitland again. He related some conversations, and confirmed that no one at *Vernon* knew of Crabb's whereabouts either. He had called in before the dive, but had not been seen since. The officer said there was a strange and subdued atmosphere but thought it was probably due to the tension of this VIP visit. The officer said if he hadn't heard by Monday, he would call the Admiralty.

Sunday 22 April: Sir Ivonne Kirkpatrick, the Permanent Under-Secretary of State for Foreign Affairs, who was staying at Chequers for the week-end, received a telephone call from a senior civil servant. The civil servant relayed him the gist of the message regarding Khrushchev and Bulganin's comments at the dinner party. There was said to be no discussion about Crabb's disappearance, and Sir Ivonne said he had no knowledge of any incident.

Monday 23 April: Prime Minister Eden was officially informed of Rear Admiral Kotov's inquiry about the frogman incident, and of his remarks to Rear Admiral Philip Burnett. He called in Sir Ivonne Kirk-patrick. He related the message from the night before, and said that he had only just been advised by a civil servant about the probable loss of Cdr Crabb.

The Portsmouth commander who had befriended Crabb the night before his mission put a call into the Commander-in-Chief's office in Portsmouth, asking if any incident had been reported. He was told nothing had been officially logged.

Maitland Pendock called the journalist, Marshall Pugh, to see if he knew anything. He asked Pugh whether he could put any pressure on the authorities to find out if something had happened to Crabb. Pugh seemed relaxed and said 'he always turned up'.

Tuesday 24 April: Maitland Pendock contacted Crabb's friend, the Commander-in-Chief at Portsmouth, again. The officer agreed to contact the Admiralty directly. The Director of Naval Intelligence was then made aware of the government's concern and about inquiries from some of Crabb's family and friends. He spoke with the prime minister and it was agreed that all parties should keep quiet until after the Russian visit was over. The government was keen for the Admiralty to put out a statement assuming full responsibility.

Wednesday 25 April: A meeting was held at the Admiralty between the Director of Naval Intelligence (DNI), the head of MI6, and other key senior naval officers. Following lengthy discussion, three main conclusions emerged.

(1)   The DNI agreed to submit to the Vice-Chief of Naval Staff, Admiral Sir William Davis, that the Admiralty should at once assume responsibility for covering the operation.
(2)   It was agreed that if the matter were put to higher authority in one department it would, at the same time, have to go up to higher authority in the other departments concerned.
(3)   It was agreed that the top priority was to prevent the story breaking while the Russians were still in England.

That afternoon, Admiral Davis agreed that the Admiralty would have to provide cover and he also agreed that Capt Richard Sarell DSO, a senior Admiralty officer who was appointed to the Deputy Chief of Staff, should visit Maitland Pendock to try to persuade him to keep quiet. This meeting also opened and established a direct line of communication to Lord Mountbatten. His interests were to be represented by Admiral Davis.

Friday 27 April: Government minutes confirm that Capt Sarell made contact with Maitland Pendock. He agreed to meet him later that day. Another high-level meeting then took place at the Admiralty between Sarell, the Director General of MI5, Dick White, and other senior officers. A brief was hastily drafted, which proposed the suggested wording to be used by the Admiralty if they had to answer any questions about Crabb's disappearance. A copy of this note released in 2006 confirms: 'Brief issued by Chief of Naval Intelligence to cover Crabb statement. Cdr L.K.P. Crabb, OBE, GM, RNVR, who was specially employed in connection with trials of certain underwater apparatus, has not returned from a test dive and must be presumed dead.'

The following instructions were attached to the statement:

(1)   The above is NOT to be volunteered to the press, but can be used in answer to any pertinent Press enquiry which may arise.
(2)   If pressed, by the enquirer, it can be admitted that the location was in Stokes Bay, Portsmouth Area.
(3)   Similarly, if pressed, it is to be admitted that he became missing, presumed drowned on 19 April.
(4)   If asked whether the next of kin has been informed, the answer is yes. CNI [Commander Naval Intelligence]

That same day, Chief Superintendent Lamport from Portsmouth police was called into the Chief Constable's office. He was passed a directive from Naval Intelligence that he was to report immediately to the Sallyport Hotel and remove pages from the register relating to Cdr Crabb and Matthew Smith's signature and details.

He attended with a uniformed officer and a CID assistant and gave the owner Edward Richman a receipt for the pages. The hotel owner was advised that the Official Secrets Act covered their actions and said he was not allowed to discuss the matter. Richman told the officers that some people, including journalists, had already noted the details from the hotel register.

Later that day, the Secretary to the Admiralty was informed, and was also asked to approve a draft brief. He said that he would decide on Monday 30 April whether or not to officially inform the First Sea Lord, Lord Mountbatten.

Capt Sarell also reported that he had informed Cdr Crabb's mother, Mrs Beatrice (Daisy) Crabb of the presumed death of her son. After discussion in Portsmouth with the Commander-in-Chief, he made the authorities aware of potential legal action from the family over this matter. The Russian ships finally left Portsmouth. Sarell visited Maitland Pendock at his office premises, Espresso Furnishings salesrooms at Seymour Place. The captain confirmed that Crabb had disappeared while carrying out underwater tests. He asked for a contact address for Crabb's ex-wife. He also inquired as to why Crabb's mother had been listed as next of kin. Capt Sarell asked Pendock to keep the matter secret.

The Admiralty had been totally unaware of Crabb's divorce about eighteen months earlier, and Pendock believed the records for his mother must also be out of date. Maitland also made the officer aware of Crabb's fiancée, Pat Rose. The journalist Marshall Pugh phoned the Admiralty and contacted the office of the Deputy Chief of Naval Staff. He then started to make calls to fellow journalists and was unhappy about the way Crabb's disappearance was being handled.

Saturday 28 April: A row broke out between Anglo-Soviet officials over press speculation concerning the dive under the Russian ships. It was claimed the two Soviet leaders and many of the delegates had clashed with Labour officials and Opposition leaders Hugh Gaitskell and George Brown. Brown was said to have been 'slightly tipsy' and made an unfortunate remark about Crabb to the Russians.

Capt Sarell travelled to interview Cdr Crabb's ex-wife. There was a discussion about possible compensation and pension rights.

The captain later met Marshall Pugh. He told him that Crabb was simply 'missing' at that stage, and claimed he did not know the full circumstances of his disappearance. He also suggested that Crabb might have been rescued by another vessel – a suggestion that took absurdity to the point of farce. Sarell also made brief contact with Pat Rose. A message was left at her rented property confirming that Lionel had 'gone missing' while on a diving mission. It was hoped he might still be found.

Maitland later telephoned Pat. From their conversation he gained a powerful sense of Pat's distress. She said she had contacted her brother in France and he had invited her for a short stay. She quickly made arrangements to travel by train and ferry. However, as she left home the following morning, she received numerous invitations from reporters to tell her story. She packed all her belongings and left without speaking to anyone, or leaving a forwarding address.

Sunday 29 April: The press had finally picked up on the probable disappearance of Cdr Crabb in Portsmouth harbour, which had coincided with the Russian warships' visit. They began to ask the Admiralty a number of embarrassing questions, which officials deemed appropriate to answer on similar lines to those of the Admiralty brief, agreed on 27 April.

Capt Sarell then told Marshall Pugh that he had met both Crabb's ex-wife and his mother, and said that a statement would soon be made available at the Admiralty. He accepted this advice and contacted his press colleagues to make them equally aware. The first report mysteriously claimed: 'Cdr Crabb was presumed drowned after failing to return from a test dive which took place in connection with trials of certain underwater apparatus in the Portsmouth area about a week ago.'

A short time later the release was amended by the duty clerk at the Admiralty to say 'Stokes Bay', rather than the Portsmouth area. This location was at least 3 or 4 miles from the actual site of his disappearance in Portsmouth harbour. This statement was perhaps introduced to distance the dive from the vicinity of the Russian ships. Some other national reporters had been hot on the trail since Pugh's first call and found out that Crabb and a 'Mr Smith' had stayed at the Sallyport Hotel for a couple of nights. The dates and details were confirmed. It was only when they were told that

Supt Lamport of Portsmouth Police had forcibly removed several pages under threat of the Official Secrets Act that alarm bells started to ring.

Monday 30 April: There were some initial reports about Crabb's disappearance in the press but most contained limited information and were considered mainly speculative. It was behind the scenes at Whitehall, however, that the real political intrigue was beginning to unfold. The Crabb affair was fast becoming a hot potato.

The Secretary to the Admiralty decided not to put the case to the First Sea Lord, Lord Mountbatten. It was thought to be a protection exercise. However, the Admiralty were forced to assume a shared responsibility, and Sir John Laing was advised that Permanent Under-Secretary of State, Sir Ivonne Kirkpatrick, had decided *not* to tell the Foreign Secretary until the Admiralty had told their minister.

Based on the available facts, he thought the risk of a controversy was relatively small. Therefore he decided to carry the responsibility himself and consequently decided not tell the First Sea Lord. Kirkpatrick felt the responsibility for the whole operation lay with the Admiralty and he explained that it was for this reason alone that the Admiralty decided to accept responsibility for the cover story. He claimed the press had not, so far as he knew, spoken to the Foreign Office about this matter. But the fact that the press had decided to put out this initial cover story suggested to him that it was primarily for them (the Admiralty) to approach their ministers. It seemed the knives were out – and were being well sharpened.

Tuesday 1 May: Another flurry of lead press stories continued, but each report contained few or no hard facts, which could give the government cause for alarm.

Wednesday 2 May: This was the day when matters came to a head. The majority of national newspapers discovered that several pages had been removed from the register at the Sallyport Hotel, where Cdr Crabb and Matthew Smith had stayed. The proprietor claimed the police had vigorously questioned and threatened him with legal action. It was also clear from the press questions asked that they were aware of the existence of another man, Smith, a possible American Intelligence Agent, who had accompanied Crabb. The next question was, who dived with him? Or at least who helped Crabb to dive that day? And why?

Thursday 3 May: Practically all the national, and several international, newspapers dedicated considerable publicity and space to the mystery of the hotel register. The more the Admiralty refused to address specific questions, the more the press dug in their heels. It was clear that a major press campaign was starting. And despite Rear Admiral Inglis's best efforts, there was acute speculation about the First Sea Lord's role in this incident. Many claimed he was one of the central figures. The government decided the matter could no longer be kept secret. That afternoon, the First Lord of the Admiralty, Viscount Cilcennin, was officially informed, and in the absence of the Foreign Secretary, Selwyn Lloyd, who was away on sick leave, the Minister of State was also advised.

Friday 4 May: Prime Minister Anthony Eden was updated on all matters.

Chapter 20

Classified Information

I now include what I consider to be vital extracts from official papers released in 2006 by the Cabinet Office, National Archives, MI6 and other intelligence agencies. They cover a crucial period, from 4 May to 14 May 1956, and concern Operation 'Claret', the official code name given to the Crabb affair.

As government ministers and top civil servants scrambled to try to distance themselves from this fiasco, the Director of Naval Intelligence, John Inglis, and the head of MI5, Dick White, listed a few home truths about Crabb's failed mission. Once again, they were determined to keep Mountbatten's name out of the frame.

They advised that immediately before Christmas 1954, the Admiralty had indeed quite clearly requested the relevant intelligence agencies to report back with information concerning the underwater noise characteristics of Russian warships. The Admiralty had indeed insisted this order be given priority.

In October 1955, the Soviet warship *Sverdlov* visited Portsmouth for the Coronation Review. An underwater examination of her hull had been ordered and successfully carried out with 'useful results'. (This included both Crabb's and Naval Intelligence's dives.) It was stated that at the same time, some of Her Majesty's ships had visited Leningrad, where they too had been subjected to intense probing by the Soviets – including the use of divers.

The report claimed that in February 1956 a meeting was held at the Admiralty to discuss a very rare opportunity for the intelligence procurement presented by the Russian naval visits to Western European ports. A month later, an important meeting was held at the Admiralty to discuss intelligence operations to be carried out against the Russian warships when they arrived at Portsmouth.

The minutes specifically confirm the use of frogmen; and suggest that contact be made urgently with Cdr Lionel Crabb, to see if he would be willing to carry out an operation against the Soviet cruiser bringing Messrs Bulganin and Khrushchev to England for a goodwill visit.

On 6 April 1956 the First Lord of the Admiralty, Viscount Cilcennin, asked Prime Minister Eden for the authority to carry out Operation 'Claret' against the Russian warships. A few days later, a minute was produced, setting out a list of possible operations to be carried out during this visit. As a result of these conversations, the head of MI6 gained the distinct impression that Foreign Office clearance had indeed been given for the proposed operations against the Soviet warships.

Nearly a week later, and after most of the arrangements had been completed, the Prime Minister minuted the First Lord of the Admiralty in connection with these proposals, claiming: 'I am sorry, but we cannot do anything of this kind on this occasion.'

Saturday 5 May: A letter of protest was sent to the Foreign Office from the Soviet Embassy. The Russian spokesman said:

The Embassy of the Soviet Union Socialist Republics in Great Britain presents its compliments to the Foreign Office and has the honour to state as follows. During the stay of the Soviet warships at Portsmouth, at 7.30hrs on 19 April, three sailors of the Soviet vessel discovered a diver swimming between the Soviet destroyers at their moorings at the South River Jetty.

The diver, dressed in a black, light diving suit with floats on his feet was on the surface of the water for the space of one or two minutes, and dived again under the destroyer *Smotryashchi*.

The commander of the Soviet warships, Rear Admiral V.F. Kotov, in conversation with the Chief of Staff of the Portsmouth Naval base, Rear Admiral Burnett, drew attention to the fact of the appearance of the diver near the anchorages of the Soviet vessels, immediately alongside the destroyers.

Rear Admiral Burnett categorically denied the possibility of a diver alongside the Soviet vessels and declared that at the time, no diving operations of any kind were being carried out. In fact, however, as appears from information reported in the British Press of 30 April last, the British Naval Authorities were actually carrying out secret diving investigations in the vicinity of the anchored Soviet vessels at Portsmouth.

Moreover, the carrying out of these investigations (tests) caused the fatality of a British diver. It is sufficient to quote that the *Daily Sketch* is reporting the loss of the diver Crabb, stated as follows. He went into the water for the last time at Stokes Bay, Portsmouth, on secret investigative work near to the anchorage of the Soviet cruiser, *Ordzhonikidze*.

Attaching as it does important significance to such an unusual occurrence as the carrying out of secret diving operations alongside Soviet warships visiting the British Naval base at Portsmouth, the Embassy would be grateful to the British Foreign Office to receive explanation on this question.

I now include extracts from papers that I believe confirm the extent of panic behind the scenes as the authorities tried to prepare a response, and their bungled attempts to keep the matter under wraps. The government's prepared replies suggest to me that despite their precise knowledge of events, the authorities still took this opportunity to try and disguise the truth of the matter. Within this brief are the government's prepared replies to questions, which again indicate a contradiction of the facts.

Monday 7 May: A top-secret report was prepared by P.H. Dean CMG, Foreign Office:

> I enclose copies of the alternative answers to the question about Cdr Crabb. In order to put an end to speculation, which the presumed death of Cdr Crabb has aroused, the Admiralty have now decided to give the known facts in full:
>
> Cdr Crabb, who was especially experienced in such operations, was engaged to conduct on 19 April last experiments with a secret underwater apparatus. The location of the trails was in the Stokes Bay area, but Cdr Crabb and his assistant were instructed to go in a boat from Portsmouth Dockyard.
>
> As soon as Cdr Crabb was dressed for diving, and shortly after the boat had left its moorings, he slipped over the side and was last seen swimming towards the Russian ships alongside and close by.

Disturbingly, the next comments include a blatant lie about Crabb's actions:

> Crabb paid no attention when recalled by his assistant, and it can only be presumed that in a spirit of adventure, he was determined on his own initiative to inspect the Russian ships. His assistant remained in the vicinity and when he failed to return after his oxygen would have been expended, carried out a search, but without result.
>
> By the time these facts were reported to the Commander-in-Chief, there could have been no hope that Cdr Crabb was still alive, and it can only be presumed that he died while diving on his unauthorised expedition.

Government officials also prepared a series of alternative answers if questioned by the press. They included the following:

> Cdr Crabb, who was an expert in shallow water diving, was engaged by a branch of the Admiralty to carry out a secret test of underwater equipment. He had been similarly engaged on previous occasions. It is not in the public interest to disclose the nature of these tests.

Cdr Crabb, who was an expert in shallow water diving, was employed by the Admiralty to carry out an inspection of the Russian naval vessels in Portsmouth harbour. This is a procedure frequently followed by naval authorities when visiting warships are in port.

Cdr Crabb did not return from this duty at the expected time and no trace of him has since been found. His next of kin were informed as soon as they were traced.

Coincidentally, on the same day, C.G. Jarrett CB, CBE, forwarded an almost identical document to his colleagues at the Admiralty, again suggesting various question and answer replies in relation to potential inquiries into Cdr Crabb's sudden disappearance. Within the batch of papers, there was clear evidence of panic and a proposed cover-up, with numerous scrawled questions, and handwritten notes, which purported to try and deal with a range of expected press demands. One key document, which featured the Admiralty stamp, was headed:

Supplementary Questions

QUESTION 1: Why did the Admiralty say that Crabb was working for them on secret trials?

ANSWER 1: Whatever may have been the Admiralty motive, it does not conflict with the answer I have given.

ANSWER 2: The Admiralty did what they thought was best in the circumstances and I am not prepared to add to the statement I have already made.

Government notes (a): Answer 1 implies that the Admiralty were responsible for the work Crabb was doing – as probably most of the public, though not the press, will believe from the fact that Crabb was a naval officer and the incident occurred at Portsmouth.

Answer 2 implies that the Admiralty had no responsibility for the work but produced a cover story when the facts were about to leak. First Lord considers Answer 1 the preferable: clearly Admiralty will have to answer subsequent complications, like compensation for death.

QUESTION 2: What efforts were made to rescue Crabb, or search for the body?

ANSWER: The nature of the operation was such that there was no hope of Crabb's survival for any length of time after he was due to surface. The responsible authority carried out a search within the means immediately available.

QUESTION 3 (a): How long was it before the next of kin were informed?
ANSWER: Eight days, because it took some time to trace them.
QUESTION 3 (b): Why did the Admiralty not take the initiative and announce Cdr Crabb's disappearance?
ANSWER: Except for casualties in action, it is not the practice of the Admiralty to take the initiative in these matters, but only to answer enquiries.

Government notes (b): The reply suggested for (b) above assumes that answer 1 is given to the first supplementary.

QUESTION 4: Why were pages torn from the hotel register?
ANSWER: The Admiralty advice is to avoid answering this question if at all possible, probably by refusing to add to the statement already made. The formula Admiralty (with Home Office support) would advise if an answer has to be given is: 'I understand that the local police thought it desirable in the public interest to remove certain pages from the local hotel register. Her Majesty's Government have no responsibility for the action of the provincial police.'

But this might lead to a second supplementary about restoring them now or making them available for any inquest. For which the answer would presumably be, that the pages were removed in the public interest and the same interest precludes them being restored.

QUESTION 5: Who is Mr Smith?
ANSWER: It would not be in the public interest to disclose the personal details of those concerned.

QUESTION 6: Possible supplementary questions implicating the Russian authorities specifically, e.g. any possibility of Crabb being in the hands of the Russians?
ANSWER: Suggest refusal to add to statement already made.

QUESTION 7: Will there be any inquiry?
ANSWER: Investigations went on for a long time after Crabb was missing and I do not consider a further inquiry would serve a useful purpose.

Tuesday 8 May: The First Lord, Viscount Cilcennin, sent a memo containing an extraordinary admission to a senior civil servant at the Admiralty:

Dear Bishop,

I told the PM that nothing had been done during the November visit. I find today that I was wrong. Unknown to the Admiralty and against our instructions the same chap did the same thing. Perhaps you should let those who should, know.

Signed, Viscount Cilcennin

Wednesday 9 May: A reply was eventually sent to the Soviet Embassy some five days later from the Government Foreign Office:

The Foreign Office presents its compliments to the Embassy of Soviet Socialist Republics and has the honour to make the following reply to the Embassy's note of 4 May 1956. As has already been publicly announced, Cdr Crabb was engaged on diving tests and is presumed to have met his death while so engaged.

The diver, who as stated in the Soviet note was observed from the Soviet warships to be swimming between the Soviet destroyers, was presumably Cdr Crabb. His approach to the destroyers was completely unauthorised and Her Majesty's Government desire to express their regret at this incident.

Signed, Foreign Office

TOP SECRET: Prime Minister. Re: Cdr Crabb

My first thought had been for a formal enquiry of this kind, might be held by Sir Ivonne Kirkpatrick and Sir John Lang.

It is, however, arguable that each of them bears some share of responsibility for the fact that Ministers were not informed earlier of what had occurred. For this reason, it would be preferable that some independent person, e.g., the Treasury Secretary, should hold the enquiry.

If you will agree, I will now ask Sir Edward Bridges to arrange for such an enquiry to be put in train. There is, of course, no question of any public enquiry. Both the proceedings and the report would be private. I think it is advisable that the enquiry should have been put in hand before the statement is made in the House of Commons.

Signed: Norman Brook (Secretary of the Cabinet)

TOP SECRET: Prime Minister's Personal Minute. Addressed to Sir Edward Bridges

I wish you to carry out on my behalf an enquiry into the circumstances in which Cdr Crabb undertook an intelligence operation against the Russian warships in Portsmouth harbour on 19 April.

Your enquiry should include the following points:

(a) what authority was given for the operation.
(b) why its failure was not reported to Ministers until 4 May.

My object is to establish, by independent enquiry, what the facts are and where responsibility lies. When the report of this enquiry is available I will consider, with the responsible Ministers, what disciplinary action, if any, should be taken.

I have asked the Ministers in charge of Departments concerned to give whatever instructions are necessary to ensure that officers in their Departments give you all the assistance you may require in carrying out this enquiry.

Signed: A.E. [Anthony Eden] Prime Minister

cc. Foreign Secretary. First Lord of the Admiralty and the Home Secretary

In the first major debate in Parliament about the Crabb affair, on 9 May, Hansard recorded the following extract:

THE PRIME MINISTER (Sir Anthony Eden):

With your permission Mr Speaker, I will make a statement on the subject raised by Question 9. It would not be in the public interest to disclose the circumstances in which Cdr Crabb is presumed to have met his death. While it is the practice for Ministers to accept responsibility, I think it is necessary, in the special circumstances of this case, to make it clear that what was done, was done without the authority or the knowledge of Her Majesty's Ministers. Appropriate disciplinary steps are being taken.

The Prime Minister's statement continued to fuel the flames of a heated exchange between Government and Opposition, with a barrage of questions fired at the Prime Minister from the Leader of the Opposition, Hugh Gaitskell, and a host of experienced parliamentarians. Despite the pressure, the Prime Minister replied that he had nothing more to add to his statement.

Thursday 10 May: A handwritten note was addressed to the Prime Minister's Office:

The FO (Foreign Office) may be asked at 12 whether we have waived any approval from the Russians about the frogman. Kirkpatrick's strong view is that they should say: 'Nothing to all – to your statement yesterday.' The Russians have not responded that they have sent us a note and may therefore want to refrain from trouble making. Do you agree that FO should take this line?

IMMEDIATE: Top Secret. Re: Frogman

Following for I. Kirkpatrick: I do not favour taking any further action. Action Note to the Soviet Embassy puts our position on record and I have no doubt that the PM's statement in the House of Commons will have been reported to the Soviet Leaders, although there has been no reference to it, or indeed to the frogman incident at all in the Soviet Press so far.

Since my return, Bulganin and Khrushchev have both been effusively friendly to me, and as late as last night, Bulganin in a short speech at the Czechoslovak Embassy dragged in a quite irrelevant friendly allusion to his UK visit. It seems therefore that they are anxious to keep up a favourable atmosphere as regards HMG, while continuing attacks on the Labour Party. And this coupled with the silence of the Soviet Press makes me think that they are unlikely to exploit the Frogman Incident and that least said, soonest mended should be our motto.

Friday 11 May: An Admiralty headed paper was sent to G.E. Millard regarding Crabb:

Dear Millard,

When the Prime Minister is considering his tactics for Monday's debate on the Crabb issue, he may like to take into account the question which stands on the Order Paper for Wednesday 15 May, i.e.: Mr Arthur Lewis: To ask Parliamentary Secretary to the Admiralty, what position Lt Cdr Lionel Crabb held in his department; where this officer was stationed; and whether he will make a statement concerning the circumstances in which he has been posted as missing.

I have discussed this with the Parliamentary Secretary and the First Lord. We doubt whether we could escape with a simple reference to the

Prime Minister's statement on 9 May because the first part of the question deals with something which can hardly be regarded as not in the public interest to answer.

We are therefore reckoning to give the reply: *None*. (Cdr Crabb was a retired officer in the R.N.V.R.) I have nothing to add to the statement made by my Hon Friend the Prime Minister in reply to the Hon Member for West Bromwich on 9 May. On the whole, we do not think this can be regarded as adding anything to the Prime Minister's 9 May, statement.

Signed: Lang [Sir John]

From Moscow to the Foreign Office – Immediate

Pravda and *Izvestiya* today carried articles by their London correspondents on Crabb. (2) Articles give accounts of the Admiralty statement and of subsequent speculation in the British press that Crabb was engaged by the Secret Service to spy on the *Ordzhonikidze*.

The articles then refer to the Prime Minister's statement in the Commons on 9 May, with *Pravda* giving it in full. *Pravda* also quotes Mr Gaitskell's supplementary on espionage. The *Pravda* article reports the British press as saying that the motive for the Labour questions on this subject is to 'hush up' the incidents during their dinner for the Soviet Leaders.

(3) The articles then describe reactions to the Prime Minister's statement in yesterday's British press, the majority of papers are said to have been critical of the incident and to have expressed the hope that it would not adversely affect Anglo-Soviet relations. *Pravda* concludes that 'the shameful operation of underwater espionage directed against those who come to the country in a friendly visit, in no way does honour to its organisers and cannot but arouse the legitimate concern both of Soviet and British public opinion.

Sunday 13 May: As the government was becoming increasingly embroiled in this scandal, the first resignation offered (but at that time rejected) was that of James Purdon Lewes Thomas, 1st Viscount Cilcennin of Hereford. He was First Lord of the Admiralty. Lord Cilcennin wrote to the Prime Minister, Anthony Eden:

My Dear Anthony,

I have been thinking, with much sympathy, about the trouble, which the frogman episode has landed you in. I forecast the debate tomorrow will take the line that while Ministers were ignorant of the frogman's action, I at least must have known about the cover plan once it had been declined.

The Admiralty (I must say this in fairness to them) under great pressure from other quarters put out the Cover Story and must therefore accept responsibility for it.

It is obvious that the affair must be brought to an end as quickly as possible. I feel most strongly that my resignation now would achieve this result. It might stop your being pressed later about the disciplinary action you promised the House, details of which you may find it impossible to give.

However, apart from this, I am the head of the Ministry most concerned and I do very firmly believe that any break in the rule of ministerial responsibility is extremely dangerous. I am sure that you will have Parliament behind you on that.

Basing my desire to go on Ministerial responsibility, it would be pleasant, however, if you could repeat in the debate that Ministers were ignorant of ALL aspects of the affair until after the story had broken and that therefore you had asked me to stay on (which I gather you feel at the moment!) but that I had insisted on going immediately. I am convinced that this is the right thing to do and I hope that you will agree with me. I am in London and shall not go to Portsmouth tomorrow as arranged, in case you want me. You will remember that the First Sea Lord (Mountbatten) was abroad throughout this episode.

Yours ever, Jim (Viscount Cilcennin – First Lord of the Admiralty)

As the days went by there were several other hastily written notes inquiring about compensation and the pension rights of Cdr Crabb's widow. Some departments were obviously not fully aware that he had been divorced for several years.

Monday 14 May: Another very long, very intense and at times heated debate took place in the House of Commons on the evening of 14 May. It lasted for an hour and thirty-eight minutes, and Members discussed a number of the key issues surrounding this controversial affair. The debate was opened by Hugh Gaitskell MP, the Labour Leader of the Opposition, who confirmed that on 29 April 1956 the 'Admiralty had announced that Cdr Lionel Crabb RNVR, was presumed dead after failing to return from an underwater trial.'

The statement went on to say that 'he did not return from a test dive, which took place with certain apparatus in Stokes Bay'. It also agreed that 'Crabb was the central figure in this strange episode' and that he wished to 'pay tribute to a very gallant officer, who had been awarded the George Medal in 1944 for gallantry and undaunted devotion to duty'. He added that 'whatever the circumstances in which he met his death, all of us agree that this country would be the poorer, if it were <u>not</u> for men like Crabb'.

Tuesday 15 May: A memo was sent from the Admiralty to Prime Minister Anthony Eden:

My Dear Anthony,

Thank you officially! On behalf of us all so much for the way you have stood by the Admiralty and its Ministers in this miserable affair. You made an excellent speech last night and turned what might have been a very nasty debate into a comprehensively mild one. We are all so grateful.

Signed: Jim (Viscount Cilcennin – First Lord of Admiralty)

With reference to Sir Edward Bridges' report, it seems quite incredible even by today's standards that Sir Edward Bridges somehow managed to conclude his detailed investigations into this complex matter within just nine days. It involved a detailed 23-page report, which helps confirm the hot potato syndrome and near panic endured by the Admiralty, Naval Intelligence, Foreign Office, Government Ministers and officials at that time. It seems that at the time he was perhaps not even aware that Naval Intelligence launched their own independent dive at the same time as Crabb's. This report was for the eyes of Prime Minister Eden. I have included some interesting extracts.

Friday 18 May: An intelligence operation against warships stated:

> Prime Minister: My terms of reference are set out in your minute of 9 May, a copy of which is annexed (Appendix 1). You asked me to carry out on your behalf an enquiry into the circumstances in which Cdr Crabb undertook an intelligence operation against the Russian warships in Portsmouth harbour on 19 April, the enquiry to include (a) what authority was given for the operation, and (b) why its failure was not reported to Ministers until 3 May. I have seen 12 witnesses. A summary of the evidence, which has been seen by witnesses, is available if required. I have tried to do this as objectively as I can, with as little intrusion as possible of personal judgement. I have also done my best to present matters, as they must have appeared to the officers concerned at the moment of action, without drawing on hindsight.

Under the heading 'The Operation', Sir Edward Bridges reiterated some of the remarks already made by Naval Intelligence chief, Sir John Inglis, and Dick White of MI5, when he agreed that since December 1954 'one of the standing intelligence requirements notified by the Admiralty had been to gain information about the underwater noise characteristics of Russian warships'. It was even listed as top of the Admiralty requirements, and stated that 'news of Bulganin and Khrushchev coming to Portsmouth in a Russian cruiser provided an important opportunity to obtain this information'.

Further, a number of objectives had already been set out and agreed, and included a frogman operation inviting Cdr Crabb to participate.

Bridges said there was 'nothing unusual about the character of the operation proposed.' And confirmed that: 'Indeed, one can go further and say that provided the operation was carried out with due precautions, there was no reason why it should be attended by any special risks.' He added, however, that 'due precautions were *not* taken in carrying out this operation. Cdr Crabb should not have been allowed to spend so much time in Portsmouth, where he was likely to meet people he knew.' The report went on:

> He was brought to Portsmouth on 17 April with a view to the operation being carried out on the following morning when the Russian ships anchored at Portsmouth . . . There is no reason why its failure should have involved the Government in any way, or caused any embarrassment.

The following is extracted from Bridges' review notes:

Why was the failure of the operation not reported to ministers until 4 May?

The answer to this question is bedevilled by the fact that the Admiralty regarded the Foreign Office as responsible for the operation, while the Foreign Office thought the Admiralty was responsible. How did it come about that these contrary views were held? It is true that the operation was carried out in response to an Admiralty requirement, but the operation of April 1956 – like the operation of October 1955 was [blank] . . . and the help given to the operation by the Admiralty was described as unofficial. In the Admiralty's view, therefore, the operation was essentially one for which the Foreign Office was responsible. After the Admiralty took over responsibility on 25 April for providing cover, they regarded themselves as having a shared responsibility with the Foreign Office. They seem to have assumed that the operation was not one for which the Admiralty was responsible.

The attitude of officials in each Department was that they would tell their Ministers as soon as the Minister in the other Department was told – but not before.

Looking back, it is perhaps a pity that the senior officials of the two Departments did not have direct discussions on this point. I am also told by officials of both Departments that they had considerable hopes that the prompt measures taken by the Admiralty from 25 April onwards in dealing with Cdr Crabb's employer and relations would prevent the matter from breaking in the press.

I found general agreement that, apart from the greater wisdom which hindsight brings, it would have been both right and prudent to tell Ministers what had happened at a considerably earlier stage than was done . . . One thing is clear, and that is that it is impossible to single out any one individual from the *dramatis personae* as deserving of special blame in this respect.

OTHER MATTERS: From Bridges to PM Eden

Two other happenings call for comment. The first concerns the action taken by the Portsmouth Police in removing two pages of the hotel register of the Sallyport Hotel, where Cdr Crabb and Matthew Smith stayed. According to the particulars, the Portsmouth Police were asked . . . [blank] to advise what action should be taken about the hotel register but were NOT authorised to act.

The discovery on 2 May that pages had been removed from the register sparked an all-out press campaign. And it is thus arguable that this action taken by the Portsmouth Police was a serious error.

The last happening which must be commented on, is one which you may be surprised that I have left to the end: the fact that your decision of 12 April against Operation 'Claret' did not become known to those who were mounting the frogman operation.

Looking at the matter now from the Admiralty end: the fact that you had ruled against Claret was notified to the Foreign Office by the Military Branch of the Admiralty. It may be asked why DNI, who knew about the plans for the frogman operation, did not also communicate the decision to . . . [blank]. The answer is that he did not regard it as any part of his business to do so.

I think it is also accepted that the failure of an operation in this country has far more embarrassing effects than failure of an operation abroad. This is in part due to the extreme vigilance of the British press and their readiness to take every advantage of any apparent slip by any Government organisation.

SUMMARY: A report of this nature does not lend itself to a summary of conclusions and what follows is more by way of an epitome of the main points. If the operation had been carried out with due precautions, there was no reason why it should have been attained by any special risk. But, in fact, those who carried out the operation failed to observe a number of precautions, which should have been taken. The main responsibility for this MUST be shared.

Failure to seek the authority of the Foreign Office for the operation was due to a misunderstanding . . . the delay in informing Ministers of the failure of the operation was largely due to the fact that the Admiralty regarded the Foreign Office as having been responsible for the operation, while the Foreign Office thought that the Admiralty were responsible.

Signed: Edward Bridges

Following the release of Sir Edward Bridges' report, there was a mad scramble to try and clear areas of responsibility. On 23 May Norman Brook wrote to the Prime Minister's office:

I have read the report of Sir Edward Bridges' enquiry into the 'frogman' incident. Sir Edward Bridges' recommendations are of two kinds: Those which apportion blame between the individuals concerned in this incident; and those which are concerned with possible changes in procedure and organisation to reduce the risk that such an incident, may occur again.

Those in group (1) are the more urgent. Those in group (2) can be considered at rather greater leisure. I therefore suggest that you send copies of this report to the Foreign Secretary and the First Lord of the Admiralty with a minute asking them to consider, in the light of the report, what disciplinary action they, if necessary, should take against persons serving in their Departments.

Signed: Norman Brook

On 27 May a draft paper for ministers added:

Two problems remain to be dealt with: The establishment of, or the presumption of, death and payment of the action involving Crabb's death.

The first is the most important. The matter cannot be left where it is because royalties for a biography about to be published will accrue to his estate, and his many creditors will want to receive their share.

There are two possible courses open. The first is that the Admiralty should formally notify the Registrar General of their presumption of Crabb's death. The second is the Government should do nothing. Leaving the initiative in the hands of the solicitors handling Crabb's affairs on behalf of his next of kin (mother). The solicitors acting for Mrs Crabb (mother) have asked the Admiralty for a certificate of this kind.

Strictly, the Admiralty should not formally presume death in this way, as Crabb was not employed as a naval officer at the time of his death. He was a temporary R.N.V.R. officer during the war, and had been re-employed for some period after the war, but had been released back to civil life for more than 12 months before the incident. On the other hand, the whole of the public references, both in Parliament and outside of it, have spoken of Crabb as a lieutenant-commander or commander.

The strictly correct procedure is the second course, leaving it to those interested in Crabb's estate to apply to the Portsmouth Coroner for an inquest. In the absence of a body an inquest can be held only if the Home Secretary directs under Section 18 of the Coroner's (amendment) Act 1926.

If an inquest were ordered, it would be the duty of the Coroner to discover how, when and where Crabb came by his death. The Home Office think they would be able to persuade him to avoid asking awkward questions, or if there was no way of avoiding awkward questions, the Coroner could, at his discretion hold the inquest or part of it in camera.

There would inevitably be some publicity, and it would be necessary to have as witnesses at the inquest the officer (Lt Franklin) who dressed Crabb and was assisting him when he went into the water, and possibly 'Mr Smith', who was also with him at the time. The Coroner could probably in his discretion hold an inquest, if one were ordered, without a jury.

Nevertheless, the first course suggested in paragraph 1. i.e., for the Admiralty to issue a certificate presuming death would involve much less publicity even if it were irregular. If Ministers decide that the second course should be followed, the question arises whether the Admiralty should make an attempt to find the body. Any thorough search, involving diving and dredging would be an extensive and expensive operation – prohibitively so – but a search by divers along the face of the jetty could be done in a week (cost about £60).

There are arguments for and against the Admiralty appearing further in the matter. If the Admiralty did so, they would identify themselves with the incident more than ever. Many officers in the Navy are critical of what happened as spoiling the good name of the Service, and the First Lord is loath to add to their embarrassment by continuing to associate the Admiralty with the incident; particularly as the public would believe, more than they possibly do at present, that the Admiralty WERE associated with the Intelligence authorities in the operation.

This document was understood to have been written by Norman Brook. On 28 May, Brook wrote again to the Prime Minister:

In addition to the action to be taken on the basis of Sir Edward Bridges' report, we have also to decide how to handle the problem of Cdr Crabb's estate. I attach a paper on this, which has to be drawn up in consultation with the Admiralty and the Home Office. Of the alternative courses there discussed, I think that the lesser evil is to commit one further irregularity and allow the Admiralty to issue a certificate presuming death. But Admiralty Ministers will <u>not</u> like this, and I could <u>not</u> advise you to authorise it without discussion with the First Lord.

Signed: Norman Brook

The following is a letter of reprimand from Prime Minister Eden to his First Lord of the Admiralty, Viscount Cilcennin. Eden confirms the areas where the Naval Intelligence Department and the Admiralty were deemed responsible for the Crabb incident.

Personal Letter: From The Prime Minister: To The Rt Hon Viscount Cilcennin

I am today sending you a copy of Bridges' report on the frogman affair, with a formal minute asking you to consider what disciplinary action should be taken within the Admiralty. In view of the terms of your latest personal letter about this, I think you should know that I do <u>not</u> at all take the view that <u>no</u> blame attaches to the Admiralty. Indeed, I think that the Naval Intelligence Division of the Admiralty have been let down rather lightly in Bridges' report.

From what I hear, there is a tendency among senior naval officers to talk as though the Royal Navy had been treated unfairly over this affair. They resent, I am told, any suggestion that the Navy could treat in this way foreign visitors, who were their guests. I read your letter as implying a hope that the Navy will be 'cleared' of this kind of imputation.

If, in fact, there is any feeling of this kind among senior naval officers, I hope that you will take such steps as may be necessary to correct it. For three things emerge quite clearly:

It was N.I.D. who asked that this information about Russian warships should be obtained.

It was N.I.D. who asked that efforts should be made to obtain it while the Russian warships were in Portsmouth.

N.I.D. knew of my direction that 'nothing of this kind should be done on this occasion' and they knew of the operation.

What follows is a copy of a second letter concerning the resignation of Viscount Cilcennin. He was First Lord of the Admiralty 1951–6. He was elected in 1931 and left the House of Commons in 1955 when he became Viscount Cilcennin. He eventually resigned, on 1 September 1956, and then immediately accompanied HRH Prince Philip on a world tour. In 1957 he became the Lord Lieutenant of Herefordshire and even attended the Olympic Games in Melbourne, Australia. He died in 1960. On 29 May, Viscount Cilcennin sent a second resignation letter to the Prime Minister:

My Dear Anthony,

Many thanks. I do view the difficulty of Ministerial responsibility after what has been said. I gather you are studying the Bridges' report now and I do hope that it may be possible to clear the Navy and the Admiralty publicly. Then I shall gladly go tomorrow! I have thought, now this weekend. What possible resignation letter I could write to you on 1 July? I'm afraid I must be tiresome and say frankly that there is absolutely none which would stand the scrutiny of Parliament in session or not, pinpoint the blame for the affair on the Navy or the Admiralty, which is after all more important than the considerable personal harm which it would do myself. 1 Sept is child's play compared to 1 July, although the earlier date named suits me personally. As you know, I would do anything for you but not at the expense to the Navy.

Yours ever, Jim (Viscount Cilcennin)

On 30 May the Prime Minister's office issued their response:

My Dear Jim,

If senior naval officers feel that the Royal Navy has been treated unfairly over this affair, there is no justification for this. We can hardly get round the fact that the Admiralty was closely concerned.

Yours ever, Anthony Eden

On 5 June, a top-secret memo was issued by the Cabinet Office:

Prime Minister: said that, of the alternatives discussed in the attached note, it seemed to him that the preferable course would be for the Admiralty to notify the Registrar General and that Cdr Crabb's death could be presumed. He would however, be glad to have the views of his colleagues on this question.

The First Lord of the Admiralty said that the Admiralty should not be associated further with this matter. Now that he had read the report of Sir Edward Bridges' enquiry, he realised that officers serving in the Admiralty had in fact been implicated in the early stages of this affair to a far greater extent than he had understood previously to be the case.

If therefore, other Ministers felt the better course was for the Admiralty to issue a certificate presuming death, he would be content that the Admiralty should hold them responsible for dealing with any consequential action.

The Home Secretary: said that there could be no doubt that the first of the alternative courses was the lesser evil. On the other hand, if the course were adopted of allowing an inquest to be held, there was no knowing what embarrassment it might involve. It would certainly give rise to further publicity. And even if the Coroner were willing to accept Home Office advice on such matters as the evidence, which should be called, the press would not fail to draw attention to the absence of any witnesses who might be withheld.

The Prime Minister: agreed that, in the light of the views expressed in the discussion, it seemed clear that the better course would be for the Admiralty to issue, in normal course, a certificate that Cdr Crabb was presumed by them for official purposes to have died on April 19th. The solicitors acting for Cdr Crabb's mother had already asked the Admiralty for such a certificate.

The Admiralty: would make a corresponding notification to the Registrar General. It would be convenient if the Admiralty would also hold them responsible for taking such consequential action as might become necessary.

Cabinet Office

On 10 June the Prime Minister's Office issued a top-secret note to J.J.B. Hunt in the Cabinet Office:

Dear John,

I enclose a minute, which the Prime Minister has received from the First Lord of the Admiralty about the responsibility of the D.N.I. over the Crabb affair. Incidentally, the Prime Minister was annoyed that the First Sea Lord had already censured Rear Admiral Inglis in view of his particular request in his minute that the meeting should be held before any action was taken.

On 25 June the Admiralty sent a memo to the Prime Minister:

May I now complete my reply to your minute of 30 May about the need for disciplinary action over the frogman episode? In my minute of 8 June, I limited myself to discussing the responsibility of the Director of Naval Intelligence; I should like now to deal with the case of Sir John Lang, the Permanent Secretary of the Admiralty.

(2) Lang was told on Friday 27 April, about the conversation, its failure, and the cover story, which would be used if the press got hold of the news, and which would involve the Admiralty in 'admitting responsibility.' It was then eight days since the operation and, as Bridges says in his report, there were considerable hopes that the measures taken by the Admiralty in dealing with Cdr Crabb's employer and relations would prevent the matter from breaking in the press. Lang took the view – correctly in my opinion – as I explained in my earlier minute – the Admiralty only took over a share of responsibility at the stage of putting out the cover story on 25 April. He knew Kirkpatrick had been

aware of the facts since the preceding Monday and that he had decided against informing Foreign Office Ministers unless the Admiralty told me. After reflecting over the weekend, he decided to carry the responsibility himself and NOT to inform me. In the next two days, the press really got their teeth into the mystery and Lang changed his mind on Wednesday when all agreed that I must be told.

(3) Bridges says he cannot think that, given all the circumstances, the mistake in NOT telling Ministers sooner was a very serious one. I think there is a good deal in this view. If Ministers had been told on 27 April, and if we had rejected the proposed cover story, and either put out another one or agreed to disown Crabb altogether, I do not doubt that the press and the public would still have connected Cdr Crabb with the Navy, and the whole incident with Naval Intelligence.

(4) However, I entirely support Bridges' view that it would have been both right and prudent to tell Ministers what had happened at a considerably earlier stage than was done. Moreover, I think Lang should have discussed the matter personally with Kirkpatrick as soon as he heard of it, in which event, any misunderstanding about the primary responsibility for the operation must have been cleared up.

(5) Lang knows already that I take this view but when he returns from leave next week, I propose to tell him specifically that *his* error of judgement was disappointing and indeed deplorable.

There is no signature at the foot of the page, but it appears to have been sent by Viscount Cilcennin, the First Lord of the Admiralty. On 26 June another top-secret memo concerning Cdr Crabb was issued:

The Prime Minister held a meeting this morning to consider what action should be taken of the enquiry held by Sir Edward Bridges. As regards the Admiralty, the First Lord said that he had NOT delivered any formal reprimands on the basis of Sir Edward Bridges' report. His admonitions to the D.N.I., mentioned in his minutes to the Prime Minister, had been given at an earlier stage.

The Prime Minister said that he did not wholly share the First Lord's view of the blame attaching to the D.N.I. He thought he was more to blame for failing to take action on learning of the Prime Minister's ruling that 'nothing of this kind should be done on this occasion:' when he knew that this ruling was given.

As regards the two Permanent Secretaries, it was agreed that they had been guilty of an error of judgement – and in particular, that they should have consulted together when they knew that the operation had miscarried. Anything in the nature of a formal reprimand would however, be inappropriate. It was agreed that the Foreign Secretary and the First Lord respectively, should now proceed to take the disciplinary steps which they proposed – subject, in the case of the Admiralty, to the adjustment noted above.

Signed: Norman Brook, Cabinet Office

Some fourteen months after Cdr Crabb's controversial disappearance in the dark, dangerous, and swirling waters of Portsmouth harbour, little or nothing had been revealed to shed any further light on the full circumstances of his final dive.

The whole incident still seemed bathed in secrecy, with the true facts deliberately buried in bureaucracy, and supported at the highest level by an incredible cover-up operation. Nothing seemed likely to break the deadlock until the headless and handless body of a frogman was suddenly found floating in the sea near Chichester harbour.

Chapter 21

Body of Evidence

Shortly before 8 a.m. on Sunday 9 June 1957 a group of three part-time fishermen working out of a boat near Pilsea Island, close to Chichester harbour, found the badly decomposed remains of a small body wrapped in a Heinke rubber diving suit. Initially, they thought it was some floating debris, until one of them, John Randall, used a hook to pull it towards his boat, and hauled it aboard.

Randall and an assistant, Ted Gilbey, said it was a 'dirty grey-coloured frogman's suit covered in seaweed, with extensive rust marks around the legs', and that 'it had deep indentations clear of undergrowth, where a breathing set may have been attached'. They confirmed the suit contained a small but badly decomposed body, with its head, hands and upper chest missing. Once on board, the men took the body to nearby Pilsea Island to raise the alarm. Understandably, the discovery of the body by the men caused some speculation, as all had been friends of Lionel Crabb. The men claimed to have had no prior knowledge or notification that anything would be found at this location, and said it was their regular fishing patch.

Rear Admiral Poland also thought it a strange coincidence that these particular men were responsible for finding Crabb's body. He says:

In a book published by Christopher Creighton, a Royal Navy Intelligence officer, Creighton alleged that Crabb was rushed ashore dying of oxygen poisoning and actually died in Creighton's arms on the King's Stairs. Creighton claims the British Secret Service kept Crabb's body for five days and then had it taken to a certain spot and dumped in the sea, calculating that it would be washed up in Chichester harbour on 9 June 1957. Of course, that was the day it was found in exactly that spot. But why pick that spot and why that date? The wild rumours and speculation about this affair might have subsided had not a similarly clad, decomposed body turned up some fourteen months later.

And instead of making a clean breast of the whole unhappy story, the government continued to prevaricate and, as if to give official blessing to the wildest of theories, the recovery, identification and burial of this body was seen to have been handled somewhat mysteriously – with undue and inexplicable haste. What might have been regarded as a rather unimportant affair was seized upon by the Press and public, and has continued to excite curiosity and generate rumours ever since.

Another interesting fact, never before revealed, is that the discovery of this frogman's corpse followed a series of other miscellaneous findings within a similar geographical area. I discovered two significant reports. The first, dated 3 November 1956, seven months after Crabb's disappearance, related to another fisherman, this time working alone at night and in rough weather, close to Chichester harbour. He said he found a similar large floating object, stating that it was also the body of a frogman in a black rubber suit. It had become entangled in his nets.

The fisherman claimed the body was still attached to some diving gear and that as he struggled to secure it, it broke free and left him holding the head, which, in acute shock, he dropped into the water. The fisherman recorded an accurate compass bearing in the fast flowing waters, but according to official records, he failed to report the matter to the police until February the following year.

And yet, recently released intelligence reports contradict this account of events. They say the fisherman's claim was investigated many months before, and that he was also asked to help to draw a diagram of the body. His identification immediately eliminated Crabb by highlighting differences in the description of Crabb's suit and diving equipment. The fisherman's diagram did, however, resemble the body of a Royal Navy diver.

This may help to explain another conundrum: that the other body was in fact that of a Navy frogman – one of four men commissioned by Naval Intelligence at the same time as Crabb's final dive. A member of their team was said to have gone missing too, but at the time, no one dared admit to the dive, never mind to another death. And it might also help explain another alleged sighting of a diver close to the Russian ships. Did the Soviets mistake the other naval diver for Crabb?

The second report is in two parts. One relates to a lost airman, the other to a skull found by another fisherman. The skull apparently ended up in the same coroner's patch as Crabb's body. However, it was never identified, although it was agreed that it probably belonged to a male in his forties, and had been in the water for about the same time as Crabb. Records of this later finding have since become unavailable. To add to the mystery, Detective Supt Allan Hoare, the officer in charge of investigating the discovery of Crabb's body, also highlighted a search for another missing man, who disappeared in October 1955.

Fisherman John Seymour Randall's statement claims:

On 9 June 1957, I was out in my fishing boat accompanied by two men by the name of Gilbey. I went down the harbour from Bosham until I got to a point where I saw a black object floating in the water about 30 yards from the boat. We circled the object on several occasions and decided it was not a buoy or a small mine which we thought at first and, upon closer examination, it appeared to be a tractor tyre because there were two large ribs showing just above the water.

I was not satisfied, and so I went alongside and pulled it into the boat with a boat hook. I immediately saw that it was the shape of a body, and on examination, formed the opinion that it contained the body of a person in a rubber diving suit. The ridges seen were the two waistband ridges. I towed the body in to Pilsea Island, and reported it to the Royal

Air Force Station at Thorney Island. I then returned and waited for the arrival of Police Constable Williams.

Detective Superintendent Allan Hoare from the West Sussex Constabulary was said to have made enquiries from all police forces along the south coast from Cornwall to Kent. He confirmed that no other person similarly dressed had been reported missing. He did admit, however, that on 23 October 1955 a man had been reported missing after diving into the River Dart, but his clothing was in no way similar to the clothing in this case. He confirmed that the frogman's suit had marks similar to rust marks on both legs, more so on the right leg, as if the body had been caught up in some metal underwater object.

Police Constable Ronald George Williams said:

I was stationed at Southbourne. At about noon on 9 June, I went to the Royal Air Force Station at Thorney Island and accompanied the station medical officer to Pilsea Island. On the beach, I saw some human remains. They were part of the body of a man dressed in a black rubber frogman's suit. The head and upper portion of the body, and the arms were missing.

The pathologist was Dr Donald Plimsoll King who confirmed that:

On 10 June 1957, I made an examination of human remains at Chichester Public Mortuary and when I saw them they were clothed in a frogman's suit. Above the waist, parts of the body, including the skull, had disappeared although certain bones, including the left humerus and both scapulae remained. The abdominal cavity was empty except below the waistband of the suit. The organs had undergone extensive post mortem change including adipocere, but they were recognisable.

He also identified a photograph of the remains and said that another was an actual size photograph of the feet. He found the measurement of the feet was 8¾in, and said that was small for an adult male. He found that there was a condition called *hallux valgus*, which was a condition of the toes in which the big toe – the *hallux* – was turned outwards. The joint of the big toe was enlarged and disjointed. He thought the deceased was a small man in the region of 5ft 6in, but he could give no more detail of his estimation.

He added: 'The legs were in a good state of preservation and I would describe them as muscular and well formed and, apart from the feet, there was no deformity. They were quite straight.' In a further statement he said: 'At 8.45 a.m. on Tuesday, 11 June, I went to Chichester Public Mortuary in company with the coroner and there viewed the part body of a man and the articles of clothing.' From the adipocere, he concluded that the body had been in the water for at least six months and could well have been in the water for at least fourteen months. On 14 June 1957, he examined the remains again. He looked at the left knee and saw a scar. A photograph was taken at Chichester Police Station in his presence of the portion of the skin bearing the scar.

Dr King later gave evidence at the inquest and was recalled after Crabb's ex-wife had given evidence to confirm that 'a hammertoe normally involves the second toe and not the big toe. The big toe might be slightly folded under the second toe giving the impression that the big toe was raised up.'

Crabb's friend and former colleague, Cdr Gordon Gutteridge, told Rear Admiral Poland that he couldn't understand why he hadn't been called as a witness to help identify the body. He says:

The bundle contained the body of a small man, which was almost bent double with the head, hands and chest missing. They dragged the body on board, took it ashore and phoned the RAF on Thorney Island. They sent over a launch but when they found it was not the body of a crashed airman they refused to accept it. Some naval people arrived in a helicopter and paid a brief visit to the scene. It eventually finished up in Chichester Mortuary, where Dr King examined it. The Admiralty hastily announced details of a Press conference, and then cancelled it. They did, however, offer to provide an officer to identify the body and Lt W.Y McLanachan of HMS *Vernon* attempted to do so on 11 June. Crabb's ex-wife also attended, at the request of West Sussex CID.

It was a little surprising that McLanachan (fondly known as Mac-hammock-lashing) who did not know Crabb that well, was chosen for this unpleasant task, whereas I, who lived in Chichester, was serving at the Underwater Countermeasures and Weapons Establishment where Crabb last served. I probably knew Crabb in his later life better than anyone, except his ex-wife, and yet I was not asked to be involved in any identification at the inquest. At the time, much was made by the Press of the fact that Crabb had a singular piece of identification in that he had hammer toes on one foot, and that none of the witnesses who viewed the body found it to have this aberration. It was subsequently explained to me that, after fourteen months in the sea, from which the suit showed clear signs of having being caught up in wreckage, the feet were both badly decomposed and distorted.

Cdr Charles Emmerson, the Executive Officer back at HMS *Vernon*, said the hullabaloo only really started when Crabb's body was found. He says: 'I was never questioned at the time he disappeared about what he was up to. It only really came to light when his body was found in Chichester harbour. It was all hush-hush I suppose, then. I had a formal meeting and a chap came down asking questions. I just told him what I knew.'

I now include extracts and information about Lt McLanachan's role from HMS *Vernon*, and from Intelligence files under the recent Freedom of Information rules, together with supporting details from Crabb's friends, family and colleagues.

In the fifteen days prior to holding the inquest, once again the wires between the Admiralty, British Intelligence, Naval Intelligence and the House of Commons were red hot. There seemed a peculiar determination to establish that this was indeed the body of Cdr Crabb. Perhaps the finding of the other Navy diver had prompted this state of anxiety and the intention to keep secret another dive and another loss. After all, it was on the same day as Crabb's failed mission and had been prohibited by the Prime Minister.

Some of the main instigators to ensure the 'correct' verdict was reached included the Director of Naval Intelligence, Rear Admiral John Inglis, Dick White, the head of MI5, and W.A. Lewis, acting head of Naval Law at the Admiralty. The identity of the body was an obvious concern for the authorities, especially as the head, hands and upper chest were missing but the lower parts remained relatively intact. By studying the clothing and undergarments, however, it was believed a 'satisfactory' result would be obtained.

In a note from Rear Admiral John Inglis, he confirmed that 'the Chief Constable and the Coroner were being most co-operative'. With a keen press interest, the Admiralty decided to keep witness identification to a bare minimum and summoned only a limited number of close associates to the inquest. The main witnesses included Crabb's ex-wife, Mrs Margaret Elaine Crabb: his diving partner, Sydney James Knowles, and his colleague from HMS *Vernon*, Lt William Young McLanachan.

The evidence of a further witness, Lt George Albert Franklin, the last man to see Cdr Crabb alive, and the man who helped him dress on his final dive, became a major cause for discussion and controversy. The authorities were keen that he should *not* be called to attend the hearing in person, and that his identity should be kept secret. Franklin had previously given two sworn statutory declarations on 19 June 1956 to William Hanna, the Notary Public.

I now include letters and notes relating to the urgent response and concern from Naval Intelligence before the inquest. Many papers have dates and other key information obliterated by official sources.

SECRET & PERSONAL: From Captain E.A. Blundell, OBE, Royal Navy. HMS *Vernon*, Portsmouth. 11 June 1957. To: Rear Admiral J.G.T. Inglis, OBE, and Director of Naval Intelligence, Admiralty

I enclose for your information a copy of the statement made by Lt McLanachan, today, Tuesday 11 June, to the Chichester Police after examination of the diving equipment and body recovered off Portsmouth harbour.

(2) The only equipment which could definitely be established as being of Service pattern were the Swim Fins which were marked pattern 3386. Lt McLanachan did not however, draw attention to this other than to state that they were similar to Admiralty pattern.

(3) Lt McLanachan understood that the police would be enquiring from Messrs Heinke, whether they had supplied a frogman's suit to Cdr Crabb.

(4) He was informed that he would probably be required later at the inquest, which is understood to be on 26 June. The press has not yet interviewed him. I have instructed him not to reveal any details of his examination should he be approached by the press, other than that he was sent to the Chichester police to assist in the identification of the diving equipment recovered.

E.A. Blundell – Captain

SECRET & PERSONAL: MI6 files. William Young McLanachan: Lt Royal Navy

I am a Lieutenant in the Royal Navy stationed at HMS *Vernon*, Portsmouth. I am a diving officer. Cdr Crabb was fairly well known to me. I first met him in 1948, when he was serving in the R.N.V.R., and he was at that time undergoing his annual training at HMS *Vernon*.

I did not see much of him until about 1955, when he had been recalled for service. He had, I think, served from about 1951. I was in his company from 1955, when we were together at HMS *Vernon*. Although I did not actually dive with him, I frequently saw him in his diving equipment.

He had small feet, but I could not say I really noticed his toes, although I did notice he was splayfooted. I did not see anything of Cdr Crabb after he left the Service. I have today (11 June 1957) attended Chichester Police Station, where I was shown by Detective Superintendent Hoare the following equipment:

1 Frogman's two-piece suit; 1pair Swim Fins; 2 sorbo pads; 1 pr bathing trunks; 1 pr nylon socks; 1 pr blue combinations (top missing); 1 pr nylon combinations; 1 piece of an under vest.

With the exception of the swim fins, I cannot identify any equipment as that issued by the Royal Navy. The swim fins are sold commercially, but are similar to Admiralty pattern. At 4 p.m. on the 11 June 1957, I viewed a body at the Mortuary. I cannot definitely identify the body as that of Cdr Crabb, all I can say is that the feet are similar in as much that they are small and appear to be slightly splayed.

W.Y. McLanachan, Lieut RN

TOP SECRET: Personal: Admiralty SW. to Director of Naval Intelligence, John Inglis

Deputy Secretary,

I enclose the two statutory declarations made by Lt George Albert Franklin, which after discussion with Mr W.H. Lewen (Head of Naval Law), I think he should retain in the Admiralty docket. I have also prepared an aide-memoire concerning these declarations, which I think should be filed with them. Possibly you may wish to add your remarks. If you agree, I will pass this to Mr Lewen.

TOP SECRET: From Admiralty SW1

AIDE MEMOIRE. Attached are two statutory declarations sworn by Lt G.A. Franklin of H.M.S. *Vernon*, concerning the presumed death of Cdr Crabb. These declarations were made before Mr W.N. Hanna, Head of Air Branch. A Notary Public. He advised as follows: 'I thought it was proper that these statements should be in the form of statutory declarations, which is the proper way of recording statements about any matter which is not the subject of legal proceedings.

If legal proceedings had been started, it would probably have been appropriate for the statements to be in the form of affidavits made in those proceedings. If it becomes necessary to file the unrestricted statement in court, it may be necessary to have it sworn as an affidavit, but I think it would have been improper to swear an affidavit in the present state of play when there are no proceedings actually issued.

(2) If at any time it appears likely that these declarations will be required in legal proceedings, the following are to be personally informed: Permanent Secretary – [all the other names are blanked out]

(3) They will consider the desirability of informing the following, other than Members of the Board, who are concerned in this case: C in C Portsmouth (Admiral of the Fleet, Sir George Creasy, GCB, CBE, DSO, MVO), C.O.S. to C in C Portsmouth (Rear Admiral P.W. Burnett, DSO, DSC), C.O. HMS *Vernon* (Captain J. Grant, DSO, RN, CNI).

(4) Throughout this incident, it was considered essential to avoid implicating the C in C Portsmouth and his staff, and other Naval authorities at Portsmouth. The main reasons were:

(a) In a bona fide Naval diving operation, immediate and extensive rescue operations would have been ordered by the C in C, accompanied by warnings to all Naval and police authorities in the area. This would have been done for humanitarian reasons even if there had been no hope of Cdr Crabb's survival.

(b) Lt G.A. Franklin, an experienced diving officer, would have taken immediate steps [blanked out] . . . the moment it became clear that a mishap had occurred and Franklin was ordered to return to his ship and take no further part in the affair. In consequence, any cover story purporting to show that this was a bona fide naval operation would only have exposed [blank] and the C in C to charges of negligence, lack of humanity and error of judgement. Even as a last resort, this was considered unacceptable.

(d) The above considerations remain extant and as far as Parliament, Press, the Fleet and the Public are concerned, no satisfactory explanation has been made of the exact circumstances. Because the incident remains an unexplained mystery, there is every probability of press publicity and public interest as a result of any legal proceedings, which may occur in the future and therefore expose him and the authorities not only to publicity in the press, but to charges outlined in Para 4(c) as well as involving further risk of compromise of the true nature of the operation.

(7) Careful consideration will therefore have to be given in the Admiralty on how the situation is to be handled, but this can only be done when the exact nature of the legal proceedings is known, as well as the part that Lt G.A. Franklin will be called upon to play in them.

I have taken the following extracts from official secret documents recently obtained from MI6 files. It seems the plot was thickening, and there was a determination to keep Franklin away from the inquest, and a renewed intention to secure an Open Verdict.

Reasons why Admiralty does not want (Lt G.A. Franklin) to appear at the Coroner's Inquest:

(1) As soon as he appears (and even if his evidence were to be given in camera), it would immediately be assumed that he was the missing 'Mr Smith' and he would become the target for all kinds of enquiry from the press and other sources.

(2) Even if he were not asked in open court to say where exactly he last saw Crabb, he would inevitably be asked this by the press. If he refused to answer, the inference would be stronger than ever that it was in the vicinity of the Russian ships. This would not only be contrary to the country's interest but contrary to what the Admiralty have already said, as a cover story, namely that it was in Stokes Bay. Similar contradictions arise only more strongly in regard to questions about the frogman, and his application, only less likely to answer.

(3) The story Lt Franklin has to tell is basically inconsistent with the impression which we have tried to convey – that this was a naval operation – because, if it had been [blank] . . . would have been reported to his superiors that Crabb had failed to reappear and there would have been a highly organised search.

(4) Even if the Press do not realise that it is unfair to Franklin . . . [and also, incredibly, to the whole of the Naval Command at Portsmouth] to give the impression that they failed in their duty to try and find him.

(5) The reason why no search was conducted can only be explained by saying that a search could not be carried out beside the Russian warships, which immediately suggests the true nature of the operation is again contrary to the public interests.

(6) [All blanked out . . .]

(7) If Lt Franklin's evidence could be confined to the fact that he saw Crabb into the water, and to identifying the clothing, it wouldn't be so bad.

TOP SECRET: Personal

From: Rear Admiral J.G.T. Inglis, CB, OBE. Intelligence Division, Naval Staff, Admiralty: The Crabb Case: 17 June 1957.

As you know, I have been in direct touch with the Captain of *Vernon* concerning some of the details of the Crabb case, but have now reached the stage where I feel you should be informed of how the affair is developing.

(2) I am afraid the lawyers have concluded that it is inevitable that Lt Franklin of the Diving School should give evidence in person at the inquest. The Coroner and the Chief Constable are however, being most co-operative. The whole of his evidence, including his taking the oath, will probably be held in camera.

(3) The Treasury Solicitor will represent The Admiralty.

(4) We hope the police will be able to get him to and from the court without the press being aware that Franklin is involved. We are particularly concerned about the necessity for keeping his part in the affair away from the press and, even allowing for the skill they have shown in the past in obtaining clues, we hope it will be possible to bring this off.

(5) Even if the press do not find out that Lt Franklin is giving evidence, there is likely to be talk in *Vernon* about his absence on that day, and this may reach the reporters. At present, only the Captain knows about Franklin's role in the affair, and to avoid any undesirable speculation and possibly open comment in *Vernon*, I am hoping that Blundell will be able to arrange some fictitious duty or possibly leave for Franklin for a few days covering the day of the inquest. I am asking Blundell to let me know what he thinks would provide the most natural cover for his absence.

(6) Even so, it will probably be necessary for him to tell some officers in *Vernon* as much as is necessary to keep their mouths shut! I suggest this should be done at the Captain's discretion.

(7) I hope the above is in accordance with your wishes? But if not, perhaps you would be good enough to inform Blundell and let me know.

(8) I might add that [blank] is being extremely robust in his approach to his unenviable situation.

(9) Sir John Lang has seen this letter and agrees.

As the date of the inquest approached, there seemed more confidence within government ranks when the extent of evidence was considered. And the evidence allegedly included a witness statement claiming Lionel Crabb had been shot in 1944, and carried a distinctive bullet wound to his leg.

SECRET: C.N.I. The adjourned inquest on Cdr Crabb will be resumed at Chichester on Wednesday 26 June at 15.00hrs

(2) The body will be identified by the evidence of the following:

    (a) Crabb's ex-wife (small feet etc).

    (b) Heinke, who will identify the frogman's suit as being similar to one which they sold to Crabb.

    (c) A man in Newcastle, who has come forward and identified a bullet wound in Crabb's leg which he knew he had received in the Middle East in 1944 (the scar is of a special shape which was mentioned in the pathologist's report).

(3) The coroner is aware of the background of the case and is <u>not</u> asking for the appearance of any embarrassing naval witness. He does however, need the Admiralty's help, because, surprisingly, none of the witnesses mentioned above can give Crabb's full names or the date of his birth.

(4) For this purpose, Mr G.W. Bostock, a temporary clerical officer, serving with A.C.R., will give evidence from Crabb's Service Record. He knows nothing of the background of the story and will not be able to answer any embarrassing questions, even if he were asked. In any case, the coroner (who is sitting without a Jury) will stop the proceedings as soon as he can, once he is satisfied of the points on which he requires to be satisfied; and there will be no adjournment during which such matters could be probed.

(5) Bostock's evidence will indicate that Crabb did not serve actively as a naval officer after April 1955. After the inquest, the Press, who will no doubt be disappointed by the lack of sensation in the proceedings, may ask questions about the capacity in which Crabb undertook the trials of underwater apparatus, on which we announced in April 1956 that he had been lost. This is not really embarrassing as we said that he had been 'specially' employed in connection with 'the trials' and those words do not suggest that he was necessarily employed as a naval officer.

(6) The answer to all questions continues to be that we have nothing to add to what the Prime Minister said in the House of Commons in May 1956.

(7) Bostock is going to finish his evidence by stating that during his service as an officer, Crabb consistently received extremely high reports from his senior officers and was regarded as a man of very high qualities, and an inspiration to those serving under him. I thought it would be pleasant for the Admiralty witness to take the only opportunity of paying tribute to him.

Regarding the claim about Cdr Crabb having a bullet wound in his leg, I have spoken with some of Crabb's associates, and all say they have no knowledge of it. It is said that this particular witness and the statement content were not mentioned at the inquest. There is another claim, however, that Crabb broke a toe at some stage in his naval career, and that x-rays may have been recorded and used to help with identification.

Again, there appears to be no record of this claim at the inquest, but Noel Cashford has found a medical note of an incident about an injury on 2 August 1943. It suggests Crabb fractured his first phalanx (left big toe). Surgeon Vice Admiral Sir John Rawlins says:

I have never heard about Crabb's bullet wound. I have no inside knowledge about it. It was all very confidential at the time. The Press seemed to have various accounts of what was going on. Some said it was hush-hush. There was a claim though, that an x-ray of the corpse matched an x-ray held by the Navy at Haslar. In fact I met a radiologist at the time from Haslar, who told me he'd seen the x-ray and said they matched.

Crabb's former diver Sydney Knowles also disputed the alleged bullet wound but was uncertain about other injuries. He says: 'All the time we spent in Gibraltar, Italy and France, we were fired at many times but never hit. As to the question of the broken toe, I was working with the commander and to my knowledge he never had a broken toe, nor was x-rayed. This again was never mentioned at the Inquest.'

Crabb's ex-wife Elaine and Sydney Knowles gave the final witness statements at the inquest. In her statement, Mrs Margaret Elaine Crabb of the Granville Hotel, Dover, a typist/barmaid, confirmed that on 15 March 1952, she married Lionel Kenneth Crabb. They lived together until April 1953. She then began proceedings for divorce against him and finally obtained a decree absolute around 1954. Crabb did not contest the proceedings. During their brief marriage, Crabb was serving in the Royal Naval Volunteer Reserve and shortly after they were married, he became a commander. Eileen described Lionel as a short man and said that he was not as tall as she, her height being 5ft 5in. His legs were straight and muscular and the hair on his body was very light brown, inclined to be ginger. His feet were very small and his big toes were very unusual. They appeared to be what she thought were hammertoes and were raised off the ground.

The photograph shown to her was not as she remembered them. She thought he took size 6 shoes. On 11 June 1957 she went to the mortuary and saw the remains of a human body. She could not identify the feet as those of her former husband, although she was unable to say definitely that they were not his feet.

A further identification witness was Sydney James Knowles of 2 Geoffrey Street, Preston. He was described as a swimming pool supervisor, and said he first joined the Royal Navy in December 1939. He met Cdr Crabb in 1941, when they carried out underwater work together. Knowles confirmed that Crabb was a small man, and said that on countless occasions when dressing to go underwater, he saw Crabb stripped. He said he had strong legs with large calves. He added that in the winter of 1943, they were serving at Leghorn in Italy, where ships were instructed to place rolls of barbed wire below the watermark for protection against Italian frogmen. One morning, he and Cdr Crabb went below the surface to search for limpet mines, and also to investigate the American ship *John Harrison* for mines. A tug threw both of them against the barbed wire. When they went back to their launch, he noticed that Crabb had sustained a wound to the side of his left knee. He dressed it for him and about three weeks later, when he was working with Crabb again, noticed a scar – in the shape of an inverted 'Y' on the side of Crabb's left knee.

After the war, Knowles said he saw Crabb from time to time and knew that he was living at 2a Hans Road, London. He was also familiar with the clothing Crabb used when diving. Crabb owned a two-piece rubber suit with a neck seal instead of a hood. He said he wore a pair of maroon swimming shorts, and two sets of combinations underwear alternatively, one was khaki, the other blue. He also used blue socks. He was not able to say from the photograph whether the feet were those of Crabb.

The identification of some of the clothing worn by the diver formed the subject of debate and examination by expert witnesses, and included reports from Colin Turner, a shoe specialist, and Eric Blake, the managing director of underwater diving suit manufacturers, Heinke & Co.

Colin Grey Turner said that a foot measuring 8¾in was rather small for a man and that if a man with that length of foot had ordinary straight feet then possibly he would wear shoes in the region of size 4 to 5. If, however, he had an enlarged joint, he would possibly take a size or two larger depending on the width of the foot. The enlargement of the joint would make the foot broader.

Eric James Blake, the managing director of Heinke & Co. Ltd, said his firm manufactured underwater swimsuits. He knew Cdr Crabb and agreed the description of him given by other witnesses. On three occasions, he said his company supplied Crabb with underwater suits, with the last one supplied on 11 October 1955. It was unusual in that it had a neck seal and did not have a hood. He confirmed that normally these suits were sold with hoods.

Blake said he had seen the suit found on the deceased and said this was designed in about January 1955. During the ten months between the time it was designed, and the time a suit was sold to Cdr Crabb in October 1955, Blake said Heinke had sold about 15 suits, identical in all respects to that found on the deceased.

He agreed that Crabb had always expressed a preference for a suit with a 'neck seal' instead of a hood. The suit seen at Chichester Police Station was identical to the one sold to Crabb but he was unable to say, of course, whether it was the same suit.

The inquest opened on 11 June. It only lasted for about a minute and was then adjourned until 26 June before the county coroner George Frederick Leslie Bridgman. The resumed inquest lasted for less than an hour. An Open Verdict was returned. In his concluding address the coroner stated:

We have all been warned from time to time in the legal profession about a chain being as strong as its weakest link, but there is also such a thing as a number of incidents which are minor indications building up to a conclusion, which I do not think can be resisted.

I think it would be beyond all our ideas of possible coincidence if all these different things, the size of the feet, the scar, the colour of hair, the supply of an identical suit, if all these things were to be put down to show coincidence.

Looking at the evidence in this case, I am quite satisfied that the remains which were found in Chichester harbour on 9 June, were those of Cdr Crabb.

The final report stated: 'Cdr Lionel Kenneth Philip Crabb was found dead in Chichester harbour on 9 June 1957. He was a male, aged 48, of 2a Hans Road, London SW3. His occupation was described as a retired commander, Royal Naval Volunteer Reserve. The cause of death was not known. An open verdict was returned.'

Cdr Crabb was given a simple send-off with his body placed in a relatively plain grave in Milton Cemetery, Portsmouth. His mother Daisy Crabb attended with just a few other family members. She said she was surprised that she was not asked to attend the inquest. Nor was she questioned about Lionel's disappearance. Daisy was never convinced it was her son's body.

The Admiralty paid for the funeral but refused Crabb full military honours. The headstone carried a somewhat brief and misleading citation: 'In Ever Loving Memory of My Son, Commander Crabb, at Rest at Last.' It was a small funeral for such a big hero. And the inscription angered Crabb's mother, who claimed his full name and war accolades had been omitted.

A mystery woman maintained Crabb's grave for more than two decades. It could well have been a member of his family who didn't want to make any fuss, although Crabb's distant cousin Charlotte Miller denies this. It may even have been the daughter of one of the crew from the Tenth Light Flotilla, who were regular visitors to London. It was also suggested that it might have been Rosa Lewis, the owner of the Cavendish Hotel, who always had a soft spot for Lionel.

Whoever was responsible, this person ensured the grave was maintained to a very high standard. In 1981, the headstone was cleaned and updated with an amended inscription. This was long after Daisy's death. It reads: 'In Loving Memory of My Son, Commander Lionel Crabb, RNVR, GM, OBE, at Rest at Last 1956.'

Current relatives present an arguable case for Crabb's grave being empty. They say that knowing the extent of cover-up by the authorities over the past fifty years, and perhaps to avoid any further controversy, they allege the government may have removed or destroyed the body. If the body still exists, then Crabb's distant cousin Lomond Handley says she is prepared to undergo DNA testing to establish its identity. She says: 'Only DNA testing from members of the Goodall, Jarvis or Crabb family might show a resemblance. It might point however, one way or the other, and I'd be happy to take a test.'

I must admit I was surprised that some sort of blood test, or analysis from Crabb's hair, blood or fibres was not taken at the time, and perhaps compared to his mother Daisy, or other family members. The coroner, however, seemed satisfied with all the other circumstantial evidence provided.

When the diver's body was first found Crabb's fiancée, Pat Rose, was adamant that it wasn't Lionel Crabb. Her testimony from intelligence files confirms: 'That was not Crabbie. It was a Russian about his build. They cut off the head and hands and dumped it there. We had experts in who studied the tides. They said the body could not possibly have been in the water for more than twenty-four hours.' She was aware of someone placing flowers on his grave, and said: 'I have a photograph of the grave. Every week, someone is said to put flowers on it. People think it is me, but it isn't, because I have always known he is alive!'

To her final days Pat Rose remained convinced that Lionel's death was faked. She said that on many occasions she had been contacted by strangers and told he was still alive, and said she was looking forward to being reunited with her husband. Pat used to tell family: 'We will soon be together. He has been training Russian frogmen in the Black Sea. He has served his purpose and wants to leave Russia now.'

Many of Crabb's relatives obviously want to believe that Crabb was probably captured, or taken against his will to live and work in Russia. Their thoughts are based on stories handed down through two generations. Charleen Miller confirms this:

Neither Kitty, Daisy, my mother [Audrey], or Eileen [Audrey's sister] believed it was his body which was washed up. At the time they believed he had been captured and taken aboard the Russian ship, and as the body wasn't his, they thought he had either been taken against his will or killed on the ship. The family believed he was probably tortured to gain information. This fact haunted my mother, and she repeated over and over again that he never would have revealed any secrets – and might have been killed by the Russians as a result.

Knowing how close Lionel was to Daisy, Kitty, Mother and Eileen, he would never have left them and gone to Russia willingly. She, Eileen and her brother Kenneth, all grew up with him. She never got over his disappearance and refused to believe that he had betrayed his country. Ma always said there was no greater patriot. She always knew his work involved spying for the government.

When the body was found without head or hands, Mother said she knew it wasn't his. The whole family had webbed feet between the second and third toes. Mother had these feet, and I've got them to a certain extent, and she said Lionel definitely had them. Ma said the feet would have been a giveaway and anyone would have had to remove the feet as well as the hands and head.

Only his mother went to the funeral. At the time, the whole family were upset, but somehow they always expected him to come home. As the years went by, and nothing happened and books were published saying he was now working for the Russian Navy, Mother just kept saying he would have known his mother had died, and supposed he had married in Russia, and had nothing to return for.

Lomond Handley adds:

> Mother [Eileen] never believed he died at Portsmouth and maintained to her death that he'd been captured and taken to Russia. Granny [Kitty] Jarvis was not well at the time. Not long afterwards, she had a major operation. Daisy never believed that Lionel was dead and at some point the inscription was changed on the headstone, but I can't throw any light on the reason. Mother believed there was a cover-up. She asked her MP, Richard Sharples, to look into it. He went through the motions but it was obvious he didn't want to rock the Tory boat.

In stark contrast to Daisy Crabb and other members of the family, Rosa Lewis from the Cavendish, and Crabb's friend Maitland Pendock were convinced Crabb died in Portsmouth harbour and was later buried in Milton Cemetery. Coincidentally, they both had strong secret service and intelligence connections, and just a few years later Maitland was supposed to have died in equally mysterious circumstances during a private business trip to Ireland.

One of the most recent and outrageous suggestions surprisingly comes from a former naval officer, who claims Crabb died aboard the Russian cruiser after suffering from respiratory problems. He says the Soviets gave Crabb a burial at sea with full military honours. I find this hard to believe. If true, why not give up Crabb's body? And why hold a private burial at sea? The Soviets could have gained a massive propaganda victory from these actions. And indeed, if true, where did the other body come from?

Certainly the majority of ex-naval personnel involved in the original and revised inquiry are fully of the opinion that Crabb died in Portsmouth harbour, either as a result of faulty equipment, a tragic accident, or murder.

Quite a few important officers involved with the case believe Soviet agents may have tampered with Crabb's equipment. The role of Soviet spymaster, Anthony Blunt, and the method of his final exposure add further credibility to this argument. But I have certainly found no reliable evidence to suggest Crabb was captured, defected, or even planned to defect – in fact quite the opposite. Murder. however, remains a distinct possibility.

I am convinced Crabb had every intention of carrying out his mission. He was due to marry Pat Rose and settle down, and loved his family and his country. I doubt that he would have done anything to jeopardise these relationships. And if he had gone to Russia under any circumstances, and particularly as a defector, I feel certain he would have been paraded through Moscow's Red Square, as some sort of trophy.

Crabb may have ruffled a few feathers in his time and was certainly on a few hit lists with terrorist groups, but I think any Soviet interference would have been subtler. That is why I feel the tampering of his oxygen tank far more likely than an attack by Soviet divers. He knew the Russians were expecting some sort of inspection, but only a handful of intelligence officers knew there would be *two* inspections that day.

Was Crabb's mission a decoy? Why was the second dive not admitted at the time, or since? And did a second diver disappear? It is highly probable that Crabb experienced technical difficulties, but it is also likely that he was betrayed and consequently could have died as the result of Soviet actions, or as a sacrificial lamb.

Chapter 22

Cold War Warriors

The Cold War lasted for more than four decades and eventually became a battle of wits between Britain's Secret Intelligence Services (SIS), Naval Intelligence, the Russian KGB and the American Central Intelligence Agency (CIA). The aim was for each to outsmart the other by gaining access to confidential information.

Soldiers were exchanged for spymasters and if Communism had not collapsed in the late 1980s, many of today's spy stories may never have come to light. Anthony Blunt was probably one of Russia's most accomplished double agents. He headed the infamous Cambridge Five, a collection of some of the most notorious Soviet agents ever to penetrate the British Secret Services, particularly MI6.

I managed to obtain an interesting insight into the activities of Anthony Blunt, Guy Burgess, Donald Maclean, and Kim Philby, from some recent Federal Bureau of Investigation (FBI) documents released in 2006. The documents confirmed Blunt was under suspicion of being a Communist agent long before 1949. Moreover, the FBI was also 'giving consideration' to interviewing him during his American lecture tour in Louisville, and in Cleveland, Ohio, in March 1956. The documents said Blunt would be staying at the Brown Hotel in Louisville. Strangely, this same town was mentioned in other secret intelligence papers, when evidence was accidentally revealed at the British Embassy in Cairo.

Initially the FBI files referred to a 'remarkable coincidence', as Blunt was about to give a lecture in Louisville during March 1956 – the very period intelligence services were planning Crabb's final dive.

The file mentioned an article in the *Louisville Courier & Journal* from their Washington reporter, dated 16 March. The piece claimed that the British Secret Service was investigating their entire Embassy staff in Cairo in an effort to track down a Russian agent. The agent was believed to have collaborated with at least one of the two spies, Burgess and Maclean, who were then working behind the Iron Curtain.

The newspaper article said the investigation had come about as the result of a coded letter from Louisville that had accidentally slipped out of a book inside the British Embassy library in Cairo. The incident was taken so seriously that American intelligence agents were brought in to investigate.

A British librarian and an American visitor in Cairo discovered a strange letter in a copy of one of Lord Cromer's books. The letter fell out when the book was opened for checking in November 1955. The letter, sent from someone in Louisville, and dated June 1951, was placed in a sort of spy's letterbox.

An extract from the letter reads: 'As I am writing, the news of Donald's disappearance is coming over the air . . . he must be given a longer breakdown period in the future . . . ten days is a long time to howl . . . Donald is very cautious about David's replacement chap and hasn't decided what he is like.' American agents claimed it was a coded message between two Communist agents reporting about Donald Maclean. Every book in the library was pulled down and searched.

The file also contained allegations of Blunt's spying activities from an unknown woman. Some additional letters also referred to an unidentified (female) associate of Blunt, who alleged that Guy Burgess, who once worked at the British Embassy in Cairo, was the individual associated with or directing Blunt.

There were also claims of Blunt's recruitment activities for the KGB at Cambridge University, many years before the Second World War. In addition, the file confirmed precise details concerning the defection of Soviet spies Burgess and Maclean, who had worked closely with Kitty Jarvis and Blunt at the War Office in London, and partied with Lionel Crabb.

The papers confirmed that Burgess's roommate in the States, Kim Philby, was the first person to contact Blunt in London, to tell him about the defections. They also contained references to the University's 'Conversazione Society', or 'The Apostles' described as an ancient, non-conformist discussion society, but not considered political in the States.

When claims against Blunt were first investigated, many years before his exposure as a spy, Crabb's distant cousin, Lomond Handley, says:

Granny Kitty was interviewed by some men from one of the official departments sometime during the early 1960s. They visited her when she was living with her daughter, Audrey. They questioned her for three days about Blunt's activities. She never believed he was involved in any wrongdoing, and died before he was publicly exposed. However, I understand she asked for my father to go with her for moral support, and to be present as a witness. Father never spoke of it. I only found out because Granny answered my questions about Blunt, Burgess, Maclean and Philby.

Her cousin Charleen Miller also recalls how she heard about the incident:

I was about fourteen and Granny Kitty lived with Mother and us in St Albans. Out of the blue, Kitty got a phone call from either MI5 or MI6, asking if they could come down and interview her about Anthony Blunt, because he had been exposed as a spy. She was shocked. She liked him an awful lot, but said she didn't particularly like Burgess or Maclean. She said they weren't in the same drawer. Kitty claimed Blunt though was charming and cultured, and she had the greatest difficulty coming to terms with the fact he was a spy.

At first, she was worried they thought she could have been a spy too. For two days and two nights, men sat in the lounge from morning till late. One man asked questions about what information and jobs she and Blunt did during the war. The other man kept writing everything down. They said she was the only person who knew what information he would have had. At the time, she and we were told not to tell anyone that they had been there, or that Blunt was a spy. So when the story broke many years later, I was quite surprised that I already knew about it.

The ongoing saga of Blunt's exposure, Soviet treachery and links with both Kitty and Lionel Crabb, continue to be a major talking point within the family. Lomond adds:

When we moved to Haslemere when I was about sixteen, Mother tried to get Sir Godfrey Nicholson MP to look into the Crabb affair. He was our Member of Parliament, and his agent was Colonel Abbot, who visited Mother at my request – including her views that Blunt might have been involved.

Mother had a letter or a copy of a letter left by Guy Burgess when he defected, which a journalist had given to her. She said it named Blunt, and claimed she was familiar with Burgess's handwriting. She showed this to Colonel Abbot, and when he left he took it with him. Many months went by, and he never returned it. Mother continued to believe that both he and the MP were doing something about it – but they obviously weren't. They were just like the others, all keen to cover it all up. Mother eventually wrote to Colonel Abbot or phoned him asking for her letter to be returned. She received a written reply saying that Sir Godfrey no longer had the letter, which by then had had a D-notice served on it, and said it had possibly been lost or destroyed.

During the 1960s, Lionel Crabb's fiancée, Pat Rose, appeared in a film along with his mother Daisy. They refused to appear together as apparently, by that time, they thoroughly despised each other. It was a documentary produced by Jim Sainsbury, a former navy diver. Several of Crabb's former diving colleagues were included, and it was loosely based on his sudden disappearance.

This film, however, never reached a mass audience. And despite a very keen public interest, it was blocked from appearing on either the big or small screen. It was technically in breach of the Official Secrets Act, and no trace of the film or Jim Sainsbury has ever been reported since.

Something similar happened with the BBC in 1967. They were blocked by the government from trying to produce another documentary about the second Naval Intelligence dive in 1956 – a fact which was kept hidden until 2006. One of their journalists claimed to have spoken to one of the divers involved. He said that *two* dives took place at the same time. They both encountered serious problems, but even to this day, the authorities have still only officially admitted to one dive – which resulted in the unfortunate loss of Cdr Crabb.

This second mission included four Navy divers from HMS *Vernon*. They dived at the same time as Crabb from a nearby location yet incredibly neither knew about the other. Rear Admiral Inglis, the head of Naval Intelligence, sanctioned the second dive, which was a near copy of his mission under the *Sverdlov* the previous year. I believe this was actually Operation 'Claret', rather than Crabb's dive, and it is said that one of their divers was also lost, presumed drowned. A limited search was ordered, on the pretext of looking for Crabb, with Inglis desperate to keep his own failure away from public knowledge and political scandal. This fact was later noticed by the First Sea Lord, Mountbatten.

Although I found clear evidence of this second mission organised by Naval Intelligence some time ago, together with allegations of a second fatality, it was only during 2006 that MI6 finally agreed to release paperwork that helped corroborate these facts. MI6 now says: 'It is a fact that a naval team from *Vernon* did dive under the Russian ships.' A letter from their secret files confirmed that Cabinet Secretary Burke Trend had sent a note to Prime Minister Edward Heath, claiming: 'The BBC now know that, in addition to the operation by Crabb, a separate diving operation was planned by the Royal Navy against the cruiser. They have also got wind of this second operation. Although officially called off, the dive nevertheless took place as an unofficial enterprise. The source for the story was said to be one of the divers.'

Some later MI6 documents confirm the extent of an additional cover-up, clearly designed to deny that a second dive ever took place at the same time, and on the same morning as Crabb's ill-fated dive in April 1956. They also blocked all the remaining divers from taking part in the BBC programme by threatening to withdraw their service pensions and by using the full force of the Official Secrets Act. Most of the paperwork and letters from the government and BBC relate to a period around March 1967, and are headed: 'BBC plans for a TV documentary.'

There was a handwritten note at the top of one of the letters, which read: 'Conum's letter from the BBC – proposing to do a half-hour programme on "Commander Crabb (The Mission)".' The BBC claimed they had found a diver who was there at the time. The BBC's diver source was concerned about his pension if he took part in the programme. It confirms:

> Having consulted the head of the Naval Pensions Panel, I will deal first with the questions of pensions mentioned in par 2 of M6, and in the BBC's letter. Under the Admiralty Pensions Act, the Department may at its discretion, suspend (and restore later) or forfeit a pension on account of:
>
> Misconduct by the pensioner.
>
> Conviction of a serious offence connected with the Service.
>
> Grave criminal offences; any other criminal offence resulting in a sentence of imprisonment exceeding six months.

It seems most unlikely that if the BBC's diver/divers took part in the proposed programme we should have any cause to take serious action concerning his pension. That said, the diver does of course, remain subject to the Official Secrets Act and depending on what he says, might lay himself open to prosecution for unlawful disclosure of information.

I suspect, however, after the passage of time and bearing in mind the Departmental view that there is no security objection to the programme, that the Director of Public Prosecutions would be unlikely to bring a prosecution.

At the inquest into the death of Cdr Crabb, the Coroner recorded an open verdict. If, therefore, the diver mentioned by the BBC has, and discloses information relevant to the death of Cdr Crabb, which he deliberately withheld in 1957, then he might find himself in trouble with the authorities on that score.

On the general question of a television programme about Cdr Crabb it is notable that the Prime Minister personally made a statement in the House of Commons on 9 May 1956, in which he said:

It would not be in the public interest to disclose the circumstances in which Cdr Crabb is presumed to have met his death.

On 14 May, on a motion by the late Hugh Gaitskell (who divided the House), the Prime Minister again refused to be drawn on the subject of Cdr Crabb's death. I do not personally know the story of the Crabb affair but if the Prime Minister's reticence was due to political reasons or diplomatic reasons or security reasons (or a combination of such reasons), then even though security reasons can now apparently be discounted, Ministers may still not wish publicity to be given to this matter and may indeed wish the BBC to be discouraged from proceeding with the proposed programme.

Signed: D.K. Bomfrey, Head of NL. 5 April 1972

Another flurry of secret letters was sent backwards and forwards between government departments. One from the Secretary of State was dated the following day and went into more detail and obvious concern about proposals and methods to try and block the programme. It was headed: 'Proposed BBC TV programme on Commander Crabb':

Any advice you may be able to give could be related only to any 'D' Notice which may be relevant to the case. If we are up against real political and/or security difficulties, I must let the Cabinet Office know as soon as possible. The draft reply to the BBC should be cleared by Head of C2 (AD) as well as CPR so that we can maintain consistency in an area with which some of us are constantly involved. Certainly, this seems to be yet another case in which the Ministry of Defence should give neither assistance nor hostages to fortune.

Signed: P.T.E. England, AUS (Defence Staff). Stamped Assistant Under-Secretary of State (Naval Staff). 6 April 1972

A confidential letter sent from Vice-Admiral Sir Norman Denning, Assistant Under-Secretary of State (Naval Staff), and dated 11 April 1972, gave a surprising and stark admission that the government had deliberately lied once again regarding the Crabb mission. For years they had consistently denied any claim that a second dive had taken place on the same day as Crabb's, and yet here, within a couple of official documents, was a top representative from the Admiralty and British government admitting that a second dive did take place under the Russian cruiser. He also corroborated the fact that it was completed under the orders of Naval Intelligence, authorised by Inglis, and included a party of divers from HMS *Vernon*.

It was agreed to block the BBC's attempt to produce the documentary by giving no assistance, and further persuaded any participants that they could lose their service pensions and faced threats of a D-notice for breaching the Official Secrets Act.

Another letter of admission was headed 'Proposed BBC TV programme on Commander Crabb':

The only D Notice relevant to the case of Crabb is D Notice No 10, British Intelligence Services. So much has already been published on Crabb, some factual, much speculative, that I doubt whether any significant new light can be cast on the affair concerning Crabb himself. However, it is a fact that a Naval team from *Vernon* did separately from Crabb, who was [blank] . . . dive under the Russian ships, and I suspect the new evidence is from one of these. The operation was kept secret and a revelation could have political/security difficulties. I agree that MOD should give NO assistance but perhaps CPR may like to suggest to Darlow that he clears the script with me.

Signed: Vice Admiral Sir Norman Denning, document stamped Assistant Under Secretary of State (Naval Staff). 11 April 1972

Over the next few days, Vice-Admiral Denning and his colleagues sent further correspondence confirming the plan to make any production almost prohibitive and suggested a suitable reply to the BBC. In these he said:

Would you please draft a reply from Director of Public Relations (Navy) to the producer of the proposed programme, Mr Darlow, and clear this draft with Mr Child of the Cabinet Office. On present advice, it seems to me that the reply should, in effect, say we are sorry there is no assistance we can usefully give but that the BBC should clear the script with Admiral Denning in case there are any D Notice angles.

Signed: P.T.E. England, AUS (Defence Staff). Stamped Assistant Under-Secretary of State (Naval Staff). 12 April 1972

Two divers known to be involved with the BBC programme included Sydney Knowles, Crabb's former diving colleague, and an Italian driver who worked with Crabb in Venice during the war. Knowles was going to talk about his mission with Cdr Crabb the previous year under the Russian warship *Sverdlov*. He was not, however, involved in the final mission. An approach was also made to Lt Franklin. When I challenged Knowles over his role in this programme, he admitted: 'Yes, I was asked to appear on television but I then had a D-notice served on me.' He was then quite unwilling to talk about the matter any further, and remained worried about the consequences.

Another (unidentified) naval diver was also apparently willing to talk at the time about the second Naval Intelligence dive, and the loss of his colleague, but he has since died. The body of this Naval Intelligence diver was almost certainly the body caught up in the nets on 3 November 1956 – about six months after Crabb's final dive – and described in detail by a fisherman, and sketched by intelligence sources.

When this other body was located, Naval Intelligence hoped it would be that of Cdr Crabb, but were surprised when it obviously resembled one of their own divers. Clearly at a loss and unwilling to give any public explanation – and possibly relieved that the body vanished back into the depths – a parallel cover-up plan was instigated. This remained in force until Crabb's body was found near Chichester harbour, some eight months later.

Recent British intelligence files suggest that in 1963, one of Blunt's so-called failed Soviet recruits, an American, Michael Straight, informed Britain's MI5, and provided evidence about Blunt's Soviet spying activities.

Blunt was initially offered immunity from prosecution, and a promise of anonymity by British Intelligence, provided he gave full details of his involvements with the KGB.

In exchange, Blunt was allowed to continue with his privileged lifestyle but apparently Lord Mountbatten intervened. He was determined to investigate Blunt's role, and to expose him for decades of traitorous activities, possibly even involving the loss of Crabb. Close colleagues of Crabb, who were also associated with Lord Mountbatten, suggest Blunt broke the 'Family' rules, and needed to be publicly exposed.

Within other important material on both sides of the Atlantic, there is now a growing belief among supporters of Crabb that Blunt may well have been responsible – perhaps inadvertently – for Crabb's death or murder in April 1956.

It is an irony that Blunt was uniquely affiliated with, and trusted by, Crabb's family. Confidential information about Operation 'Claret' was definitely leaked to Soviet sources, who were also made aware of a second Naval Intelligence dive. Meanwhile, at the time it would seem Lionel Crabb and the First Sea Lord, Louis Mountbatten, were not informed.

The claim of Blunt being a long-term Russian agent was eventually leaked by Naval Intelligence sources to Andrew Boyle, a journalist who had previously worked within the intelligence network, and was also known to Mountbatten. Boyle published a book in 1979, some thirteen years after evidence of Blunt's spying activities had first been revealed. In *The Climate of Treason* Blunt's story is revealed in a character called Maurice. The book attracted considerable attention and was even discussed in the House of Commons by Prime Minister Margaret Thatcher. She shared Mountbatten's concern and deliberately asked who this Maurice really was, finally revealing his identity as none other than Anthony Blunt on 27 August 1979. Blunt subsequently lost his knighthood and all his privileges. He died in disgrace about three years later.

In a macabre twist of fate, 1979 turned out to be a tragic year for the Mountbatten family, too. While on holiday at his summer residence near the quiet fishing village of Mullaghmore in County Sligo, Lord Mountbatten and some members of his family were murdered by the IRA. A bomb had been planted aboard Mountbatten's boat, the 30ft vessel *Shadow V*, moored in the small harbour. The device, like many others that Crabb once intercepted in Haifa, was detonated by remote control shortly after the party left the harbour in Donegal Bay. The blast killed Lord Mountbatten, one of his twin grandsons, his mother-in-law, and a fifteen-year-old local boy. To add to the bloodshed, just a few hours after this attack, eighteen soldiers from the Parachute Regiment died in another IRA attack at Warrenpoint, County Down. One other strange coincidence regarding this tragedy was that the explosives used were reported to have been of Russian origin.

Chapter 23

Secrets and Lies

Apart from the occasional Sunday newspaper story or work of fiction, the nearest anyone has ever come to making sense of Crabb's life as a possible defector to Russia came many years ago, when a young Israeli journalist, Igal Sarna, made some controversial public statements.

Sarna claimed a former Russian Naval Intelligence officer had contacted him in Tel Aviv. He said one of the officer's junior colleagues had served on the Russian cruiser *Ordzhonikidze*, or on one of its attendant destroyers that brought the Russian leaders to Britain in 1956. He alleged that he saw Crabb surface between the two destroyers early on the morning of 19 April. He said the Russians were on the lookout for him and shot him dead. He said that he sank, and was never seen again. As a result of this claim, many years later, Sarna travelled to England to meet a journalist from the *Daily Telegraph*, and Crabb's friend, Cdr Gordon Gutteridge.

Gutteridge told Rear Admiral Poland that his account was brief. He explained: 'Although the officer seemed to be honest and reliable, he was not actually there, he didn't fire the gun, and I said I wouldn't have believed the story, even if he had been.' I believe all reports concerning

Crabb's alleged Russian experiences are pure fiction, and were just part of a clever strategy instigated by Lord Mountbatten and his counter-intelligence operatives to muddy the waters.

This misinformation was calculated, manipulated and force-fed to seek out other Soviet infiltrators. The KGB fell for it, hook, line and sinker, and unwittingly enhanced it. And although the precise details are likely to remain on the classified list for some while yet, correspondence between Cdr Gordon Gutteridge, Rear Admiral Nicho Poland and several other high-ranking former naval officers suggests Crabb's role in 1956 could be compared to the plot of *The Man Who Never Was*. The 1954 book by Ewen Montagu, which was later made into a film, tells the story of how the British devise an intelligence scam using a dead body to trick the Nazis into thinking the Allied invasion of Sicily will happen elsewhere.

Crabb's fiancée, Pat Rose, became a typical example of Mountbatten's counter-espionage process. She believed Crabb went to Russia, either voluntarily, or as a hostage, and that consequently he didn't die in Portsmouth harbour. She remained convinced about Crabb's whereabouts, always believing he was working somewhere in the Soviet Union. What better champion could Mountbatten have had to sing Crabb's praises? She naturally wanted to believe that Lionel was still alive, and became completely fooled, especially when handed a unique coded message with 'the most definite proof of all.' It included Crabb's pet name for her as the 'Old Grey Witch'. She explained:

> No one else knew it, and no one else does. And I have not told anyone else about it since . . . After he disappeared, I went to the South of France for a time to avoid the publicity. When I had been there for about two weeks, a friend showed me a German magazine with a story about Crabbie in it. There was a photo of my brother, my sister-in-law, and myself. Only three copies of that photo existed. I had one, the photographer had another, and Crabbie the third. I traced the other two. That was the first proof he was still alive.

Pat's pet name, though, was known to some of Crabb's family, and close associates. Pat also believed Crabb held the only remaining private photograph of her, as she could account for two others. Again, not true. This photograph appeared in his cabin at *Vernon*, and was copied. All Pat's details were registered as a matter of course for anyone associated with an intelligence agent. After all, she too could have been a Soviet spy. Confidential information was meat and drink to intelligence personnel, and the introduction of 'secrets' often helped persuade sceptics. It was a tactic often used during the war to help establish a person's credibility.

It was not Crabb's death that was faked but his life in Russia, thanks to Her Majesty's Secret Service. Regrettably, and despite decades of hope and patience, Pat Rose never received an invitation to travel to the Soviet Union. I feel certain that if Crabb had been living in Russia, a way would have been found, or Crabb would have made a very public appearance and statement. After all, it happened with Maclean, Philby and others. It was all part of a very convincing deception plan, and when Mountbatten felt he had exhausted the idea, and stories began to recede, so did Pat's passion and belief in any subsequent reunion. Finally, she died broken-hearted.

I would like to draw some conclusions about the life and death of Lionel 'Buster' Crabb. Cdr Crabb worked for Lord Mountbatten in a number of roles from 1943. He was Britain's most experienced and highly decorated diver. His lifelong hatred of Communism was known to a few, including his Commander-in-Chief, and Crabb's unique family connections gave him the perfect cover to work as an agent.

During and after the war, Crabb was encouraged to attend meetings and supper parties with suspected Communists, including Blunt, Burgess, Maclean, Philby and Cairncross. Winston Churchill knew Burgess from the 1930s, and as the wartime prime minister, he regularly discussed his concerns about Communist infiltration into the Intelligence networks with Mountbatten. Both remained suspicious of rival British intelligence organisations.

Mountbatten was always a master meddler. He was outspoken and loved interfering in government policies. At times, he even clashed with Churchill, his great political friend – particularly over India. But when Mountbatten's involvement over the Crabb affair seemed likely to go pear-shaped, with his name already shouted across the House of Commons, and with the press baying for his blood, Mountbatten looked for a lifeline. The lifeline came from an equally concerned ally, Rear Admiral John Inglis, the head of Naval Intelligence.

The Freedom of Information Act, and some expert digging, are finally beginning to loosen the government's grip on this bizarre episode. Despite advances in information technology, however, many pages relating to this case remain defaced, with key facts blanked out. The complete file is still banned until 2057. Why? What is still considered by the government to be so sensitive or against the national interest that officials still feel the need to keep matters secret for another fifty years? I have discussed these points with a number of senior naval officers, including many of Crabb's friends and colleagues. The same name crops up each time – Lord Louis Mountbatten.

So what do we really know about Lionel Crabb the man? Or about Cdr Crabb the spy and wartime diving hero? What do we know about Crabb's final dive, who sanctioned it, who briefed him and what was expected of him? Perhaps more importantly, who instigated and maintained a cover-up that has lasted for five decades, and looks likely to continue for five more?

My inquiries reveal what happened to Crabb throughout most of his life and what made him such rich source material for Ian Fleming's Cold War secret agent, James Bond. Crabb was a man of many parts: adventurer, odd-job man, undertaker, chaperon, model, salesman, entrepreneur, mercenary, sailor, navy diver, war hero and then spy. And certainly his heroics must have provided a mine of intrigue from which to quarry countless adventure stories. His underwater exploits were innovative and revolutionary, being involved at the very early stages of undersea warfare and photography, even beaming back to a surface ship the very first pictures of a daring rescue attempt on a stricken submarine.

Crabb was a genuine hero, a fearless diver able to undertake the most dangerous of missions in extreme temperatures. But my investigations have also revealed a flawed, more human and vulnerable side. Crabb was a man who liked to drink and smoke to excess, to gamble, and, according to his ex-wife, to have had a sexual fetish for rubber.

Crabb left very little in the way of letters, notes or any written evidence. He was either loved or loathed for his sometimes over-the-top antics. He hated exercise. He found difficulty in building relationships, and preferred the company of strangers. His life was also tainted by family tragedy and he constantly veered between the high life and penury, and a desire to please his widowed mother. He frequently suffered ill health and several failed relationships.

In 1918, when he was nine, Crabb lost his father in the First World War. In the late 1920s, when sailing the South American seas, Crabb gave up his Merchant Navy apprenticeship when he learned of his cousin, Kitty Jarvis's, affair with the best friend of her husband, Frank – Lionel Crabb's guardian and mentor, who died suddenly in 1932. In October 1949 Crabb lost his best friend and cousin, Kenneth Jarvis, in a racing car accident, and in the early 1950s another friend and diving partner, Jimmy Hodges, was killed.

Add to all this Crabb's wartime experiences fighting the Communists in the Far East around 1937, his demanding exploits in many other theatres of war, his associations with the Cambridge Five Soviet spy ring, and a variety of secret espionage duties for his country, and you begin to understand the complex motives that drove the man. Lionel Crabb remained highly vulnerable, but also able. His dependence on drink and nicotine, a lack of fitness, and a constant shortage of money, made him susceptible to exploitation.

The key question, of course, is what happened on Crabb's final dive. Discussions with service personnel give a clear indication of who was really behind Crabb's final mission. My inquiries over four years have helped to separate fact from fiction. Crabb was used regularly by the Admiralty for a series of underwater missions. From 1943, he worked on retainer for a 'special branch' of the Admiralty, being called into action on numerous occasions, as we have seen in earlier chapters.

Crabb's overall supervisor was the First Sea Lord, Lord Louis Mountbatten. And on the final dive, his operation was shared with MI6 and the CIA. Crabb still operated under the direct orders of Mountbatten, but this time he also worked with Sir John Sinclair, the head of MI6; Nick Elliott, his London station manager, and an American Intelligence liaison officer from the CIA, Matthew Smith. Each shared a responsibility for the planning and subsequent fiasco of the failed mission.

Crabb had in fact worked with the same party the previous year, when examining the hull of the Russian warship, *Sverdlov*. His duties in April 1956 were to utilise a special underwater camera developed at the Admiralty Research Laboratories and to photograph the underside of the Russian cruiser, *Ordzhonikidze*. There is still some debate about why this action was requested, as much was already known. When news of Crabb's demise was relayed to Mountbatten, he feared the worst, not only for his colleague, but also for his own naval career.

Mountbatten's name was already starting to appear in headlines as the man most likely to be responsible, and several national newspaper editors started gunning for him. The First Sea Lord was at a loss to explain, when suddenly his own intelligence contacts offered him an extraordinary Get Out of Jail Free card. They advised that Rear Admiral Inglis from Naval Intelligence was heading for a similar manure heap, particularly if news of *his* failed dive, and the loss of *his* diver became known. With a huge sense of relief and an eye to the great escape of which Houdini himself would have been proud, Mountbatten was soon back in command. The public and political consequences would have been horrific for Inglis, Eden, Anglo-Soviet relations, and Mountbatten, if confirmation of a second, unauthorised mission, and another fatality, had been publicly revealed at that time.

Mountbatten was soon able to formulate a plan to cover his back, keep his name out of the papers, direct scrutiny towards MI6 and the CIA, and lay partial blame on the Admiralty. The deal and subsequent cover-up would also give Inglis's failure complete anonymity. Mountbatten met Inglis and contacted Dick White, head of MI5, whom Mountbatten had asked to keep an eye on Crabb's mission. It was probably White's men who tipped off the First Sea Lord about this second failure. They made a formidable trio and soon a plan was hatched, with Inglis agreeing to oversee the expected government inquiry, with a determination to keep a firm lid on matters and to reveal as little as possible. Part of the plan was to leak potential defection stories to the Soviets to see if they took up the slack. Lionel Crabb in effect became part of the bait to expose the extent of Soviet infiltration within the British Intelligence Services. And although Crabb's loss probably came as a something of shock, it stimulated Mountbatten's insistence on justice and revenge.

When the Soviets found out that they had been hoodwinked, they dared not admit to their vulnerability, as they had unknowingly been sucked into a circle of deceit. As the years passed, the Soviets could not admit their true role, or any knowledge of the Crabb affair. Coincidentally, during the many decades of Soviet dominance and KGB successes, they have never once boasted of Crabb as a defector, or produced any reliable supporting evidence to confirm he went to Russia.

Mountbatten had always maintained regular contact with Crabb and probably warned his diver the 'mission' might be compromised. Certainly Mountbatten and Naval Intelligence sources knew that the Russians knew, and later realised the Soviets expected Crabb to take part. Mountbatten and his senior officers probably didn't know whom to trust, and Crabb's death simply served to weed out enemy agents.

My feeling is that Soviet spies probably murdered Crabb. It may have been in relation to Crabb's undercover work at the Communists' supper parties, or for his own spying work on the *Sverdlov*, or in Israel, or just to stop him from doing anything more. It could also have been Anthony Blunt's alleged tip-off about Operation 'Claret' that cost the life of Crabb and perhaps the other navy diver. Someone could easily have tampered with Crabb's equipment. Crabb and his colleague Lt Franklin were warned to be on the look-out for some sort of intervention.

Unusually, Crabb queried his oxygen flow on returning to his launch. He was 'anxious and out of breath'. And when the problem finally kicked in, Noel Cashford says he wouldn't have known much about it. If he was underwater, Cashford said Crabb would have lost consciousness almost immediately from carbon monoxide poisoning. It would have been a quick, and – for the perpetrators – very convenient death. And ironically, it may have been the way Crabb would have wanted to go – at the height of his powers, and in the service of his country.

My investigations have consistently exposed a deliberate, clumsy and continuous cover-up by the government and the intelligence services. This has now been supported by a mini-series of intelligence releases, and helps to fill in the last few pieces of the jigsaw. In the years I have spent unpicking the threads of this complex espionage plot, I have been most fortunate to work with experienced former naval officers. They tend to support my theories, name similar names, and have given their own valuable opinions in relation to my inquiries.

Crabb's former Commanding Officer and diving colleague, Cdr Gutteridge, tried for years to investigate the circumstances behind Crabb's final dive. He too came very close to solving the problem. In correspondence with one of Mountbatten's senior support officers, and a former head of Undersea Warfare, Rear Admiral Nicho Poland, Gutteridge said:

The only part of the Crabb puzzle about which I am not certain is not *who* sent him – we know the answer to that – but *why on earth* he was sent, possibly at considerable risk? The Admiralty already knew what was under the cruiser; it had already been well photographed in dry dock and while it was being built. What made MI6 do this?

We know that the Admiralty already knew everything there was to know about the underside of that ship. This raises the question of why there is this nonsense of reclassifying the Crabb story. It was MI6, not MI5, working under Mountbatten's direction, who sent Crabb on his abortive mission. Nick Elliott, the head of the London station, was directly responsible. His boss, Sir John Sinclair, was away at the time. MI6 were full of traitors and Dick White was soon moved from MI5 to take over and clean it all up.

It follows that the 'true mission' did not have to be endorsed. There was no need to worry about the Commander-in-Chief's threat [not to cause any problems after being warned off a dive on the *Sverdlov*]. Someone extremely important had the authority and used it to cause MI6 to behave as it did, and to be able to assure them of immunity if things went wrong. This could only be Mountbatten, who was the First Sea Lord, and in any case he would have had access to Naval Intelligence on this subject.

I once had drinks with Admiral Peter Hill Norton, who was working at the Admiralty on an intelligence committee at the time. He unequivocally stated that the Admiralty were quite unaware of this escapade until after the event. While the Admiralty claim to have had no idea of what was going on, the First Sea Lord did. This also fits with Crabb's meeting with

Mountbatten at Cowdray Park shortly before his fatal dive. Moreover, Nicholas Elliott of MI6 confirmed that it was done at the request of the Admiralty. There is ample evidence that Elliott and company from MI6 were a bunch of loose cannons and quite capable of mounting this type of operation with or without the backing of Mountbatten, or any mandate under their terms of reference. And what other reason could Crabb have had for seeing the First Sea Lord?

If we assume that MI6 did not initiate this adventure, there is very strong evidence that only someone as arrogant, as well connected and wielding as much power as Mountbatten could have been responsible. On the face of it, this is the last piece of the jigsaw but there is still the question of why. Why would he use MI6, whose job it wasn't? And why use Crabb? And why even contemplate such a pointless activity?

Surgeon Vice Admiral Sir John Rawlins gave his considered opinion on this matter to Cdr Gutteridge, and more recently to Noel Cashford. He told Gutteridge in correspondence a few years ago:

Crabb had applied to the Commander-in-Chief for permission to carry out an investigation on the *Sverdlov*. According to the Supt of Diving at that time, he had been told by the Admiralty that he'd have to put him in irons if he did [investigate the *Sverdlov*], because the two ships were on a diplomatic visit, and were therefore sacrosanct. He must have obtained the authority of some person who reckoned he could override the C-in-C's authority.

Well, the only person that I can think of who might have been able to do that was Louis Mountbatten, who was always a maverick. He also reckoned he knew something about diving. But that was typical of Dickie MB. Mountbatten would certainly reckon he could override the Commander-in-Chief, who was junior to him in rank. And that would, or could, account for the delay in revealing the Crabb story. And because the royal family have had enough problems with the press, a revelation that Mountbatten had been behind the Crabb escapade would have been disastrous.

Rawlins remains puzzled about why the government has continued to block the Crabb files for another fifty years, and he recently told Noel Cashford:

> If the situation was simple, why bother to re-classify the material? And I wonder if DNA testing could be carried out on the remains? It was a trivial and absurd mission and technically cannot be a matter of national security today. So why is there still a substantial ban? There has to be some aspect which might cause embarrassment. There appears to be nothing special about the *Ordzhonikidze* that might have been revealed by an inspection in zero visibility. Regarding my own speculations about the Crabb affair, the only one I can think of who can fit the bill as I set it out, was a very senior officer, who could have done a bit of escorted sport diving when he came out to Malta aboard *Vanguard*. At that time, I was the young doctor on *Triumph* and I was told that the big Cerna [octopus-like creature] that inhabited the wreck of the Breconshire was reserved for the Admiral.
>
> I could well believe that Crabb had managed to convince someone from MI5 or perhaps the CIA, that there was something to be learned from an underwater survey of the Russian cruiser. And that he managed to convince the aforesaid gentleman – who evidently considered himself knowledgeable about diving – and told him to go ahead and not to worry about the Commander-in-Chief. If I am right, the very good reason for still keeping it under wraps is the undoubted embarrassment to certain people in high places, even though the gentleman in question has been dead for many years.

Naval Intelligence and Inglis were responsible for the second dive under the *Sverdlov*, and were closely associated with Crabb's final dive. The papers relating to the proposed BBC programme highlight some important points in the cover-up, and Bridges' report to the Prime Minister reveals a specific and deliberate plot to mislead the press and public – with later, even proposals to interfere with the inquest. This scandal, closely followed by the Suez crisis, did exactly what Lord Mountbatten intended. It led to rebukes for Cabinet Ministers, the resignation of the First Lord of the Admiralty, and a massive shake-up of MI6, whereby their chief, Sir John Sinclair, was forced to resign, to be replaced by Dick White of MI5. This was followed just a few months later by the downfall of Prime Minister Eden and the Conservative Party. It also involved a humiliating review of national security matters that was to cost countless more jobs, yet probably saved many thousands of lives, by the further exposure of Soviet double agents.

It is my understanding, as stated, that following discussions and correspondence with many of Lord Mountbatten's former aides, he was completely unaware of the second Naval Intelligence dive, until advised of another debacle. Information received by the author confirms Mountbatten used this 'second dive' information to secure a deal with NI chief Rear Admiral Inglis. The First Sea Lord turned this incident to his, and Britain's, advantage by using the Crabb fiasco to introduce an innovative propaganda exercise, to expose further Soviet infiltration. This way, by feeding false details into a corrupt system, his trusted intelligence colleagues could manipulate the information to their best advantage, to see just who bought what, when and where.

The Intelligence Services in 1956, and even today, still control government policy and knowledge, and between them, Mountbatten and Inglis, together with Dick White from MI5, managed to suppress the release of facts about Crabb's mission in order to contain Soviet sources.

Initially, I must admit to being puzzled about the extent of the cover-up by the authorities, the precise reasons for any denial in April 1956, and indeed the continued blocks until 2057. Crabb's story deserves to be told. The Cold War has been over for decades, so what harm can it do?

Until I fully examined Mountbatten's role in the final dive, and in many of Crabb's other missions, I found it difficult to put the First Sea Lord's master plan into perspective. However, Mountbatten and his 'special branch' team of operatives were indeed a law unto themselves, working quite independently of MI5, MI6 and Naval Intelligence. When Mountbatten's own interventions and failed actions under the Russian warships seemed likely to become exposed, he naturally did the only thing possible in the circumstances: he negotiated a brilliant deal, which not only protected his interests, but also allowed Inglis to disguise his own equally flawed operation.

Until that time, and despite technically having clearance to examine Russian ships at will, the fact that Naval Intelligence inspected the *Sverdlov* and the Soviet vessels, in addition to Crabb, was unknown to most. Mountbatten's idea ensured secrecy and anonymity. It was a superb plot, and allowed the unfortunate loss of Crabb to be put to good use. Not only did his death help rid the country of a large contingent of Soviet spies, but it also cleared or helped to expose numerous other double agents. In addition, and with the help and support of Inglis from Naval Intelligence, and the promotion of Dick White from MI5 to MI6, Mountbatten's actions urgently helped to reorganise Britain's Intelligence Services. It became an important factor when the real Cold War began to hot up, with the rest of the free world threatened by a constant build-up of Russian nuclear armoury.

If Lionel Crabb had had any notion of the furore his death would cause for the authorities, or that it would still capture the public imagination more than fifty years on, I think he would be amazed and amused. I can picture him raising a glass to his continued notoriety in a tale worthy of an Ian Fleming novel. Like the best 007 plotline, it is the story of an extraordinarily adventurous, brave yet flawed individual, whose destiny was to become embroiled in forces far greater than himself. With another half century to go before the government agrees to release all the official papers, our compulsion to understand and explain who played which part, and why, in this bizarre story of Anglo-Soviet relations, British Intelligence, the CIA and Cold War espionage, is likely to continue.

Note on Sources

I would like to thank the following individuals for their assistance in my research for this book: Lt Noel Cashford MBE, RNVR; Rear-Admiral E.N. Poland CB, CBE; Cdr Gordon Gutteridge OBE, FRSA, RN; Cdr Charles Emmerson RN; Sydney Knowles BEM; Lt G.A. Franklin; Cdr W.B. Filer OBE, RN; Admiral of the Fleet Lord Hill Norton; Miss Lomond Handley; Mrs Charleen Miller and family; Surgeon Vice-Admiral Sir John Rawlins; Stuart Ulph; and Patricia Milligan.

The following organisations have also been extremely helpful:
Royal Naval Museum
Imperial War Museum
The National Archives and the Public Record Office
MI5 and MI6 Archives
Federal Bureau of Investigation (FBI)
The BBC
Hansard
Churchill College Archives
Ministry of Defence
Getty Images

Further Reading

Readers who have enjoyed this book may find the following books of interest:

Binding, Tim, *Man Overboard*, London, Picador, 2006

Hutton, J. Bernard, *Frogman Extraordinary: The Commander Crabb Case*, London, Neville Spearman, 1960

Pugh, Marshall, *Commander Crabb*, London, Macmillan, 1956

Welham, Michael G. and Welham, Jacqui A., *Frogman Spy*, London, W.H. Allen, 1990

Index